TRANSACTIONS

of the

American Philosophical Society

Held at Philadelphia for Promoting Useful Knowledge

VOLUME 81, Part 5, 1991

The Huguenot Population of France, 1600–1685: The Demographic Fate and Customs of a Religious Minority

PHILIP BENEDICT

THE AMERICAN PHILOSOPHICAL SOCIETY

Independence Square, Philadelphia

Reprinted, 1994

Publication of this book has been subsidized by the Haney Fund
of the American Philosophical Society.

Library of Congress Catalog
Card Number: 90-56477
International Standard Book Number 90-56477
US ISSN 0065-9746

To the Memory of my Father

So often recalled as I worked on this
exercise in historical spectroscopy

TABLE OF CONTENTS

TABLES

MAPS

FIGURES

ABBREVIATIONS

A.C.	Archives Communales (followed by locality)
A.D.	Archives Départementales (followed by department)
Annales: E.S.C.	*Annales: Economies, Sociétés, Civilisations*
Arsenal	Bibliothèque de l'Arsenal (Paris)
B.N.	Bibliothèque Nationale (Paris)
B.P.F.	Bibliothèque de la Société de l'Histoire du Protestantisme Français (Paris)
B.S.H.P.F.	*Bulletin de la Société de l'Histoire du Protestantisme Français*
Haag	E. and E. Haag, *La France protestante,* 10 vols. (Paris, 1846–59)
L.D.S. film	Microfilm in the collection of the Genealogical Society of Utah

ACKNOWLEDGMENTS

Carrying out this project has taught me just how fully the world of scholarship is indeed an international republic of investigators willing to place their findings at the disposition of fellow *chercheurs*. Not only did Jean-Nöel Biraben display unstinting generosity in sharing the evidence of his ongoing *enquête* with me. Yves Gueneau, Denis Vatinel, Jean-Louis Calbat, Isabelle Michalkiewicz, Jacques Frayssenge, Brigitte Maillard, and Gregory Hanlon all proved to be equally open-handed when approached and asked to share data about individual Protestant congregations which they had gathered in the course of their research. My friend Jean-Pierre Bardet and his son Guillaume were kind enough to take time out from a vacation to count baptisms in several churches for me, while Elisabeth Labrousse responded graciously to my queries about the parish records of Mauvezin. In many ways, this is as much a collective volume as an individual one. The full extent of my debts to these individuals is made clear in the Appendix. Needless to say, I am deeply grateful to them all.

I would also like to record my gratitude to Naomi Lamoreaux, Giovanni Levi, Burr Litchfield, and Anthony Molho for offering valuable suggestions concerning earlier drafts of this study, as well as to Alden Speare for expert statistical assistance. A significant chunk of this research was done while I was a Member of the Institute for Advanced Study. I owe special thanks to that impeccable institution for the assistance it was willing to provide in enabling me to begin working with the extensive microfilm collection of the Mormon Genealogical Society. And I would like to express similar thanks to the staffs of the numerous archives, libraries, and *mairies* which I visited in the course of this project for their cooperation, most especially to Mme Francine Ducluzeau, directeur des services d'archives de la Charente.

PROLOGUE

During his travels in France between 1676 and 1678, John Locke, that concerned Protestant, frequently asked the people he met about the situation of the local Huguenot community. The entries in his diary show a particular interest in possible changes in the number of Protestants. Thus, an entry of February 1676 notes about the Huguenots of Montpellier:

> . . . they and the papist laity live togeather friendly enough in these parts. They sometimes get and sometimes loose proselytes. . . . The number of Protestants in these latter years neither increases nor decreases much.

Another entry offers an even more optimistic view of the recent fate of the city's Huguenots. "They tell me that the number of Protestants within these twenty or thirty last years are manifestly increased, and doe dayly."[1]

Locke's interest in the numerical evolution of the Protestant community that made him something of a pioneer in the study of Huguenot demography is readily understandable. In many southern French towns with a substantial Protestant population, the local *consulat* was divided between Huguenots and Catholics according to a numerical formula roughly linked to each confession's strength. Here, changes in the relative size of the two communities were matters of immediate political import, so much so that after Montauban's population was decimated by the terrible plague of 1653, the city's ministers wrote to their fellow pastors throughout the country urging them to encourage young people in their congregation to move to Montauban. Only thus could efforts by "our adversaries" to fill the void with Catholic immigrants be forestalled.[2] Even where the political stakes were not so pressing, to know how many Huguenots lived within a given part of France was—and still is—to begin to understand their place within that region. To know whether this minority grew or shrank over the course of the period which ran from the Edict of Nantes to its Revocation, and to understand the causes for any changes in the size of different Protestant communities, are to begin to probe the faith's vitality and its ability to withstand the growing pressure toward religious conformity exerted by a resurgent Catholic church and an increasingly powerful state. Most broadly of all, to determine the numerical fate of this one post-Reformation confes-

[1] John Lough, ed. *Locke's Travels in France 1675–1679* (Cambridge, 1953), 28, 41.

[2] B.N., Ms Nouvelles Acquisitions Françaises 22702, fols. 15–16, Verdier to Paul Ferry, Jan. 3, 1654.

sional community is to add to our understanding of the tenacity and character of confessional attachment within the larger universe of European states within which the religious upheavals of the sixteenth century gave rise to a measure of religious toleration and pluralism. In brief, establishing the Huguenot community's numerical evolution is a necessary prologue to any more detailed investigation of its experience in this period, as well as a contribution in its own right to the study of confessional attachment in the century following the Reformation.

Locke did not just ask about the number of Protestants. He was also curious about their religious practice and moral behavior, especially whether or not they could truly be said to be the "Reformed." Here, his informants were more pessimistic. "Mr. Bertheau told me that there was little piety or religion among their people and that the lives of the Reformed was no better than that of the Papists," one entry notes. Echoes another, "The Protestants live not better than the Papists."[3]

Although Locke did not use the techniques of historical demography in investigating the comparative morality of Protestants and Catholics, that other, funnier historical demographer *avant la lettre*, François Rabelais, had already realized a century earlier that parish registers could be used to determine how closely people cleaved to the teachings of the church. "In the baptismal register of Thouars," notes Pantagruel, "the number of children is greater in October and November than in the other ten months of the year; and so by retrospective computation we find that they must all have been made, conceived, and engendered in Lent."[4] Of course, the significance of this (miscalculated) observation was not easy to decipher. Pantagruel and Friar John disagreed as to whether the more numerous conceptions resulted from the kinds of food consumed during Lent, which stimulated sexual activity, or from the preaching of the season, which shamed husbands into abandoning their maidservants and returning to their wives. Whatever the difficulties in determining the meaning of the patterns thus revealed, modern historical demographers have followed these *doctes* in realizing that the statistical tendencies which can be deduced from parish register investigations bring to light otherwise unobservable patterns of social and religious behavior. Not only does the seasonal movement of baptisms and marriages illuminate the extent to which people adhered to, or broke, the Catholic church's calendar of Lenten and Advent prohibitions. Rates of illegitimate births and premarital conceptions can indicate how strictly standards of sexual morality were followed, while the length of time people waited before having their infants baptized after birth sheds light on prevalent attitudes toward the sacrament of baptism. The sober statistics of historical demography provide a valuable complement to the study of religious history.[5]

---

3 Lough, ed. *Locke's Travels*, 28, 94.

4 François Rabelais, *The Histories of Gargantua and Pantagruel*, tr. J.M. Cohen (Harmondsworth, 1955), book V, ch. 29, p. 673.

5 As has been strongly argued by E. William Monter, "Historical Demography and Religious History in Sixteenth-Century Geneva," *Journal of Interdisciplinary History*, IX (1979), 399–427.

The questions which Locke asked of his hosts in France define the two goals of this study. Its primary aim has been to assemble the surviving information that can be used to trace reliably the numerical evolution of France's Calvinist minority between 1600 and 1685. Part I analyzes the pattern of change brought to light by this evidence. In the course of gathering this information, it was also possible to accumulate material that sheds interesting light on aspects of Huguenot piety and behavior, the focus of Part II.

Like many historical investigations, this one took shape only gradually, and some explanation of its genesis may help readers understand the extent of the information it presents. When, over a decade ago, I began research on the social history of seventeenth-century French Calvinism, I had no intention of carrying out an extended demographic investigation. Both the authoritative opinion of Samuel Mours and some acquaintance with the experience of the Protestant congregation I knew best, that of Rouen, led me to believe that after the often violent fluctuations in size experienced by many Huguenot communities over the course of the later sixteenth century, the years from 1600 to 1685 formed a period of calm during which the Protestant population evolved along lines essentially similar to those of France as a whole. Exceptions might exist, notably the dramatic fate of La Rochelle brought to light by Louis Perouas, but this was surely an extraordinary case, tied to that city's tragic experience during the siege of 1628–29.[6]

As I began to explore the changing sociological composition of several large urban congregations, I discovered that my original presuppositions were wrong. To take the case of Montpellier, it turned out that Locke had not been misinformed; the number of Huguenots there remained remarkably stable from the 1640s through the 1670s. But this was at a level close to thirty percent lower than that of the first decade of the seventeenth century, for the number of Protestants living in the city had been substantially reduced by siege during the revolt of 1621–22 and by plague in 1629. Meanwhile, Montpellier's total population had grown significantly from the time of Henry IV to that of Louis XIV, with the result that while the Huguenots formed 60 percent of the city's inhabitants in the 1610s, they were reduced to a minority of 30 percent by the 1660s. Most of the other urban communities I first looked at experienced a comparable, if often more gradual, decline in size.

As I discovered more and more such cases of decline among the communities I studied, I grew increasingly curious. Was the phenomenon of diminishing numbers confined to the congregations located in larger cities, or was it more generally typical of the fate of Protestant communities over the course of this period? Was it sharper in certain regions of the country than in others? And what accounted for it? Was this a confirmation of the "lethargy" and "spiritual sickness" which certain distin-

[6] Perouas, "Sur la démographie rochelaise," *Annales: E.S.C.*, XVI (1961), 1131–40.

guished historians of French Protestantism have diagnosed as afflicting the cause in this period? Or were there simpler political or demographic causes?

At this point, I began to investigate Huguenot demography seriously, working in two directions. First, I carried out a detailed study of a single community which experienced a significant decline in size, using the techniques of family reconstitution in order to probe in depth the causes of decline. I chose Alençon for this purpose, since the time-consuming process of reconstituting its Protestant families was greatly facilitated by the existence of an excellent set of genealogies for all its Huguenot inhabitants.[7] The long delay between my completion of this research and the publication here of its results has deprived this work of some of its novelty, for family reconstitution studies of other urban Huguenot communities have appeared in the interim.[8] This delay stems from the unexpectedly ambitious expansion of the second half of the project, the accumulation of aggregate data about the evolution of enough different Protestant communities throughout France so that the overall movement of the Huguenot population and its chief regional variations could be traced with some reliability from 1600 to 1685. Two events were particularly important here. First, in 1985, after I had assembled enough information to write an initial version of this study, I learned that the important investigation undertaken by Jean-Noël Biraben of the Institut National d'Etudes Démographiques to reconstruct the movement of France's total population from the first widespread establishment of parish registration through 1670 had engaged him in a parallel venture. We entered into contact and agreed to share the data about the Huguenot population each had gathered to date and to coordinate further archival work. Then, after a first version of Part I of this study, incorporating data provided by Dr. Biraben, was published in 1987,[9] the Archives Nationales completed a guide to all known demographic sources concerning France's Huguenot population.[10] This revealed that we had already accumulated so much evidence about the numerical evolution of the Protestant community in the seventeenth century that the examination of all surviving sets of Huguenot vital records covering a long stretch of the seventeenth century had become an obtainable goal. That became the objective of a final archival push.[11]

---

[7] These genealogies were drawn up by the pastor and local historian Benjamin Robert, and are now conserved along with the rest of his notes at the B.P.F.

[8] Jean-Pierre Bardet, *Rouen aux XVIIe et XVIIIe siècles. Les mutations d'un espace social*, 2 vols. (Paris, 1983), esp. I, 216ff, 276, 314ff, 325; Brigitte Maillard, "Religion et démographie: Les Protestants de Tours au XVIIe siècle," *Annales de Bretagne et des Pays de l'Ouest*, XC (1983), 550–6.

[9] Philip Benedict, "La population réformée française de 1600 à 1685," *Annales: E.S.C.*, XLII (1987), 1433–65.

[10] Gildas Bernard, *Les familles protestantes en France, XVIe siècle–1792. Guide des recherches biographiques et généalogiques* (Paris, 1987).

[11] Biraben and I initially envisaged the joint publication of our results, with an extensive section on the Protestant population under my authorship being included within his

This volume has thus come to be built upon all of the known parish register and census evidence bearing upon the changing size of France's Huguenot population over the course of the period between the Edict of Nantes and its Revocation—specifically, upon census figures or annual totals of baptisms for any Protestant church or community for which such evidence spans forty or more years of the century. It is important to point out that I take France to refer here to that territory under the control of the French crown for the full period 1600–1685. Although Reformed congregations also existed in this era in certain other communities located within the modern boundaries of France (e.g., Colmar, Mulhouse, Sainte-Marie-aux-Mines, Sedan, and the principality of Orange), and although Louis XIV's annexation of Alsace incorporated an important Lutheran population into the kingdom as well, the history of these communities obeyed a different logic from that of the Reformed churches subject to the control of the Bourbon monarchs throughout the century. Its reconstruction and explanation are best left to local historians of those communities.

While this study is built upon evidence gathered for over six score congregations or localities, it is also important to stress that the extent of the information assembled about each one varies considerably. Reconstructing the secular trend of the Protestant population in the community in question has always been the first priority when gathering data about a given locality. Where time and the sources permitted, such matters as the seasonal movement of marriages, the evolution of the Catholic population in the same community, and (most time-consuming and hence rarest of all) rates of illegitimacy or prenuptial conceptions have also been explored. While the basic sample retained for use in analyzing the secular trend of the Protestant population concerns 120 localities, the discussion of certain issues rests upon just two to two dozen cases.

However extensive the archival base upon which it rests, a national survey such as this, based upon the often summary exploitation of a restricted group of sources, necessarily has one further limitation. The methods employed here can provide a sound basis for generalizations about the aggregate experience of the group being studied. As will be seen, they bring to light numerous hitherto unsuspected regional variations in its destiny and behavior. They can even suggest some of the causes of the trends they uncover. Often, however, they raise as many questions as they answer. Time and again, in carrying out the research for this project, I have had to suppress the urge to settle down in an in-

much longer monograph dedicated to reconstructing the movement of France's population as a whole. With time, however, we increasingly recognized the difficulties of close trans-Atlantic collaboration and came to see that a study whose chief goal in utilizing demographic data was to shed light on the history of seventeenth-century French Protestantism required sufficiently different techniques and involved a sufficiently different set of questions from one whose chief goal was to reconstruct and analyze France's population history as a whole to warrant separate publication. The additional material gathered since 1987 has led to some modification of the findings published in that year, while further reflection has also permitted me to refine aspects of my analysis.

dividual archive or region in order to do the extensive digging necessary to explain some intriguing trend or pattern brought to light by the evidence, lest this project take even longer to complete than it already has. Time and again, in consequence, it has been possible for me to do no more here than offer hypothetical explanations for important phenomena brought to light and to urge more research on the topic. It is increasingly apparent that great regional variations characterized both the sociology of seventeenth-century French Protestantism and the patterns of co-existence and confessional identity formation which governed Catholic-Protestant relations in this period. This national investigation is offered in the hope that it can help to stimulate more of the detailed local studies of individual Protestant communities and of the relations between their members and their Catholic neighbors that are so desperately needed to illuminate these variations, as well as to highlight those regions where such studies might be particularly fruitful.[12] When more such studies have been carried out, not only the explanations offered here, but indeed many of the findings themselves, may look very different.

[12] Important local studies are currently in progress about Mauvezin by Elisabeth Labrousse and Layrac by Gregory Hanlon. I am working on a thematic investigation of the social history of the urban congregations.

PART I
A DECLINING MINORITY

A. The Size and Distribution of France's Protestant Minority, ca. 1660–70

Any examination of Huguenot numbers in the seventeenth century must begin from the work of Samuel Mours. In a series of books and articles culminating in his *Essai sommaire de géographie du protestantisme réformé français au XVIIe siècle* of 1966, this dedicated pastor-historian drew together the information contained in the scattered surviving regional censuses of Protestantism, the immense and highly uneven monographic literature on the local history of the religion, and a few original baptismal registers in order to build up, case by case and region by region, the best picture of Protestantism's numerical strength and geographic distribution available to date.[1] Earlier estimates of Huguenot numbers had ranged as high as two million. Mours's patient investigation showed that a figure on the order of 850,000 was far more probable. His breakdown of Protestantism's strength by region (provided in Table 1) also highlighted the most striking characteristics of the cause's geographic dispersion: the clustering of over four-fifths of the country's Huguenots within the crescent of provinces running from Dauphiné across Languedoc and Guyenne and up the west coast into Poitou; and the disproportionately urban nature of the faith, especially in the northern half of the kingdom. Even though Mours appears to have used rather unsystematic criteria to classify different communities by size and character, his figures suggest that over 40 percent of the Huguenot population of this latter portion of France lived in towns, whereas the percentage of the country's total population living in communities of two thousand inhabitants or more around 1700 stood between 15 and 19 percent.[2] Mours's estimates, his 1958 work makes clear, apply to the period

---

[1] Mours, "Essai d'évaluation de la population protestante réformée aux XVIIe et XVIIIe siècles," *B.S.H.P.F.*, CIII (1958), 1–24; reprinted in *Les Eglises réformées en France: Tableaux et cartes* (Paris-Strasbourg, 1958), 157–68; "Essai sommaire de géographie du protestantisme réformé français au XVIIe siècle," *B.S.H.P.F.*, CXI (1965), 303–21; CXII (1966), 19–36, also separately published (Paris, 1966).

[2] Jacques Dupâquier, *La population française aux XVIIe et XVIIIe siècles* (Paris, 1979), p. 40; Dupâquier ed., *Histoire de la population française*, II *De la Renaissance à 1789* (Paris, 1988), p. 87; and Philip Benedict, "Was the Eighteenth Century an Era of Urbanization in France?" *Journal of Interdisciplinary History*, XXI (1990), 196, 211, all provide estimates of the percentage of the population living in communities of two thousand or more inhabitants. Deciding just what attributes qualified a locality as a city is, of course, one of the most delicate problems facing students of Ancien Régime French society. While claiming, "nous prenons

TABLE 1. The Reformed Population of France, ca. 1660–70, According to Samuel Mours

Synod	Number of churches	Total Protestant population	Urban population	"Mixed" population	Rural population
Six Northern Synods					
Ile-de-France–Champagne–Picardy	45	48,000	19,000	19,000	10,000
Normandy	43	59,000	33,000	14,000	12,000
Brittany	11	6,000	4,000	2,000	
Anjou–Maine–Touraine	21	13,500	8,800	4,700	
Orléanais–Berry	23	15,500	5,500	7,500	2,500
Burgundy	26	17,000	1,800	8,500	6,700
Total	169	159,000	72,100	55,700	31,200
Ten Southern Synods					
Poitou	49	90,000	15,000	26,000	49,000
Saintonge–Aunis–Angoumois	60	98,000	18,000	37,000	43,000
Basse-Guyenne	72	100,000	19,000	31,000	50,000
Béarn	46	30,000	8,000	10,000	12,000
Haut-Languedoc–Haute-Guyenne	64	80,000	23,000	20,000	37,000
Bas-Languedoc	63	88,000	27,000	16,000	45,000
Cévennes	59	82,000	12,000	9,000	61,000
Vivarais	29	48,000	3,500	5,500	39,000
Provence	12	9,000	400	4,600	4,000
Dauphiné	67	72,000	16,000	16,000	40,000
Total	521	697,000	141,900	175,100	380,000
Grand Total	690	856,000	214,000	230,800	411,200

NOTE: These figures do not include the Reformed churches of Metz, Alsace, Sedan, or the Valcluson. By "mixed" churches, Mours means those numerous congregations located in market towns which included a large component of artisans, merchants, and noblemen.
SOURCE: Mours, *Essai sommaire*, 41.

1660–70, years for which evidence about the strength of the faith in different regions is abundant, but before the increasingly harsh measures of discrimination leading up to the Revocation had begun to take their toll on the size of the Protestant community.[3]

Mours's work represents a monument of modest and patient scholarship, but subsequent investigations of Protestantism's strength within certain regions have indicated that his figures may still exaggerate slightly the size of the community to which he was so attached. This is partic-

le mot ville dans son acceptation la plus large, y comprenant des petites villes, telles que Sainte-Foy, en Guyenne; Anduze, en Cévennes; Die, en Dauphiné," (*Essai sommaire*, p. 40), Mours nonetheless does not appear to have bestowed urban status on other localities of roughly equal size which contemporaries also considered cities, such as Barbézieux and Cognac.

[3] Mours, *Les Eglises réformées de France*, 158.

ularly true of his estimates for those regions where he had to build up his figures on a case-by-case basis. Thus, after a very careful review of all the evidence available about the vast *province synodal* of Orléanais-Berry, Yves Gueneau arrived at a figure of between 10,750 and 11,400 Protestants within this region, where Mours had suggested 15,500.[4] A similar investigation of the colloquy of Moyen-Poitou yielded an estimate of 40,000 souls, where Mours had placed the number at 50,000.[5] By no means are all Mours's figures equally inflated. For much of the Midi he was able to rely on the censuses of Protestants drawn up by the local authorities in many regions after 1661, and a comparison of his figures with the original sources indicates that he usually, although not always, respected the accuracy of these documents, which are unquestionably the best available sources for this purpose. A thorough review of Mours's sources and of the corrections of his figures which have been offered since their publication yields the revised estimates set forth in Table 2, which also modify his figures to make them refer to France's boundaries of 1610 and to a more systematic division of the communities within which the Protestant churches were located according to their total size.[6] As can be seen, a more accurate approximation of the total number of Protestants living within these confines in the years 1660–70 might place the figure at just under 800,000 people. These revised figures offer us a starting point for the backward extrapolation of the Huguenot population and a context for judging how representative is the sample of congregations on which this study rests.

B. The Sources and the Sample

Two kinds of sources exist which enable one to trace the movement of the Protestant population within given localities between the promulga-

---

[4] Gueneau, "Protestants du Centre 1598–1685," unpub. *thèse de troisième cycle*, Université François Rabelais de Tours, 1982, 103–29.

[5] André Benoist, "Les populations rurales du 'Moyen-Poitou Protestant' de 1640 à 1789," unpub. *thèse de troisième cycle*, Université de Poitiers, 1983, 469.

[6] In classifying churches or localities according to size, I have placed those churches or censuses which encompassed people inhabiting a wide geographic area in the category of community from which the majority of those concerned were drawn. Although contemporaries considered many localities of less than 2,000 inhabitants to be cities, I have chosen a population of 2,000 as the cut-off point to define cities for the sake of facility. Population estimates of community size have been drawn from a wide range of sources, most notably Jacques Dupâquier, *Statistiques démographiques du Bassin Parisien 1636–1720* (Paris, 1977); Paul Bairoch, Jean Batou, and Pierre Chèvre, *La population des villes européennes de 800 à 1850/The Population of European Cities from 800 to 1850* (Geneva, 1988); René Le Mée, "Population agglomérée et population éparse au début du XIXe siècle," *Annales de Démographie Historique*, 1971, 467–94, extrapolated backward on the basis of eighteenth-century trends in the urban population of the region as set forth in Benedict, "Was the Eighteenth Century an Era of Urbanization?" and the parish register information examined in the course of this study. It goes without saying that the classification decisions contain a risk of error. Most particularly Anduze, Alès and Uzès, which have been placed here in the category of small towns, all fell very near the cut-off point of 5,000 inhabitants and may have exceeded it for at least part of the period in question. Recalculating all statistics with these cities placed in the larger rather than the smaller category introduces only minor changes into the results.

TABLE 2. The Reformed Population of France, ca. 1660–70, Revised Estimates

Synod	Number of churches	Total Protestant population	Cities of 5,000+ inhabs	Cities of 2–5,000 inhabs	Rural population
Six Northern Synods					
Ile-de-France–Champagne–Picardy[1]	47	51,000[2]	21,650	4,500	24,850
Normandy	43	42,200	21,000	2,400	18,800
Brittany	11	3,500[3]	1,900	300	1,300
Anjou–Maine–Touraine	21	10,200	5,525	600	4,075
Orléanais–Berry	23	15,500[4]	2,500	5,000	4,000
Burgundy	26	17,000	1,800	1,200	14,000
Total	171	134,900	53,375	14,000	67,525
Ten Southern Synods					
Poitou	49	77,500[5]	11,000	2,000	64,500
Saintonge–Aunis–Angoumois	60	93,500[6]	16,000	7,500	70,000
Basse-Guyenne	72	97,000[7]	14,000	5,000	78,000
Béarn	46	25,000[8]		6,500	18,500
Haut-Languedoc–Haute-Guyenne	64	80,000	15,500	7,500	57,000
Bas-Languedoc	63	81,000[9]	16,500	12,000	52,500
Cévennes	59	74,000[10]		18,000	56,000
Vivarais	29	48,000		3,500	44,500
Provence	12	8,000[9]	400	400	7,200
Dauphiné[11]	71	78,000	4,500	7,000	66,500
Total	525	662,000	77,900	69,400	514,700
Grand Total	696	796,900	131,275	83,400	582,225

NOTE: These estimates refer to the Reformed population living within France's borders of 1610.

1 Plus Metz and Pays Messin.

2 Comparison of certain of Mours's estimates of the size of individual churches with the size suggested by the number of baptisms celebrated within them indicates that he overestimated their ranks. His estimate has been reduced accordingly.

3 The number of baptisms in Vitré's church suggests that it had about 500 members in the 1660s. According to a visitor to Rennes in 1636, cited by Alain Croix, *La Bretagne aux 16e et 17e siècles. La vie, la mort, la foi* (Paris, 1981), 98, that city had no more than 200 Protestants. Roger Joxe, *Les Protestants du Comté de Nantes* (Marseille, 1982), 295, puts the number of Huguenots in Nantes at 1,000 or more. As these were among the province's most important churches, 3,500 seems a reasonable estimate of the total number of Protestants in this synod.

4 Accepting the corrections of Gueneau.

5 Accepting the corrections of Benoist for Moyen Poitou and using the average of Mours's estimates for the province's other two *colloques*, rather than the higher number.

6 Figures for the *colloque* of Aunis corrected on the basis of Louis Perouas, *Le diocèse de la Rochelle de 1648 à 1724: Sociologie et pastorale* (Paris, 1964), esp. 130–3.

7 Modified in light of Lucile Bourrachot, "Démographie et société dans les documents ecclésiastiques du diocèse d'Agen au XVIIe siècle," *Annales du Midi*, LXXVI (1964), 215–22.

8 Splitting the difference between the two censuses of Béarn's Protestant population in 1665, rather than accepting the higher estimates provided by the Reformed church itself. On these, see pp. 71–2.

9 Mours's estimate of 1956, which seems more accurate when checked against his sources than his subsequent evaluation.

10 Figures for the *colloque* of Saint-Germain-de-Calberte corrected on the basis of J.R. Armogathe, "Le diocèse de Mende au 17me siècle. Perspectives d'histoire religieuse," *Revue du Gévaudan*, n. s., XVII (1971), 92.

11 Excluding the principality of Orange but including the Valcluson.

tion of the Edict of Nantes and its Revocation. The first, censuses or other enumerations of Protestant households within a certain area, offers the most convenient, and probably also the most accurate, gauge of the size of individual Huguenot congregations. Such documents are fairly abundant for the years after 1661, when central government surveillance of what the authorities termed the "Religion Prétendue Réformée" intensified. Except for the closely watched towns and regions close to France's eastern border, however, it is uncommon for such estimates to have survived from the earlier part of the century. It is more uncommon still for several such estimates to have survived for a single community at widely spaced dates between 1600 and 1685. For this reason, it has been possible to rely here on census information for only a handful of localities.

By contrast, Protestant vital records provide a far more widely available gauge to the changes which might have occurred in the size of individual Protestant communities between 1600 and 1685. The very first national synod of the French Reformed church, held in 1559, decreed that all congregations of the newly established church should maintain a record of the baptisms and marriages celebrated within them, and the obligation to note burials as well was added in 1584. Although some churches were clearly delinquent about maintaining such registers, although many were lost when the Revocation precipitated the dispersion of the papers belonging to the Reformed churches, and although others have succumbed to the vicissitudes which winnow with time the availability of all historical documents, a large corpus of such registers nonetheless exists today in France's national, departmental, and communal archives and in private hands or libraries in France, Switzerland, and even South Carolina.[7] If these documents are particularly abundant for the years after 1667, when royal legislation dictated new standards for maintaining all parish registers in the kingdom and required copies to be turned over annually to the king's officials, no less than 126 sets of registers stretch back for thirty years or more prior to 1667 and span, albeit often with lacunae, at least four decades of the century. Two other good sets of such registers were destroyed during the Second World War, but the number of acts in them was fortunately counted by scholars who worked before that time. The number of acts in still another lost set can be reconstructed from tables in the community's Catholic parish registers.[8]

Occasionally kept in the same volume as the minutes of the church's

---

[7] Bernard, *Les familles protestantes*, now provides a full guide to these registers. For their history, see B. Faucher, "Les registres de l'état civil protestant en France depuis le XVIe siècle jusqu'à nos jours," *Bibliothèque de l'Ecole des Chartes*, LXXXIV (1923), 304–46; Jacques Fromental, *La Réforme en Bourgogne aux XVIe et XVIIe siècles* (Paris, 1968), 113.

[8] Full references to all archival and printed sources concerning the communities retained for final analysis in this study may be found in the Appendix. The registers destroyed in the Second World War were those of Caen and Saint-Lô, while Loudun's registers must be reconstructed from tables in the city's Catholic registers.

consistorial deliberations, these registers were typically maintained by either the pastor or a lay member of the consistory, often on the basis of "billets" or "cartelz" which the interested parties or designated officials turned over to them following the celebration of a baptism, marriage, or burial.[9] Marginal notations occasionally betray the imprint of Protestant theology and devotional practice. Thus, Bellême's register begins with citations of the Biblical passages relating to baptism, while the keeper of Saint-Jean-du-Gard's register implored, "May God guide my hand."[10] An elder of Rochechouart, a congregation troubled by both internal conflicts and the hostility of the local seigneur, included a passionate prayer for the survival and concord of his church,[11] while the cover of Fraissinet's register is graced by moralizing verses that combine a range of injunctions—use your time well, speak and deal honestly, don't forget your friends, be a gay host—which neatly confound overly simple interpretations of Protestant ethics.[12] Not all of the marginalia is religious in character. The doodling pen of Jean de Castorret of Lagor, the Cassius Clay/Muhammad Ali of scribes, could not refrain from recording, amid elaborate curlicues, "My first time when I wanted to write, I wrote as sweetly as a fly."[13]

---

[9] This can be inferred from marginal comments within the registers themselves.

[10] A.D. Orne, I 43; A.C. Saint-Jean-du-Gard, GG 20. Similar sentiments in A.C. Montpellier, GG 321, "A Dieu seul sage soit honneur et gloire en siecles des siecles"; "Louange a Dieu."

[11] "Mon Seigneur et mon Dieu, mon Createur, mon Redempteur et mon Consolateur, ie te prie de tout mon coeur, pour l'amour de ta gloire et de ton fils nostre Seigneur Jesus, qu'il te plaise de recueillir tousjours en ce lieu une Eglise jusqu'a la fin du monde, par la voix de l'Evangile, donne luy des pasteurs fidelles et un troupeau tout remply de zele et de concorde, principalement en ce qui regarde ta gloire. Beny les Princes et Seigneurs qui maintiennent tes Eglises, et renverse les desseins de ceux qui ont resolu la ruine et la persecution de ton troupeau, et nous fais la grace que nous t'invoquions tousiours en verité, et que nos pensées, nos parolles et nos actions n'ayent autre but que la gloire de ton grand nom par J.C. ton fils nostre Seigneur. Amen."

Bienheureux est quiconques,
Sert à Dieu volontiers.
Et ne se lasse onques
De suyvre ses sentiers.

A.D. Haute-Vienne, Etat civil protestant, Rochechouart, 2nd register.

[12] L'homme se plaint de sa trop court vie
Et cependant n'emploie où il devroit
Le temps qu'il a qui suffice pourroit
Sy pour bien vivre avoit de vivre envie.

Maudit celuy qui fraude la semence
Ou qui retient le salaire promis
Au mercenaire, ou qui de ses amis
Ne se souvient sinon en leur presence.

En ton parler sois toujours véritable
Soit qu'il te failhe en tesmoignage ouir,
Soit que parfois tu veuilhes resjouir
D'un gay propos tes hôtes à table.

B.P.F., MS 422. Other moralizing remarks: "Communement et souverainement tant que un homme a de l'argent il est aymé de toutes gens puis quand son argent est finy on luy dit adieu mon Amy." A.D. Vaucluse, E, Lourmarin. "L'homme n'est pas pleutot né qu'il faut qu'on le Baptise. Lorsqu'il a la connoissance il faut pour lors qu'il faut se disposer pouvoir faire une belle mort." A.C. Montpellier, GG 353.

[13] A.D. Pyrénées-Atlantiques, 4 E 301.

Despite the provisions of the national synods, burial registration is manifestly incomplete or entirely non-existent in the great majority of registers prior to 1667, and it is not uncommon for these registers to omit marriages as well. Although this diminishes the potential of many sets of Protestant vital records as sources for calculating sophisticated demographic statistics, the copious series of baptisms still offer an acceptable source for tracing fluctuations over time in the Protestant population, since changes in the level of baptisms offer a rough guide to the overall trend of the population as a whole—so long as fertility rates or the ratio between births and baptisms did not change markedly over time (possibilities that will be explored in the sections to follow), and so long as the baptisms were recorded continuously and scrupulously.

The best maintained of the Huguenot "parish" registers are unquestionably among the richest and most informative sets of all such records from this early period of the French *état civil*, and the reconstitution of Alençon's population suggests that baptisms within that church were recorded with care. Nonetheless, in reading through certain of the baptismal registers, it is difficult to avoid the suspicion that acts have been overlooked or omitted. In certain cases, it is clear that the normal pattern of celebrating baptisms was interrupted for stretches of several months or even years at a time because of the absence of a pastor. Often in such cases, baptisms were performed at irregular intervals by ministers visiting from nearby localities. Still, we would expect the number of baptisms to be abnormally low in these years since more children would die before they were able to receive the sacrament. Since my goal in this study has been less to achieve a year-by-year count of the number of vital events occurring among France's Huguenots than to assemble the best evidence possible about the overall size of different Protestant congregations at different eras, such years have been omitted from consideration in the calculations which follow.

In other cases, negligent record keeping produced longer periods of deficient registration. Some scribes were considerate enough of future generations to note shortcomings, as did the elder of Saujon who wrote in the margin of his register, "Those hereafter interested in seeking the names of the children baptized . . . since I was received as elder and elected to keep the present baptismal paper shall remain advised that several parties received the sacrament of baptism without being registered for lack of having . . . delivered note of their names and of the said children in conformity with the order."[14] Cases such as these have naturally been eliminated from consideration here for the length of the period for which registration appears incomplete. So too have registers characterized by abnormally large fluctuations in the number of acts from year to year where these fluctuations cannot confidently be ascribed to normal demographic events or political perturbations. But what is one to do with

[14] A.C. Saujon, état civil, culte réformé, fo. 217. Similar explanations of defective or missing registration in A.D. Landes, 1 J 468; L.D.S film 687553 (A.C. Lasalle, GG 13).

registers of smaller churches where the number of acts fluctuates sharply from year to year (something which may simply be a function of their size rather than any deficiencies in registration), or with registers which contain large gaps between acts without the movement of the dates suggesting that registration ceased for a certain period of time? I must admit that I have not been able to develop a hard and fast set of criteria which could be consistently applied to determine deficient registers. Instead, I have tried to remain suitably vigilant about the quality of the registers examined, without being so exigent as to rule out potentially significant information every time the least suspicion about the quality of registration arose. The reliability of certain sets of figures retained for this study is unquestionably less great than that of others.

Beyond these problems in assessing the completeness of individual registers—problems which, it must be admitted, are typical of any study based upon the parish registers of this era—the Huguenot baptismal registers also pose one special problem of interpretation which rarely arises when dealing with other contemporaneous vital records: that of fluctuating boundaries. The limits of most parishes in seventeenth-century Europe were fixed by centuries-old custom and rarely altered. France's Reformed temples, on the other hand, often attracted worshippers from well beyond the immediate locality in which they were located and not infrequently saw a change in the area from which they recruited their members, either as annex churches were created nearby, or, as happened with increasing frequency after 1661, as neighboring temples were closed down for being in violation of the terms of the Edict of Nantes interpreted *à la rigueur.*

Faced with this problem of shifting church boundaries, historians seeking to aggregate information about many such churches can choose one of two courses of action. They may either try to make the data about each church refer to a stable geographic area, by introducing appropriate corrections, or they may accept all the evidence in the raw state in which it has come down to us and assume that in aggregating the information the cases where the number of baptisms has swelled over time because a nearby temple was closed are counterbalanced by others where the series of acts ends because it comes from a temple that was itself closed and where the number of subsequent baptisms may consequently be reckoned as zero. The former course is unquestionably preferable. It makes each individual church or locality an illuminating unit of analysis, while at the same time enabling one to skirt the necessity of determining, for each gap in a church's records, whether the church was closed during the years for which the registers are deficient or whether the gaps derive from the subsequent loss of its records, something which frequently cannot be done on the basis of the surviving evidence. But this methodological choice does mean that one must be able to detect and correct for any changes which might have occurred in the catchment area of the churches studied.

In most cases, this is not difficult. Many of the registers note, at least intermittently, the place of residence of the families bringing their children to be baptized. Where this information indicates that people from a certain locality suddenly began to attend services at a temple which they had not previously frequented, the acts concerning these newcomers can be eliminated so that all figures continue to refer to a fixed geographic area. Where the registers fail to note the parish of residence, striking changes in the number of acts from one year to the next can still serve as a warning that the church's boundaries may have changed. In these cases, histories of Protestantism in the region or the published lists of Reformed churches which existed at different dates in the century often clarify whether or not these changes indeed stemmed from fluctuations in the church's boundaries.[15] Once it has been determined that this was indeed the case, a comparison of the level of baptisms for the five-year periods before and after the neighboring church opened or closed can provide an approximate indication of the magnitude of the change in the number of baptisms induced by this event. The figures can then be corrected accordingly.[16] In certain cases, however, it is simply impossible to determine an accurate correction factor for boundary changes known to have occurred. Such cases have been eliminated from consideration here.[17] Of course, the possibility remains that certain boundary changes may also have gone undetected, particularly in the case of registers which do not record the place of residence of those bringing their children to baptism.

Once all registers marked by apparently deficient registration or uncertain boundary changes have been eliminated from consideration, apparently reliable evidence remains about a sample of 120 geographic entities, or roughly 17 percent of the total number of churches in existence around 1660.[18] Map 1 indicates the location of these communities. As

---

[15] In tracing the fate of different churches, I have relied especially upon the lists of the Protestant churches existing in 1603, 1620, and 1626, and of those closed between 1656 and 1685 in Haag, I, 269–73, 315–34, 378–81; on P. Gachon, *Quelques préliminaires de la Révocation de l'Edit de Nantes en Languedoc (1661–1685)* (Toulouse, 1899); and on the lists of churches sending delegates to provincial synods of the Reformed church to be found in the records of these synodal assemblies, most notably the Auzière collection of the B.P.F.

[16] All such corrections introduced into the raw data are explained in the Appendix.

[17] Registers of the following churches were examined and rejected because of either apparent deficiencies in registration or insurmountable problems in relating the figures to a fixed geographic area: Crocy (Calvados; B.P.F., MS 209 and L.D.S. film 660382 [A.C. Crocy]); Falaise (A.D. Calvados, I 48); Marchenoir-Lorges (A.D. Loir-et-Cher, I 16–30); Mareuil-Bessay (Vendée; Arsenal MS 6553); Chizé (Deux-Sèvres; A.N., TT 241 [2]); Niort (A.D. Deux-Sèvres, 4 E2 202); Aytré (A.D. Charente-Maritime, I 88–101); La Tremblade (A.D. Charente-Maritime, I 140); Saujon (Charente-Maritime; A.C. Saujon, état civil, culte réformé); Montagnac-sur-Auvignon (Lot-et-Garonne; A.D. Gers, Archives de l'Hospice de Condom, H 27); Labastide d'Armagnac (A.D. Landes, I J 468); Sarpourenx (A.C. at A.D. Pyrénées-Atlantiques, "Protestants"); Mazamet (Tarn; A.C. Mazamet, GG 13bis–14bis); Pranles-Tournon (L.D.S. film 1069214 [A.D. Ardèche, 5 E 90–93]); Pont-de-Veyle (A.C. at A.D. Ain; A.D. Ain, Archives de l'Hôpital de Pont-de-Veyle, C 5; A.D. Ain, 2 E 30602); and Reyssouze (A.D. Ain, Archives de l'Hôpital de Pont-de-Veyle, C 5; A.D. Ain, 2 E 32301).

[18] The percentage is approximate and the term "geographic entities" used advisedly, since not all of the entities analyzed are similar in nature. Most of the evidence concerns individual churches, which of course recruited members from more than a single local-

MAP 1. Congregations and Localities Examined in this Study

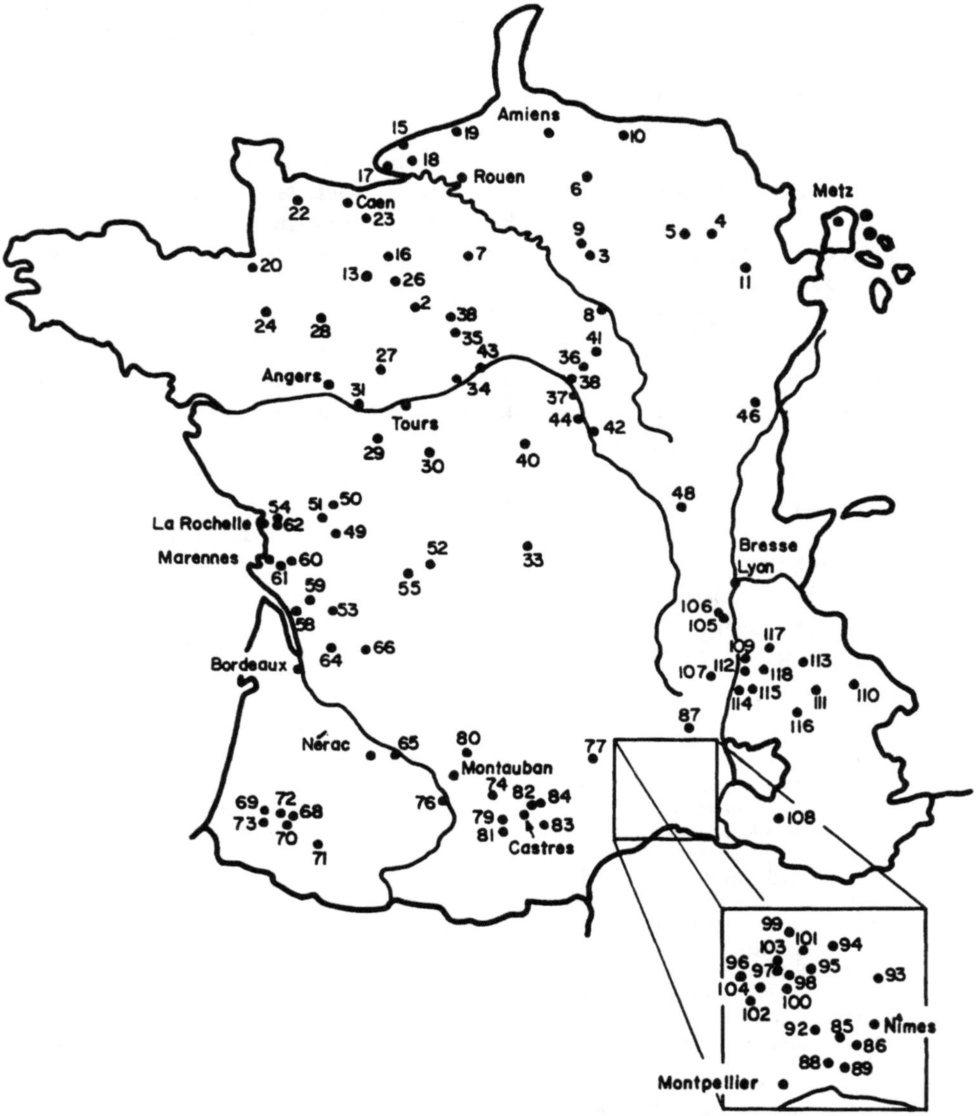

MAP 1. Congregations and Localities Examined in this Study

KEY

Localities arranged by synod.
The numbers refer to the map on the facing page.

Ile-de-France–Champagne–Picardy
Amiens
2 Authon-du-Perche
3 Chalandos
4 Châlons-sur-Marne
5 Chaltrait
6 Compiègne
7 Fontaine-sous-Prémont
8 Landreville
9 Meaux-Nanteuil
10 Saint-Quentin-Lehaucourt
11 Wassy
[Metz]

Normandy
13 Alençon
Caen
15 Fécamp
16 Laigle
17 Le Havre
18 Lintot
19 Luneray
20 Pontorson-Cormeray
Rouen
22 Saint-Lô
23 Saint-Pierre-sur-Dives

Brittany
24 Vitré

Anjou–Touraine–Maine
Angers
26 Bellême
27 Château-du-Loir
28 Laval
29 Loudun
30 Preuilly-sur-Claise
31 Saumur
Tours

Orléanais–Berry
33 Aubusson
34 Blois
35 Châteaudun
36 Châtillon-sur-Loing
37 Châtillon-sur-Loire
38 Dangeau
39 Gien
40 Issoudun
41 La Celle-Saint-Cyr-Dollot
42 La Charité
43 Mer
44 Sancerre

Burgundy
Bailliage de Bresse
46 Is-sur-Tille
Lyon
48 Paray-le-Monial

Poitou
49 Chef-Boutonne
50 La-Mothe-Saint-Héray-Exoudun
51 Mougon
52 Rochechouart

Aunis–Saintonge–Angoumous
53 Barbézieux
54 Dompierre-Bourgneuf
55 La Rochefoucauld
La Rochelle
Marennes
58 Mortagne-sur-Gironde
59 Pons
60 Saint-Jean-d'Angle
61 Saint-Just
62 Salles

Basse-Guyenne
Bordeaux
64 Coutras
65 Layrac
66 Mussidan
Nérac

Béarn
68 Arthez
69 Bellocq
70 Lagor
71 Nay
72 Orthez
73 Salies

Haute-Guyenne–Haut-Languedoc
74 Briatexte
Castres
76 Mas-Grenier
77 Millau
Montauban
79 Puylaurens
80 Réalville-Albias
81 Revel
82 Roquecourbe
83 Saint-Amans
84 Vabre

Bas-Languedoc
85 Aigues-Vives
86 Codognan
87 Les Vans
88 Lunel
89 Marsillargues
Montpellier
Nîmes
92 Sommières
93 Uzès

Cévennes
94 Alès
95 Anduze
96 Aulas
97 Lasalle
98 Monoblet
99 Saint-Etienne-Vallée-Française
100 Saint-Hippolyte-du-Fort
101 Saint-Jean-du-Gard
102 Saint-Laurent-le-Minier
103 Soudorgues
104 Sumène

Vivarais
105 Annonay
106 Boulieu
107 Privas

Provence
108 Lourmarin

Dauphiné
109 Beaumont-lès-Valence
110 Embrun
111 Gap
112 Loriol
113 Mens-en-Trièves
114 Montélimar
115 Montjoux
116 Orpierre
117 Pont-en-Royans
118 Vercheny

can be seen, the sample communities are scattered across the breadth of the country with the exception of the northern and central Massif Central and the Breton peninsula, where Protestantism never took deep root. Every one of the sixteen *provinces synodaux* into which the French Reformed churches were grouped is represented by at least one church, as are 51 of the 61 *colloques* into which the churches were further sub-divided.[19]

Despite the extensive geographic spread of this evidence, the surviving evidence does not constitute a perfect sample of the universe of Protestant churches existing in the seventeenth century. At least three biases can be detected. First, and most important, records of urban congregations are considerably more likely to have come down to us than those of rural churches; the survival rate for rural baptismal records is particularly poor in the Midi and Center-West. As a result, the sample contains 46 percent of the churches located in the larger cities of northern France, 36 percent of those in its smaller cities, and 20 percent of its rural churches, while for the Midi and Center-West the comparable figures are 38, 38, and 9 percent respectively. Since urban-rural and North-South differences were highly significant, the analysis to follow will examine the churches of each broad community type and region separately before combining the results obtained in a manner which accords due weight to the relative importance of each category.

Second, the sample is particularly thin in evidence about certain smaller regions of Protestant strength, most notably the Pays de Gex, the heartland of the Protestant Vivarais around the valley of the Ardèche, and the entire synod of Basse-Guyenne. To judge by the broader regional patterns which will emerge in the subsequent pages, it seems unlikely that this substantially skews the results obtained, but readers should keep this pattern in mind in evaluating the evidence presented.

Finally, as might be expected, there is a clear tendency toward disproportionate survival of records from the larger and more important churches within each category. Assuming that the total population of the churches in the sample can be estimated by multiplying the number of baptisms in the urban and small town churches by 25, the number of baptisms in the rural churches by 30, and the number of families or hearths in census data by 4.5—all standard assumptions about this period that will be used throughout this work—it can be computed that fully 25 percent of the estimated total Protestant population of 1660–70 lived in the sample localities, even though these represented only 17 percent of the

---

ity. In certain cases, the analysis bears only upon a stable sub-unit of the full geographic region served by a given church. Where the available evidence is composed of census data, the figures refer to the population living within a given bailliage or town. Finally, in two cases (Metz and Saint-Quentin-Lehaucourt), I have analyzed separately the rural and urban dwellers of a single church.

[19] The *colloques* which are not represented in the sample are those of the Pays de Gex, Bas Poitou, Saint-Jean-d'Angély, Haut Agenais, Vic-Bihl, Oloron, Haut Quercy, Pays de Foix, Baronnies, and Valcluson.

TABLE 3. Percentage Decline in Baptismal Levels to 1660–70 by Size of Church

<table>
<tr><th rowspan="2">Character of Church</th><th colspan="4">Estimated Size of Church in Earliest Period for which Data Available</th></tr>
<tr><th><500</th><th>500–1,000</th><th>1,001–1,500</th><th>>1,500</th></tr>
<tr><td>Rural</td><td>−11%</td><td>−13%</td><td>−10%</td><td>−18%</td></tr>
<tr><td>n</td><td>(15)</td><td>(9)</td><td>(20)</td><td>(16)</td></tr>
<tr><td>Small Town</td><td>−31%</td><td>−18%</td><td>−11%</td><td>−25%</td></tr>
<tr><td>n</td><td>(7)</td><td>(3)</td><td>(3)</td><td>(16)</td></tr>
<tr><td>Big Town</td><td colspan="2">−5%</td><td>−11%</td><td>−36%</td></tr>
<tr><td>n</td><td colspan="2">(9)</td><td>(5)</td><td>(14)</td></tr>
<tr><td>Overall</td><td>−7%</td><td>−16%</td><td>−10%</td><td>−30%</td></tr>
<tr><td></td><td>(26)</td><td>(17)</td><td>(28)</td><td>(46)</td></tr>
</table>

NOTE: For precise details of how these figures have been computed, see pp. 28–9.

number of churches existing at the time.[20] The increased likelihood of survival of records from the larger churches introduces a degree of bias into the sample, since, as Table 3 reveals, the largest congregations tended to experience a greater decline in size over the course of the period analyzed here than did the smaller ones. The sample will thus exaggerate slightly the extent of Protestantism's decline over these years. The extent of this distortion is small.[21]

C. Precocious "Malthusianism"?

As has already been suggested, the method which our sources oblige us to adopt to trace changes in the size of many congregations, that of following the movement of baptisms within them, is reliable only if the ratio between the number of baptisms and the total membership of these churches remained relatively constant over time. Some investigation of possible changes in this ratio is thus clearly necessary before we turn to look at the movement of baptisms in our sample communities. This means seeing first of all whether or not the Huguenots began to practice birth control on a large scale in this period, for if they did, this would sharply depress the number of acts in the baptismal registers even in the absence of any dropoff in the total Protestant population.

Reason certainly exists to suspect that France's Protestants might have begun to control their fertility in the seventeenth century. Jean-Pierre

---

20 The estimated percentage of the total population in 1660–70 breaks down by category as follows:

N. big cities: 47 percent	S. big cities: 60 percent
N. small towns: 48 percent	S. small towns: 51 percent
N. rural: 31 percent	S. rural: 11 percent

21 The extent of the distortion may be estimated by introducing a correction factor into the back-projection of the total Protestant population that accords the churches of below average size within each category sufficient additional weight so that the average size of the sample churches becomes equal to the average size of all churches within each category. Such a correction reduces the unweighted estimate of the total Protestant population ca. 1600–10 by 1.4 percent.

Bardet has recently shown conclusively that French towndwellers began to practice family limitation on a significant scale from the end of the century onward, while Alfred Perrenoud has demonstrated that Protestant regions of Switzerland were more precocious than Catholic ones in adopting such practices in early modern times, a development which he attributes to the Reformers' more positive evaluation of marital sexuality, which in their estimation need not aim strictly at procreation.[22] Furthermore, sociologists of contemporary societies have observed that religious minorities which are objects of discrimination often have fewer children than their neighbors of the dominant faith.[23] Indeed, one local study of a Norman Protestant community, finding a declining ratio of baptisms to marriages in the years prior to 1685, has already suggested that the Huguenots began to limit family size as the Revocation approached.[24]

The best evidence, however, indicates clearly that France's Huguenots were not pioneers in birth control. In his massive study of the Rouennais population, Bardet examined the behavior of that city's sizeable Protestant minority and found only a slight difference in fertility between Protestants and Catholics. The typical couple married between 1640 and 1669 within the Roman church could expect to bear 7.32 children over the course of a life together unbroken by the death of either partner prior to age 45. The comparable figure for Protestants married between 1640 and 1685 was 7.14. By way of comparison, the probable number of offspring of a Catholic couple married in the middle of the eighteenth century, when birth control practices had spread, was just 5.44 children.[25] Similarly, Brigitte Maillard's reconstitution of Tours's Protestant families finds extremely high age-specific fertility rates and very short intervals between the birth of successive children into the 1670s.[26] My own family reconstitution study of Alençon's Protestant community, an elite urban congregation, likewise reveals none of the signs historical demographers have developed to detect the practice of family limitation within marriage, even in the period after 1661, when royal policy toward the Huguenots became harsher and Bollon suggests that birth control practices began to spread as a consequence. Women marrying young did not cease bearing children markedly earlier than those marrying later in life, the

[22] Bardet, *Rouen*, I, 263–88; Perrenoud, "Malthusianisme et protestantisme: un modèle démographique wéberien," *Annales: E.S.C.*, XXIX (1974), 975–88. For more on the views of the leading Protestant theologians and their relationship to earlier Catholic teachings about sex, see James Brundage, *Law, Sex and Christian Society in Medieval Europe* (Chicago, 1988), 447–53, 551–3, 555–7.

[23] Calvin Goldscheider and Peter R. Uhlenberg, "Minority Group Status and Fertility," *American Journal of Sociology*, LXXIV (1969), 360–72. Specifically, the authors argue that this is the case where the group facing discrimination shares the values of the larger society and seeks the advancement of its children within it. Groups rejecting the culture of the larger society may become more concerned with group preservation and quantitative strength and hence seek to have more children. Clearly, the situation of the Huguenots most closely approximates the former case, although we have seen that their official spokesmen also shared elements of the latter attitude.

[24] Gérard Bollon, "Minorité broyée et Malthusianisme: Saint-Sylvain-Falaise-Saint-Pierre-sur-Dives au XVIIe siècle," *B.S.H.P.F.*, CXVI (1970), 489–508.

[25] Bardet, *Rouen*, I, 271 and 276.

[26] Maillard, "Religion et démographie," 550–6.

spacing between births did not increase abnormally as women approached the birth of their last child, and age-specific fertility was quite high, the reflection of a prosperous urban population that probably put a large percentage of its infants out to wetnurse and was not consciously controlling fertility.[27] Since it is known that family limitation began to be

[27] In carrying out this family reconstitution study, as in all demographic calculations throughout this study, I have followed the methods developed by Louis Henry. Those unfamiliar with the technical aspects of historical demography will find a good discussion of them in the classic monograph of Etienne Gautier and Henry, *La population de Crulai, paroisse normande: Etude historique* (Paris, 1958), which may be usefully supplemented by Michel Fleury and Louis Henry, *Nouveau manuel de dépouillement et d'exploitation de l'état civil ancien* (Paris, 1965) and Henry, *Manuel de démographie historique* (Geneva, 1967). Since the techniques of family reconstitution depend upon knowing the birth dates of a group of women and then being able to follow them through the full course of their child-bearing years, full demographic statistics can only be calculated for Alençon for couples married between 1635 and 1661. (Alençon's Protestant registers begin only in 1616; they end, of course, in 1685.) This sample yields 84 "type I" families, that is to say, families for which both the wife's date of birth and the date when the couple was broken by the death of one spouse or the other is known with certainty. The following tables present the results of this investigation alongside comparable statistics concerning nearby Catholic populations and the Genevan bourgeoisie of the eighteenth century, a group known to have been practicing birth control.

Mean Age at Last Birth (Women Surviving to Age 45)

		Comparable Figures	
		Genevan bourgeoisie	Tourouvre-au-Perche
Age at Marriage			
15–19	38 (n=4)	30.9	38.4
20–24	38.1 (n=15)	33.3	40.2
25–29	39.1 (n=15)	37.4	40.0
30–34	42.3 (n=15)	38.8	39.8

Age Specific Fertility

Age at Marriage	15–19	20–24	25–29	30–34	35–39	40–44
15–19 (n=15)	(.297)	.514	.406	.347	(.169)	(.125)
20–24 (n=31)	–	.590	.385	.335	.296	.128
25–29 (n=19)	–	–	.489	.446	.328	.179
30–34 (n=13)	–	–	–	(.543)	.773	(.300)
35–39 (n=5)	–	–	–	–	(.413)	
All Ages (n=83)	(.297)	.549	.411	.391	.384	.179
Comparable Figures, All Ages:						
Paris Basin	.375	.465	.431	.383	.307	.157
Bayeux, 1640–1700	.333	.414	.404	.381	.367	.070
Geneva bourgeoisie	.383	.450	.434	.308	.181	.078

Mean Intervals Between Births
(Families of 6 or More Children, in Months)

	1–2	2–3	3–4	4–5	5–6	6–7	ante-penult.	penult.	last
	17.2	22.4	23.4	25.1	21.8	26.2	22.6	27.8	32.1
Comparable figures:									
Geneva bourgeoisie	20	20	20.7	23.5			25	30.9	40.7
Crulai	22.4	25.3	27.2	28.6			28.7	30.9	33

SOURCES FOR COMPARISONS: Alfred Perrenoud, "Variables sociales en démographie urbaine: l'exemple de Genève au XVIIIe siècle," in *Démographie urbaine, XVe–XXe siècle* (Lyon, 1977), 154, 160–1; Hubert Charbonneau, *Tourouvre-au-Perche aux XVIIe et XVIIIe siècles: Etude de démographie historique* (Paris, 1970), 141; Jacques Dupâquier, *La population rurale du Bassin parisien à l'époque de Louis XIV* (Paris, 1979), 353–5; Gautier and Henry, *Crulai*, 141.

For the period after 1661, when royal policy toward the Huguenots became harsher and Bollon suggests that birth control practices began to spread as a consequence, Protestant widely practiced far earlier in France's cities than in the surrounding countryside, and that Normandy was a region of particularly precocious "Malthusianism," the lack of evidence of birth control practices within these congregations argues powerfully against the hypothesis that any decline in the baptisms celebrated in the Protestant churches to be examined here might have stemmed from the conscious limitation of marital fertility within this increasingly beleaguered minority group. And yet, a declining ratio of baptisms to marriages can also be detected in both Alençon's and Rouen's Protestant communities in the years prior to 1685.[28] This appears to have been due to the increase in both emigration and conversion among young couples in prime child-bearing age during the years immediately prior to the Revocation.[29]

D. Other Factors Affecting the Level of Baptisms

While France's Protestants do not seem to have begun to limit their marital fertility significantly before 1685, other developments can be observed whose effect would have been to alter slightly the relationship between recorded baptisms and the total size of the Huguenot community. The first concerns the changing delay between birth and baptism—a

---

fertility is harder to measure because the registers cease in 1685. Again, however, it appears unlikely that the Huguenots were practicing family limitation. One highly atypical group of 33 type I families married after 1661, primarily spouses wed late in life or couples broken early by the death of one partner, can be reconstituted following standard criteria. To supplement this sample, all cases of couples whose child-bearing career was interrupted *in medias res* by the Revocation have also been reconstituted. Such a sample obviously cannot be used to calculate age at last birth, but it does reveal birth intervals that were even shorter than those found in the pre-1661 cohort:

Mean Interval Between Births among Alençon's Protestants,
Two Generations Compared

	1–2	2–3	3–4	4–5	5–6	6–7
Cohort married 1635–61	17.2	22.4	23.4	25.1	21.8	26.2
Cohort married 1661–85	18.1	17.3	22.6	18.2	20	21
Cases:	(35)	(35)	(28)	(20)	(18)	(14)

Age-specific fertility was slightly lower than in the earlier cohort, but this results primarily from an abnormally large percentage of totally infertile couples.

Age Specific Fertility among Alençon's Protestants,
Two Generations Compared
(All ages at marriage combined)

	15–19	20–24	25–29	30–34	35–39	40–44
Cohort married 1635–61	(.297)	.549	.411	.391	.384	.179
Cohort married 1661–85	(.194)	.405	.425	.405	.357	.235

Cases: 63.

[28] Ratio of Baptisms to Marriages

Rouen		Alençon	
1630–59	5.33:1	1626–60	4.64:1
1660–85	4.88:1	1661–85	4.39:1

[29] See pp. 44–5, 48. Using the records of Châtillon-sur-Loire, Gueneau, "Protestants du Centre," 244, shows a significant increase in the average age of those receiving burial in the years just prior to the Revocation.

topic whose examination also exemplifies how parish register evidence can speak to questions of religious behavior and practice.

From the late Middle Ages onward, the Catholic church placed great emphasis on the absolute necessity of baptism as a precondition for salvation. Church synods urged the faithful to be sure that the sacrament was administered as quickly as possible after birth, lest newborns die without receiving it and be barred from having their bodies buried in hallowed ground. The extent to which concern about the danger of allowing babies to die unbaptized came to be shared among the faithful is attested by the multiplication of "sanctuaires à répit," shrines which became celebrated for their power to effect a miraculous resuscitation of stillborn babies long enough for them to receive the sacrament.[30] Early Catholic parish registers that note the date of both birth and baptism generally reveal the majority of newborns to have been baptized within twenty-four hours, although the sense of urgency was less great in the Midi.[31]

The Reformation, of course, marked a rupture with the Catholic doctrine that baptism was absolutely necessary for salvation. In Protestant dogma, baptism was a token of future mercy and a symbol of initiation into the community, not a *sine qua non* of redemption. According to decisions taken at early national synods of the Reformed church and reiterated consistently thereafter, parents were not to imitate their Catholic neighbors and call upon a clergyman or, in extremis, the wet-nurse to baptize their newborn as soon as possible, but were to wait until a regularly scheduled church assembly to present the infant for the sacrament before the entire congregation. But this was an element of Protestant doctrine which clearly encountered resistance among converts to the new faith, for throughout the later sixteenth century and into the first third of the seventeenth, local and national synods of the French Reformed church took up issues raised by the requests of parents to allow their newborns to be baptized at times or places other than the twice- or thrice-weekly services at the temple.[32]

---

[30] Jacques Gélis, "La mort et le salut spirituel du nouveau-né. Essai d'analyse et d'interpretation du 'sanctuaire à répit' (XVe–XIXe s.)," *Revue d'Histoire Moderne et Contemporaine*, XXXI (1984), 361–76; Jeanne Ferté, *La vie religieuse dans les campagnes parisiennes 1622–1695* (Paris, 1962), 294–300; Jacques Toussaert, *Le sentiment religieux en Flandre à la fin du Moyen Age* (Paris, 1963), 90–2.

[31] For studies of seventeenth-century Catholic parish registers that compute the median delay between birth and baptism and reveal a majority of newborns baptized within a day after birth, see Marcel Lachiver, *La population de Meulan du XVIIe au XIXe siècle (vers 1600–1870): Etude de démographie historique* (Paris, 1969), 70; Ferté, *Vie religieuse dans les campagnes parisiennes*, 300; and Denise Turrel, *Bourg-en-Bresse au 16e siècle: les hommes et la ville* (Paris, 1986), 18. Since the great pioneers of demographic studies on the basis of parish register evidence, Louis Henry and Pierre Goubert, both declared that the registers they had looked at showed the overwhelming majority of children baptized almost immediately after birth, it has become so axiomatic within French historical demography that this was the rule that most French local parish register studies do not even compute birth-baptism intervals. But cf. John Bossy, *Christianity in the West 1400–1700* (Oxford, 1985), 14, whose suggestion that "tomorrow would usually do" for baptizing newborns in southern Europe appears to be confirmed by the evidence to be presented in the paragraphs to follow.

[32] Jean Aymon, *Tous les Synodes Nationales des Eglises Réformées de France* (The Hague,

While the synodal records testify to the survival of concern about the urgency of baptism, the baptismal registers suggest that, by the seventeenth century, the great majority of Huguenots accepted the church's rules about the sacrament. In my admittedly hasty reading of numerous Protestant baptismal registers, I noticed just one entry which indicates an emergency baptism in violation of the decisions of the national synod: the "presentation" to Laval's church of a newborn girl of noble parentage who had already been baptized by "a pastor of the Roman church, in fear for her death." The alibi offered was that this was the doing of the family's servants.[33] More tellingly, the average delays between birth and baptism that can be calculated from the registers indicate, with just one exception, that by the seventeenth century a broad willingness had taken hold within Protestant ranks to wait a half a week or more before the administration of the sacrament. Over the first two-thirds of the century, furthermore, the trend was to wait longer and longer before baptism.

Only a fraction of all Huguenot baptismal registers note the date of both birth and baptism, and then often for brief periods only. The first register to do so, that of Gien for the years 1570–71 and 1580–81, reveals a median delay of 2.5 days between the two events.[34] Table 4 marshals evidence about this question from the reign of Henry IV onward. During the period 1595–1633, the interval most commonly ranged between 4 and 7 days north of a line running from Bordeaux to Lyon and between 5 and 17 days south of that line, although in Niort in 1628—a time of civil war and thus heightened inter-confessional tension—the majority of the faithful had their newborns baptized within twenty-four hours. By the middle third of the century, the median delay had increased to 3–11 days across northern and central France, to 10–29 days across most of the Midi, and had attained fully 34 days in Saint-Etienne-Vallée-Française, in the upper reaches of the Cévennes. Although information is available for the same church in both of these periods for just four cases, the trend was for the median delay to increase in three of them. Interestingly, a similar willingness to postpone baptism can be detected among the Catholics living in heavily Protestant regions in the later seventeenth century as well. In Marennes, Nérac, Montpellier, and Lodève, the median delay between birth and baptism for children born to Catholic parents ranged between 5 and 9 days in the 1660s and 1670s.[35] By contrast, the figure

---

1710), 19, 446–57; Paul de Félice, *Les Protestants d'autrefois*, 3 vols. (Paris, 1897–99), I, 182–6; Fromental, *La Réforme en Bourgogne*, 91; Janine Garrisson-Estèbe, *Protestants du Midi, 1559–1598* (Toulouse, 1980), 247–8; Gueneau, "Protestants du Centre," 262.

[33] André Joubert, *Histoire de l'Eglise réformée de Laval* (Laval, 1889), 68. While this was the only such case I encountered, I should stress that my chief concern in working through the baptismal registers was always to count the number of acts quickly and accurately. I did not read every entry closely.

[34] B.P.F., Ms 1082 (1). *n* = 122.

[35] For Marennes, median delay 9 days 1668 (n=120; A.C. Marennes, état civil, St. Pierre-de-Salles); Nérac median delay 5 days 1671–72 (n=89; L.D.S. film 730822); Montpellier median delay 7.5 days 1664 (n=376; A.C. Montpellier, GG 16); Lodève median delay 7 days 1670 (n=141; Mireille Laget, "La naissance aux siècles classiques. Pratique

TABLE 4. Intervals Between Birth and Baptism

	Evidence from 1590–1633	Evidence from 1634–67	Evidence from 1667–85
A. Median delay between birth and baptism			
Amiens	1624–6: 7 days (n = 132)		
Bellême		1639–50: 3 days (n = 117)	
Châlons-s/Marne	1612–15: 5 days (n = 98)	1641–3: 4 days (n = 71)	
Pont-de-Veyle	1604–6: 5 days (n = 97)		
Mougon	1603: 6 days (n = 151)		1677–8: 7 days (n = 148)
Niort	1628: 1 day (n = 104)		
Rochechouart	1605–8: 4 days (n = 104)		
Saujon		1640–41: 11 days (n = 105)	
Anduze	1609–11: 17 days (n = 587)	1656–60: 29 days (n = 786)	1682–83: 7 days (n = 286)
Briatexte	1595–99: 5 days (n = 55)	1654–59: 24 days (n = 44)	
Labastide d'Armagnac	1616–22: 19 days (n = 101)		
Mas-Grenier		1637–41: 10 days (n = 81)	
Mens-en-Trièves	1618–24: 10 days (n = 100)		
Montagnac-sur-Auvignon	1610–40: 8 days (n = 105)		
Montpellier	1613: 7.5 days (n = 357)		
Orpierre		1633–5: 10.5 days (n = 112)	
Saint-Etienne-Vallée-Française		1634–7: 34 days (n = 103)	
B. Percentage of Newborns Baptized Within First Week of Life			
La Rochelle	1626–30: 86%	1661–5: 61%	1681–4: 90%
Saint-Jean-du-Gard		1663–7: 16%	1681–4: 56%

SOURCES: La Rochelle—Katherine L.M. Faust, "A Beleaguered Society: Protestant Families in La Rochelle, 1628–1685" (Ph.D. dissertation, Northwestern University, 1980), 33, 46; Saint-Jean-du-Gard—Didier Poton, *Saint-Jean-de-Gardonnenque. Une communauté réformée à la veille de la Révocation (1663–1685)* (n.p., 1985), 23. All others—as given in note 30 or Appendix.

des accouchements et attitudes collectives en France au XVIIe et XVIIIe siècles," *Annales: E.S.C.*, XXXII [1977], 965); Carcassonne median delay 2 days 1684 (n=131; L.D.S. film 1217814); Narbonne median delay 2 days 1661–66 (n=106; L.D.S. film 1175673). In Agen, the median delay was 4 days in 1670–72 in the parish of St. Caprasy (n=104; L.D.S. film 786940).

was just two days in such strongholds of Languedocian Catholicism as Carcassonne and Narbonne. The Protestants' more casual attitude toward prompt baptism appears to have been communicated to their Catholic neighbors in regions where the Protestants set the tone.

Then, in the years just prior to 1685, the trend for the Protestants to wait longer to bring their children for baptism reversed itself, as Louis XIV permitted stronger measures to be taken against the heretics. No matter how much the behavior of ordinary Catholics might have been modified by the Protestant example, the Huguenots' willingness to postpone the baptism of their newborns for a week or longer appeared to certain devout members of the Roman church to betoken a dismaying lack of concern for the fate of their newborns' souls. In several parts of the country, forcible Catholic baptisms were administered to sickly Huguenot newborns or to infants who had not received a church baptism.[36] To prevent their children from receiving such unwanted baptisms "à la papaulté," Protestant parents began to bring their infants to the temple for christening far more expeditiously, and Reformed synods even took up once again the issue of whether private baptisms at home might be permissible. As can be seen, the median delay between birth and baptism in Anduze fell to 7 days in 1682–83, where it had attained 29 days in 1656–60. Where more than twenty percent of all that community's families had waited over two months before having their newborns baptized in this earlier period, less than one percent now did so. Similarly, the percentage of Protestant newborns baptized within a week now rose from 16 to 56 percent in nearby Saint-Jean-du-Gard, and from 61 to 90 percent in La Rochelle.

One might wonder if the fluctuations just revealed concerned exclusively those newborns who appeared healthy and consequently able to survive a wait of several days or weeks before baptism. Perhaps sickly babies were always rushed off to the sacrament at the first available opportunity, even while the ceremony was delayed for more robust ones. Alençon's excellent burial registers show that this may have been the case early in the seventeenth century, but that by the middle of the century it was not so. (See Table 5.) Increasingly, the town's Huguenots were willing to see offspring of theirs die without baptism. One result of this, of course, would have been that a small but growing fraction of births would go unrecorded in Protestant registers of baptism. The increase in this percentage observable in Table 5 corresponds with what could be deduced from theoretical calculations from the era's demographic rates. Given the high rates of infant mortality prevailing at the time and the particular vulnerability of newborn babies to disease, each additional week of delay between birth and baptism should have added from one to three percent to the ranks of those newborns who would be expected to die

---

[36] Katherine L.M. Faust, "A Beleaguered Society: Protestant Families in la Rochelle, 1628–1685 (Ph.D. dissertation, Northwestern University, 1980), 40–51. This valuable dissertation contains a great deal of demographic information.

TABLE 5. Recorded Cases of Burial of Unbaptized Infants in Alençon, 1626–85

Years	Cases	Cases as per cent of total baptisms
1626–46	3	0.2%
1647–67	13	1.2%
1668–85	5	0.8%

before baptism.[37] The gradual internalization of a Protestant understanding of baptism revealed by the evidence of birth-baptism delays was thus a development that could have accounted for a decline of one or more percentage points in the number of baptisms recorded in the Reformed church's records between 1600 and 1670, even in the absence of any other changes in the size of the community.

While the tendency to postpone baptism for longer periods of time was an exclusively Protestant phenomenon, broader changes in marriage behavior that were occurring throughout France in this era would also have reduced with time the ratio of baptisms to total population. Numerous demographic studies have shown a tendency for young people in most, although not all, regions of France to postpone marriage until a slightly later age over the course of the century.[38] Since calculating age at first marriage accurately requires a lengthy process of record linkage, I have explored this question for just one Protestant community, Alençon. (See Table 6.) In this city, the increase which occurred was so modest among women that one hesitates to place too much weight on the finding. Nevertheless, the tendency for the age of first marriage to increase among women appears to have been general enough in France in this era for one to suspect that a similar evolution occurred in many Protestant communities in this period, especially when it is recalled that the Huguenots faced increasing difficulties in establishing themselves in many crafts as the century progressed.

TABLE 6. Mean Age at First Marriage among Alençon's Protestants

	1645–67		1668–85	
	men	women	men	women
	27.5	25.7	28.8	26.1
Cases	(85)	(125)	(48)	(53)

[37] Calculated on the basis of the mortality rates presented in Lachiver, *La population de Meulan*, 197.

[38] The best summary of the evidence is to be found in Jean-Louis Flandrin, *Familles: Parenté, maison, sexualité dans l'ancienne société* (Paris, 1976), 183. Cf. Alain Croix, *La Bretagne aux 16e et 17e siècles: La vie, la mort, la foi* (Paris, 1981), 194, for a region unaffected by this trend.

At the same time, in what was almost certainly a related development, there is evidence that the percentage of women who never married also increased in this period, at least in the towns. Katherine Faust has documented such a trend among the Protestants of La Rochelle, where the percentage of never-married women among those dying at age 40 or above increased from 1.3 percent in 1636–60 to 6.9 percent between 1661 and 1683.[39] A similar trend emerges in predominantly Catholic Rouen, and an increase in the number of unmarried female heads of household can be detected in Dijon's tax rolls.[40] Both of these developments, of course, would have had the effect of depressing gross fertility rates.

For three reasons, then, the movement of baptisms over time exaggerates slightly the fall which occurred in France's Huguenot population between 1600 and 1685. The evidence is not extensive enough to permit the calculation of a precise correction factor to compensate for the distortions introduced by such trends.

E. The Pattern of Decline

Having explored the nature and limitations of the available evidence, it is now time to see what it suggests about the fate of the individual congregations comprising the sample and the movement of France's Huguenot population as a whole between the Edict of Nantes and its Revocation. As has already been explained, the congregations in the sample have been divided into categories according to their geographic location and the size of the localities from which they drew their members. To make comparisons possible between a large number of churches for which the data often cover quite different years within the period 1600–1685, the dates from 1660 to 1670 have been taken as the standard point of reference for all churches. These years are those for which data exist for the largest number of churches. Their use also facilitates comparisons with the overall figures on the Protestant population derived from Mours.

For each church, a base index was computed using the average number of annual baptisms celebrated in those years between 1660 and 1670 for which evidence was available. Where no figures were available for these years but data survive from the decades both preceding and following them, a straight-line method of extrapolation was used to calculate the base index. Where figures were available only for years either preceding or following 1660–70, these figures were extrapolated forward or backward to the base period on the assumption that the church evolved along the same lines as the constellation of nearby congregations closest to it in character and location. In the case of those churches whose evolution is known from censuses rather than the movement of bap-

---

39 Faust, "Beleaguered Society," 229.

40 Bardet, *Rouen*, I, 322; James R. Farr, "Consumers, commerce, and the craftsmen of Dijon: The changing social and economic structure of a provincial capital, 1450–1750," in Philip Benedict, ed., *Cities and Social Change in Early Modern France* (London, 1989), 158. Bardet does not analyze the rates of permanent celibacy by confession.

tisms, the population estimates have been transformed into an approximate level of baptisms using the standard assumptions of 4.5 people per household and a birth rate of 40 o/oo. For each congregation, the base index was then compared against the average number of baptisms per year in the earliest period of the century for which reliable figures have survived in order to measure the community's evolution over the course of the years prior to 1660–70, and all of the cases within each category have been aggregated to calculate the overall movement of the churches within the category. Similarly, any surviving figures from the 1670s and 1680s have been compared with the base index to calculate the evolution over the last fifteen years of the period of legal toleration. To obtain a rough indication of shorter-term trends within each category prior to 1660–70, decade-to-decade comparisons have also been made, using figures from all those congregations for which data are available for at least three years of each decade being compared and extrapolating figures for the remaining congregations for which the evidence suffers from larger gaps according to the most probable assumptions about each church's evolution in light of what is known about its history.

Analyzed in this fashion, the data reveal significant variations, not only between the churches of northern France and those located in the Midi and Center-West, but also among those situated within each half of the kingdom. In view of the complexity of the pattern, the evidence will be examined here initially by category and region, before the results obtained are combined to estimate the overall evolution of the Huguenot population. Readers interested in following the fate of individual congregations in even greater detail are referred to the Appendix, where annual figures and decennial averages are provided for each congregation.

i. Northern France

Throughout northern France, the Huguenots generally comprised a small and powerless minority. To be sure, the congregations of certain major provincial cities, notably Metz, Caen, and Dieppe, still counted their members in the thousands and comprised a significant fraction of the total city population; a few smaller towns in Western France or along the Loire (e.g., Saumur, Loudun, Jargeau) were Huguenot *places de sûreté;* and scattered concentrations of rural Protestants could be found in regions such as Normandy's Pays de Caux, parts of the Blésois, or the formerly Genevan Pays de Gex. For the most part, however, the urban congregations had seen their numbers greatly reduced by persecution and violence from the levels attained during the first flush of Protestant expansion in the 1560s—such proud centers of Huguenot strength during the First Civil War as Lyon and Orléans now housed a thousand Protestants or less—while few rural or small town congregations had ever extended their membership much beyond the local nobility or a smattering of small town craftsmen and professionals. Acutely aware of past atrocities and the present insecurity of their position, the Huguenots of these regions kept a prudent distance from the agitation of their southern co-religionists in the 1620s, seeking above all to live in peace with their Catholic neighbors. Even so, many congregations were shaken by periodic fears of renewed violence against their members, and when civil war broke out again in the south in 1621–22, many Norman ministers thought it prudent to flee to England.[41]

Within such a context, the fate of the churches in this region was to experience a long, gradual decline that accelerated as the Revocation drew nearer. This decline was slightly more marked in the churches located in towns of more than 5,000 inhabitants than in those located in smaller towns or rural areas, especially when the movement of the number of Protestants is compared with the broader demographic evolution of the communities in question.

Figure 1 sets forth in graphic form the available evidence about the movement of the Protestant population in the nineteen larger northern cities in the sample, plus a cumulative decade-by-decade index of the their fate, while Table 7 presents the data about each church in a manner designed to reveal the long-term trend as clearly as possible. In this, as in all of the other categories of churches, the evolution was by no means uniform. As can be seen, the number of Protestants living in one city, Saint-Quentin, increased quite substantially over the course of the century. This was truly a special case, in that Protestantism took only feeble root here during the late 1550s and early 1560s (the great age of the faith's expansion elsewhere in France), no church was "planted" in the vicinity until 1570, and the foundations for a significant Huguenot community only came with the arrival of a growing stream of textile workers and manufacturers in the seventeenth century, who immigrated from regions just across the border in the Spanish Netherlands, notably Cambrai.[42] A significant number of other churches also saw their ranks increase or remain stable, at least until the 1630s or 1640s, when a downward trend set in in many of them that appears to coincide with a general *renversement* of the demographic *conjoncture* in these towns. In Lyon, Rouen, Issoudun, Châlons-sur-Marne, and Angers, the congregation was in the 1660s as large as, or larger than, it had been at the earliest period in the century for which information is available. In the majority of churches, however, the level of baptisms had declined by this time to a point below its initial level. This fall was particularly marked in Caen, Metz, Loudun, and a few of the smallest churches, such as Laval or Châteaudun, all of which witnessed the level of baptisms celebrated within them sink by 38 to 50 percent between the early years of the century and 1660–70. Overall, the

---

[41] B.P.F., Ms 209, provides a particularly vivid echo of the attentiveness of one Protestant minister to the local circulation of news and rumor of all sorts and to the recurring fear of developments which might provoke "remuments." Excerpts from this document have been published by A. Galland, "Un coin de province (Falaise et ses environs) à l'époque de l'Edit de Nantes," *B.S.H.P.F.*, IIL (1899), 12–29. On the flight of Protestants to England in 1621–22, see F. de Schickler, *Les Eglises du Réfuge en Angleterre*, 3 vols. (Paris, 1892), I, 390–1.

[42] Alfred Daullé, *La Réforme à Saint-Quentin et aux environs du XVIe à la fin du XVIIIe siècle* (Le Cateau, 1905), passim.

FIGURE 1. The Movement of the Protestant Population: The Cities of Northern France

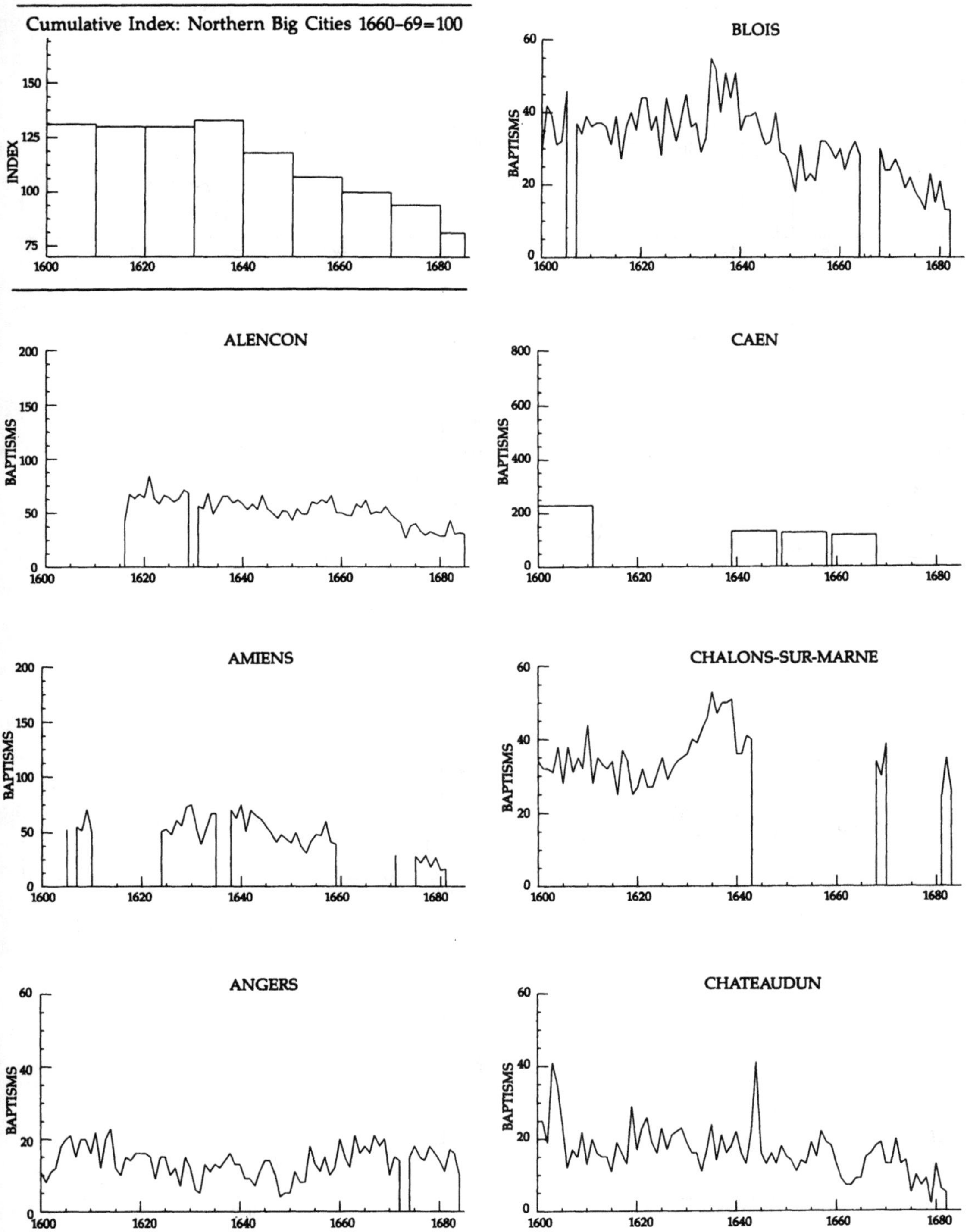

FIGURE 1. *(continued)*

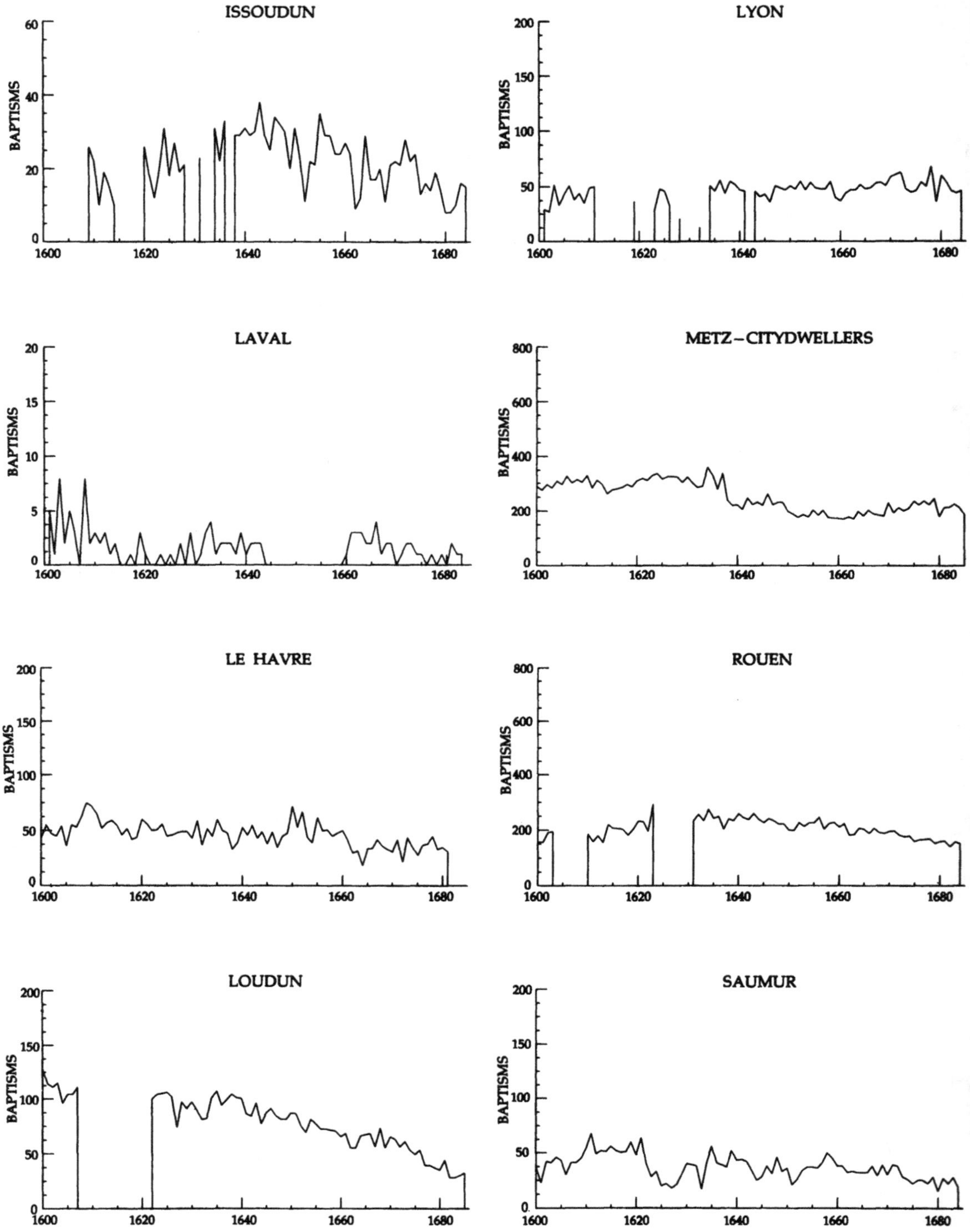

FIGURE 1. *(continued)*

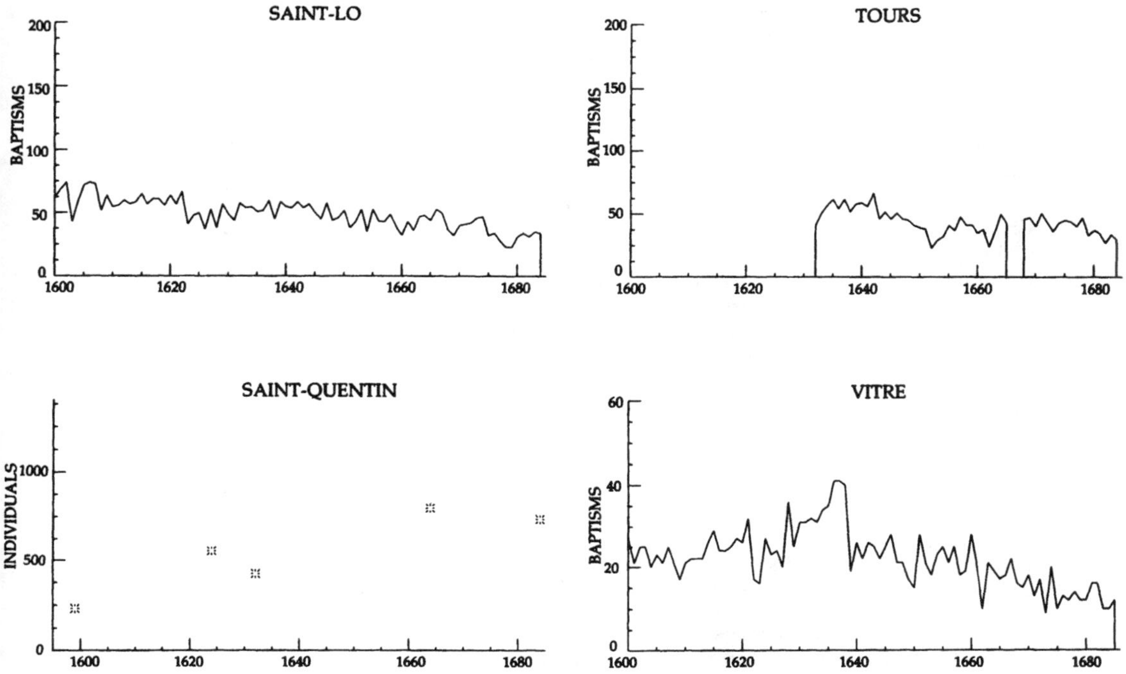

size of these churches fell by 25 percent between the earliest years of the century for which figures are available in each case and the period 1660–70 (an average span of 57 years). If it is assumed that the 19 cases in the sample represent a random sample of the total universe of churches located in larger northern cities, the standard error for this figure is ±5 per cent. As the aggregate figure for this category of churches shows, the decline was concentrated in the last three and a half decades prior to 1685 and assumed particularly accentuated dimensions in the years just before the Revocation. Between the 1660s and early 1680s, baptismal levels fell a further 19 per cent from their 1660–70 plateau.

Protestantism's numerical decline within this category of localities is even more marked when the ranks of the Reformed are compared to the total population of the cities in question. Table 8 sets forth the evidence for those towns in the sample whose general demographic evolution is known. As can be seen, most grew in size, a trend in keeping with the findings of recent studies that reveal that France's cities as a whole grew more rapidly than its total population in this era.[43] This increase in the

[43] Dupâquier et al., *Histoire de la population française*, II, 87–8; Philip Benedict, "French Cities from the Sixteenth Century to the Revolution: An Overview" in Benedict, ed., *Cities and Social Change*, 28.

TABLE 7. Secular Trends: The Cities of Northern France

	Earliest period for which data available (with dates in question)	1660–70	1670–79	1680–85
Alençon	65 (1616–29)	52	37	31
Amiens	56 (1605–10)	[35]	26	16
Angers	16 (1600–09)	18	15	14
Blois	37 (1600–09)	28	20	16
Caen	229 (1600–11)	119	–	–
Châlons-s/Marne	33 (1600–09)	34	–	28
Châteaudun	24 (1600–09)	12	10	8
Issoudun	17 (1609–14)	18	19	11
Laval	4 (1601–09)	2	1	1
Le Havre	53 (1600–09)	35	36	33
Loudun	110 (1600–08)	63	52	33
Lyon	41 (1601–11)	49	53	50
Metz	299 (1600–09)	187	220	205
Rouen	175 (1600–03)	198	174	153
Saumur	39 (1600–09)	33	28	22
Saint-Lô	64 (1600–09)	42	36	33
Saint-Quentin	233 people (1599)	130 families		"nearly 120" families
Tours	55 (1632–39)	40	43	33
Vitré	23 (1600–09)	19	14	13

All figures represent the average number of baptisms per year in the period in question unless otherwise indicated. Figures in brackets represent extrapolations.

overall population of these cities meant that the Protestants' place as a percentage of the total population declined even more significantly than the absolute number of Huguenots living within them. This table also calls attention to what appears to be a consistent and significant pattern within this category of churches: the larger the percentage of Protestants living within a given city at the beginning of the seventeenth century, the greater the decline in the absolute number of Protestants over the course of the century. As a result of this pattern, the Huguenot minorities of Metz, Loudun, or Alençon bulked far smaller within the walls of those towns in the age of Colbert than they had in the time of Sully.

The twelve small town congregations of northern France experienced slightly less of an aggregate decline in their numbers between the earliest years of the century and 1660–70: 20 percent, over an average span of just 45 years.[44] Many of these churches were small, and broader trends within them are occasionally difficult to discern amid the large annual fluctuations in the number of baptisms visible in Figure 2. The decline was nonetheless particularly accentuated in the congregations located in western France—Fécamp, Laigle, Bellême, and Château-du-Loir—and in

[44] Again assuming that these are a random sample of the total universe of churches located in communities of this size, this figure can be computed also to have a standard error of ±5 percent.

TABLE 8. Importance of the Huguenot Minority within Sample Cities of Known Total Population: Northern France

Alençon		1625–34	1650–59		1675–84
estimated population		9,900	11,250		12,700
percent Huguenot		15.5	12.2		6.5
Angers	1600–11		1652–63		
estimated population	24,800		31,800		
percent Huguenot	1.6		1.1		
Blois	1600–09	1620–29	1640–49	1660–69	1680–84
estimated population	16,300	16,200	18,600	16,200	14,800
percent Huguenot	5.7	5.9	4.7	4.3	2.6
Châteaudun	1600–04			1666–70	
estimated population	7,5–8,500			7,500	
percent Huguenot	7.5			5.6	
Le Havre				1665	
estimated population				6–7,000	
percent Huguenot				13.5	
Loudun	1603–08		1645–55	1660–69	
estimated population	6,500		10,000	8,750	
percent Huguenot	41		21	18	
Lyon		1636	1650–60		1679–88
estimated population		42–49,000	67,500		97,750
percent Huguenot		2.9	1.8		1.2
Metz		1635			1684
estimated population		19,092			20,710
percent Huguenot		33			21
Rouen	1600–09	1620–29	1640–49	1660–69	1680–84
estimated population	60,233	73,096	88,953	82,642	69,518
percent Huguenot	6.2	6.9	6.6	5.8	5.3
Saumur	1611–24				1690–1701
estimated population	9,625				10,075
percent Huguenot	14				
Tours					1675–80
estimated population					46,000
percent Huguenot					2.2
Vitré	1600–09	1620–29	1640–49	1660–68	
estimated population	8,000	8,000	9,500	9,000	
percent Huguenot	7.2	7.8	6.2	5.3	

SOURCES FOR POPULATION ESTIMATES: Alençon: B.P.F, fonds Robert; A.C. Alençon, 11 E 1–2, 12 E 1–8, 21, 26–39; Angers: François Lebrun, *Les hommes et la mort en Anjou aux XVIIe et XVIIIe siècles: Essai de démographie et de psychologie historiques* (Paris, 1971), 162; Blois: baptismal figures kindly furnished by Jean-Noël Biraben; Châteaudun: Marcel Couturier, *Recherches sur les structures sociales de Châteaudun, 1525–1789* (Paris, 1969), 89, 104–5; Le Havre: André Corvisier et al., *Histoire du Havre* (Toulouse, 1983), 80; Loudun: A.C. Loudun, GG 184, 187–8, 245; Lyon: Olivier Zeller, *Les recensements lyonnais de 1597 et 1636: démographie historique et géographie sociale* (Lyon, 1983), 331–7; Maurice Garden, *Lyon et les lyonnais au XVIIIe siècle (Paris, 1970), 31–2;* Metz: Jean Rigault, "La population de Metz au XVIIe siècle: quelques problèmes de démographie," *Annales de l'Est*, 5th ser., XI (1951), 309; Rouen: Jean-Pierre Bardet, *Rouen aux XVIIe et XVIIIe siècles. Les mutations d'un espace social* (Paris, 1983), II, 34; Saumur: Lebrun, *Les hommes et la mort en Anjou*, 159; Tours: Alexandre Giraudet, *Recherches historiques et statistiques sur l'hygiène de la ville de Tours et sur la mouvement de sa population depuis 1632 jusqu'à l'époque actuelle* (Tours, 1853), 81; Vitré: Alain Croix, "La mort quotidienne en Bretagne (1450–1670)," unpublished thèse de doctorat d'état, typed copy conserved at A.D. Ille-et-Vilaine, vol. 5. All estimates of total population derived from baptismal levels have been calculated using a multiplier of 25. Where possible, the percentage of Huguenots has been calculated on the basis of a comparison of the number of Catholic and Protestant baptisms celebrated within the city.

FIGURE 2. The Small Towns of Northern France

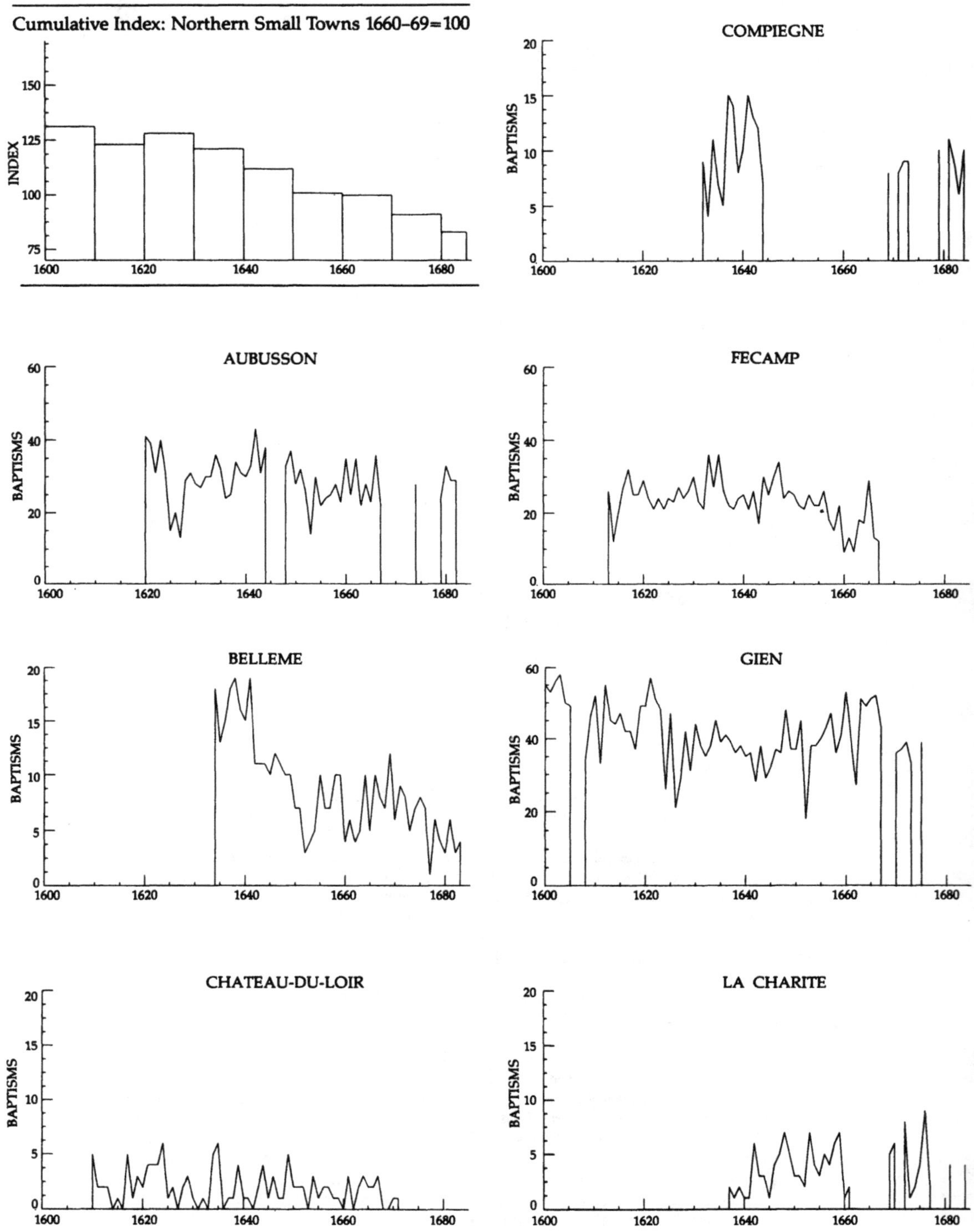

FIGURE 2. *(continued)*

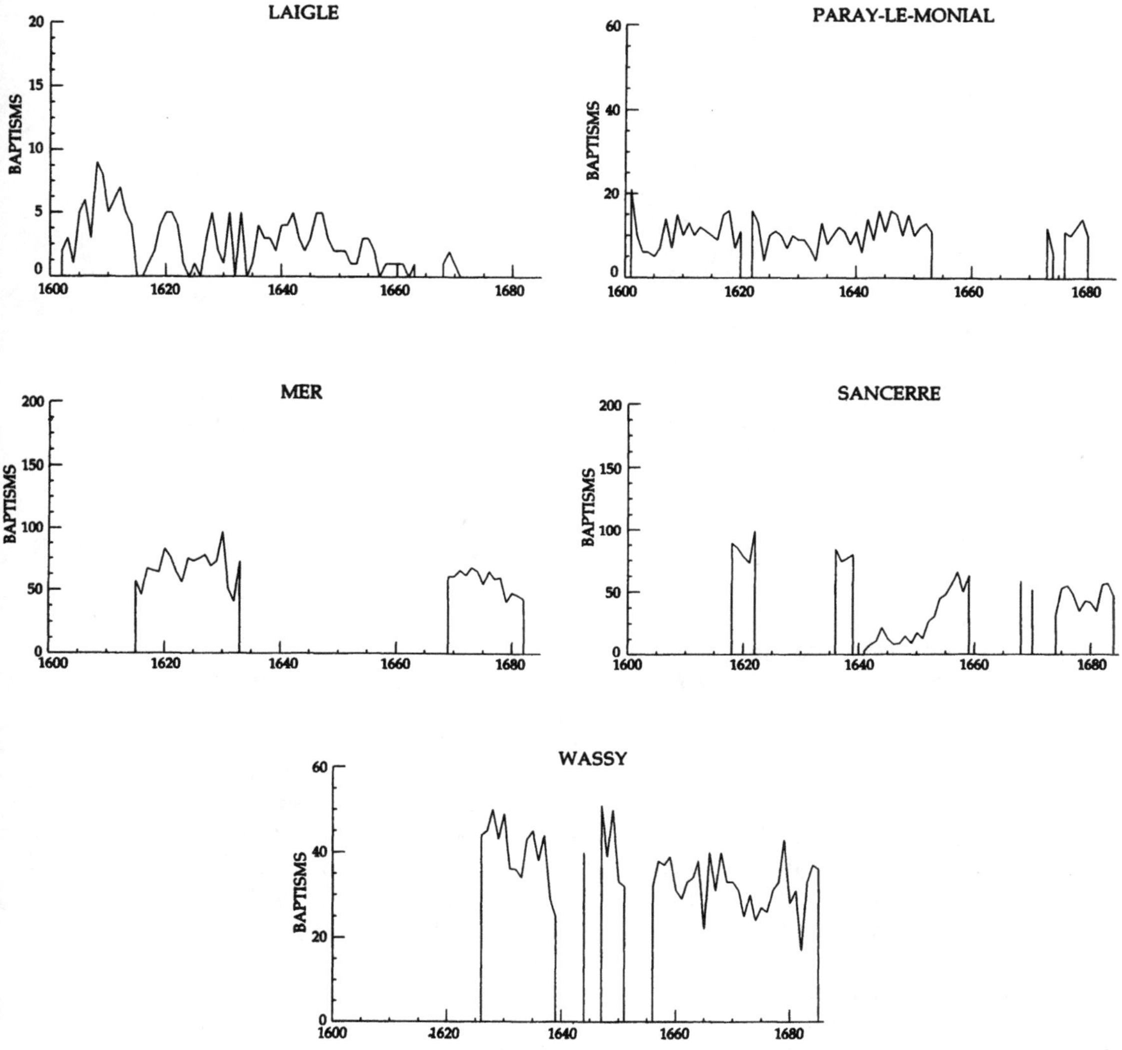

the erstwhile Loire valley citadel of Sancerre. By contrast, the other small town churches of the upper Loire valley lost no more than ten percent of their numbers over the years prior to 1660–70, and the same rough stability prevailed within the small churches of Compiègne and Paray-le-Monial. The cumulative decade-by-decade trend shows that the overall level of baptisms within this category of churches headed gradually and virtually uninterruptedly downward over the course of the century. Once again, the decline accelerated in the period just prior to the Revocation, and baptismal levels in the 1680s were 83 percent of what they had been in 1660–70. Unfortunately, total population figures are not available for

TABLE 9. The Small Towns of Northern France

	Earliest period for which data available (with dates in question)	1660–70	1670–79	1680–85
Aubusson	29 (1620–29)	28	26	30
Bellême	16 (1634–39)	7	6	4
Château-du-Loir	2 (1610–19)	1	1	–
Compiègne	9 (1632–39)	8	9	9
Fécamp	24 (1613–19)	15	–	–
Gien	50 (1600–09)	45	37	–
La Charité	2 (1637–42)	4	5	4
Laigle	5 (1602–09)	1	–	–
Mer	65 (1615–24)	61	60	46
Paray-le-Monial	9 (1602–09)	[11]	11	–
Sancerre	85 (1618–22)	56	45	47
Wassy	43 (1626–32)	33	30	29

All figures represent the average number of baptisms per year in the period in question unless otherwise indicated. Figures in brackets represent extrapolations.

any of these communities, thus ruling out comparison between the general evolution of these communities and the fate of their Huguenot minority.

The nineteen congregations of northern France which have been labeled here as "rural" (many were located in cities or market towns of less than 2,000 inhabitants and included among their members a large percentage of artisans or bourgeois) experienced an aggregate decline over the years prior to 1660–70 that differs little from the preceding two categories—minus 22 percent for an average period of 52 years.[45] Once again, significant variations emerge from case to case, as can be seen from Figure 3. While the important churches of Luneray and Meaux-Nanteuil (composed predominantly of *vignerons* and other agricultural workers from the *plat pays* around Meaux and hence classified here as a rural church) and the small ones of Châtillon-sur-Loing and Dangeau grew ever so slightly in size, the number of Protestants fell by a third or more in the Bresse, the Pays Messin, and the little churches of Authon-du-Perche, Pontorson, and La Celle-Saint-Cyr-Dollot. Map 2 brings to light a clear geographic pattern to the fate of these churches and their small town cousins. Those located west of Paris, particularly in the region running from Normandy south through the Perche and Maine to the Touraine, appear to have been far more likely to have experienced above average declines than those located in the east and southeast of the Paris Basin. As with the small town churches, the erosion in the ranks of these congregations appears to have been gradual from the first decade of the century onward. Still again, the hemorrhage intensified in the years just

[45] Standard error of this figure as an estimate for the total category of churches: ±3.5 percent.

FIGURE 3. The Rural Congregations of Northern France

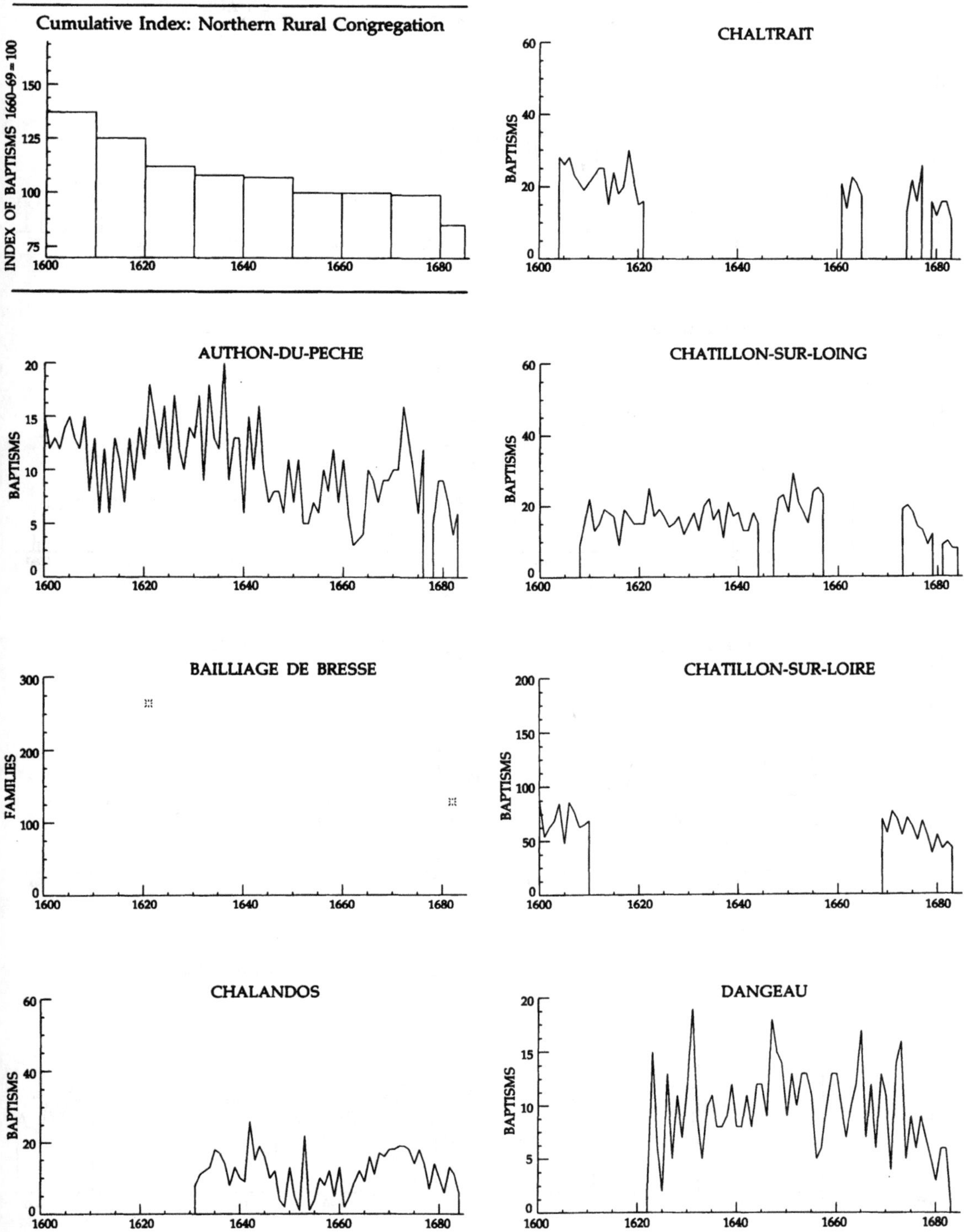

FIGURE 3. *(continued)*

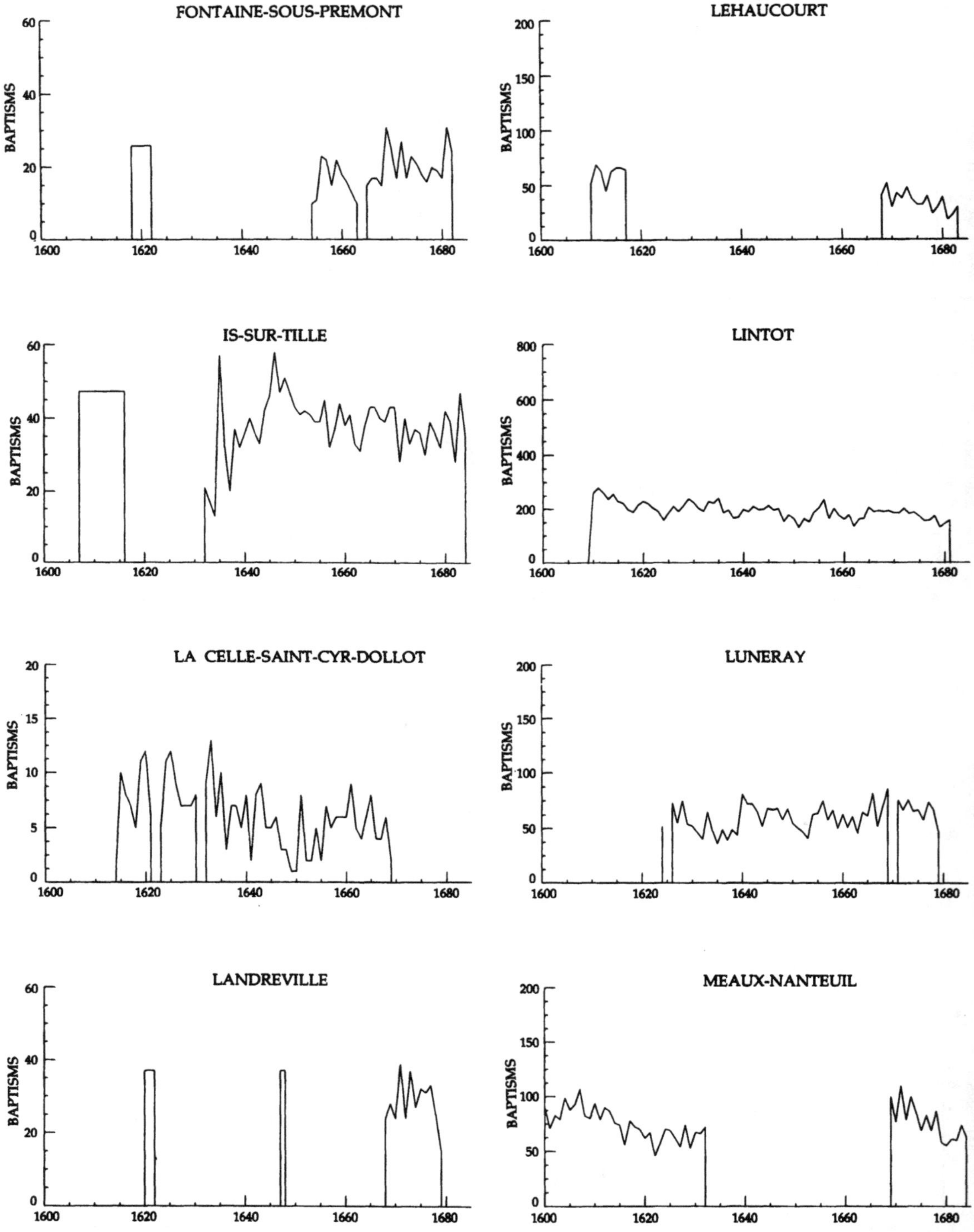

Figure 3. *(continued)*

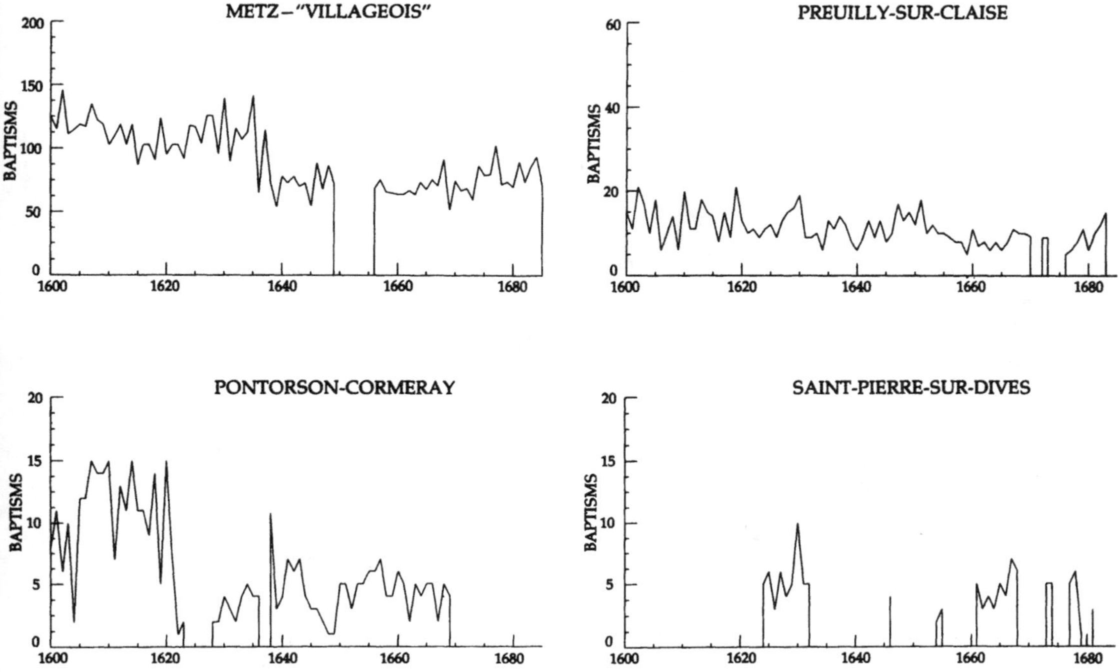

Table 10. The Rural Congregations of Northern France

	Earliest period for which data available (with dates in question)	1660–70	1670–79	1680–85
Authon-du-Perche	13 (1600–09)	8	10	6
bailliage de Bresse	265 families (1621)	–	–	129 families
Chalandos	13 (1631–39)	12	16	9
Chaltrait	24 (1603–12)	19	19	14
Châtillon-s/Loing	16 (1608–19)	[18]	15	9
Châtillon-s/Loire	70 (1600–10)	64	61	47
Dangeau	8 (1622–29)	11	9	4
Fontaine-Prémont	26 (1618–22)	18	20	24
Is-sur-Tille	47 (1607–16)	39	35	38
La Celle-St-Cyr	8 (1614–21)	5	–	–
Landreville	37 (1620–22)	25	29	–
Lehaucourt	60 (1610–15)	41	35	28
Lintot	237 (1609–19)	177	173	150
Luneray	62 (1624–29)	64	66	–
Meaux-Nanteuil	87 (1600–09)	89	82	63
Metz "villageois"	122 (1600–09)	70	77	81
Pontorson	10 (1600–09)	4	–	–
Preuilly-sur-Claise	13 (1600–09)	9	9	11
St-Pierre-sur-Dives	6 (1624–32)	5	4	–

All figures represent the average number of baptisms per year in the period in question unless otherwise indicated. Figures in brackets represent extrapolations.

MAP 2. The Pattern of Decline

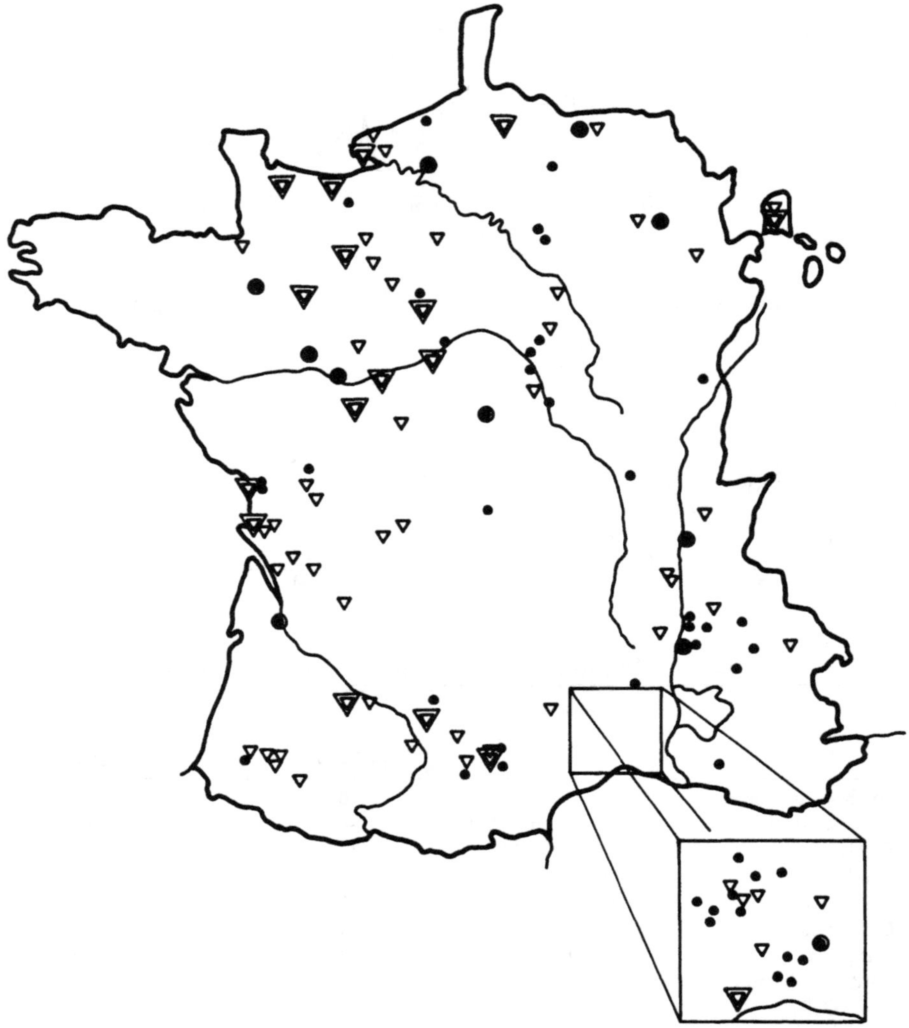

KEY

▽ Locality whose Protestant population declined more than the average of all communities in sample.

● Locality whose Protestant population grew, remained stable or declined less than the average of all communities in sample.

● ▽ City of 5,000+ inhabitants.

• ▿ Small town or rural.

prior to the Revocation. Baptisms among this category of churches in the 1680s stood at 85 percent of the level of 1660–70.

While the northern urban congregations in the sample drew their members predominantly from growing cities, some of the more important centers of rural Protestantism were located in demographically stagnating or declining regions. The Pays de Caux housed probably the largest concentration of rural Protestants north of the Loire, and two large rural churches represent it within the sample. This appears to have been a region of general population decline, for the level of baptisms in eleven Catholic parishes was five percent lower in the 1660s than at the beginning of the century.[46] Similarly, the "villageois" of the Pays Messin worshipping at Metz and the numerous inhabitants of the rural Vermandois who shared the temple of Lehaucourt with the residents of Saint-Quentin both lived very close to France's borders in regions which suffered considerable devastation during the Thirty Years' War, an event which depressed population levels more generally throughout eastern France.[47] In all four of these cases, which together account for roughly half of all rural baptisms in the sample, some, if not all, of the numerical decline must be attributed to the broader economic and demographic fate of the region, rather than to any decline particular to the Huguenot community. Pending the completion of Biraben's investigation of the movement of France's population as a whole prior to 1670, it is harder to compare the other rural churches in the sample with the broader demographic evolution of the regions in which they were located, but the work to date about the broad region around Paris suggests only moderate growth during this era.[48] In short, unlike the urban churches, many of the largest rural churches were located in regions whose general demographic vigor was limited.

The patterns revealed in this survey of all three categories of northern churches help to illuminate the causes of these churches' decline. One cause has already been mentioned: the general demographic stagnation

---

[46] Jacques Bottin, *Seigneurs et paysans dans l'ouest du pays de Caux (1540–1650)* (Paris, 1983), Appendix A, 1–10; Jean-Noël Biraben, "Population et économie en pays de Caux aux XVIe et XVIIe siècles," *Population*, LXI (1986), 937–60. Here once again, Dr. Biraben was kind enough to furnish me with his raw figures, which supplement those published by Bottin.

[47] Charles Abel and E. de Bouteiller, eds., *Journal de Jean Bauchez greffier de Plappeville au dix-septième siècle* (Metz, 1868); Stephane Gaber, *La Lorraine meurtrie* (Nancy, 1979); Marie-José Laperche-Fournel, *La Population du Duché de Lorraine de 1580 à 1720* (Nancy, 1985), 106; Dupâquier, *Population rurale du Bassin Parisien*, 191; Jean-Noël Biraben and Alain Blum, "Population Trends in France, 1500 to 1800. Comparison with Other Western and Eastern Countries," unpublished paper, 46th session of the International Statistical Institute, 1987, 8.

[48] Dupâquier, *Population rurale du Bassin Parisien*, 190–92; Pierre Goubert, *Beauvais et le Beauvaisis de 1600 à 1730: Contribution à l'histoire sociale de la France au XVIIe siècle*, 2 vols. (Paris, 1960), I, 612–16, II, 50–53; Jean Jacquart, *La crise rurale en Ile-de-France, 1550–1670* (Paris, 1974), 597–609, 680–85; Jean-Marc Moriceau, "Mariages et foyers paysans aux XVIe et XVIIe siècles: L'exemple des campagnes du sud de Paris," *Revue d'Histoire Moderne et Contemporaine*, XXVIII (1981), 483; Biraben and Blum, "Population Trends in France, 1500 to 1800," 7–8.

or decline of certain regions of important rural Protestant strength. Beyond this, at least four other factors contributed to the erosion of Huguenot numbers.

Emigration abroad was unquestionably the least important of these factors until the years just before the Revocation. While a trickle of emigration may be detected in the direction of such neighboring Protestant regions as England, Switzerland, and the Low Countries over the first six decades of the century, perhaps widening into a thin flow after Louis XIV assumed personal rule in 1661 and began what Lavisse has so aptly labeled his policy of "persecution sournoise" (it was precisely in 1661 that the French church of Berlin was founded), evidence from the French Church of London, long one of the greatest centers of refuge for France's Protestants and hence perhaps the best barometer of long-term trends in emigration, suggests that the outflow was only large enough to maintain the church at a steady size until 1681. Only after that date, when the first dragonnades in Poitou provoked a sharp upsurge in emigrants fleeing France, did the number of new members admitted to the church begin to increase. (See Table 11.) Protestants were also well represented among the merchants and indentured servants who settled the French Antilles in this era, and again the number of Huguenot migrants appears to have increased after 1681. Nonetheless, the total outflow of migrants to both Europe and the Caribbean cannot have amounted to more than a few hundred people per year prior to the 1680s, a tiny fraction of the total Huguenot population. The majority of the refugees who made the Huguenot exodus from France the largest intra-European mass migration of the era did not leave the country until after the Edict of Nantes was revoked.[49]

Of equally modest importance in this part of France was the direct impact of political and military events. Two communities in the sample did experience a significant reduction in size as a result of changes in the structure of local authority. The sharp drop visible in the number of baptisms in Sancerre after 1639 stemmed from the acquisition of the county

---

[49] De Schickler, *Les Eglises du Réfuge en Angleterre*, I, 376, 390–401: II, 8–9, 311; Robin D. Gwynn, "The Arrival of Huguenot Refugees in England, 1680–1705," *Proceedings of the Huguenot Society of London*, XXI (1969), 366–73; Gwynn, *Huguenot Heritage: The History and Contribution of the Huguenots in Britain* (London, 1985), 35; Gabriel Debien, "La société coloniale aux XVIIe et XVIIIe siècles. Les engagés pour les Antilles (1634–1715)," *Revue d'Histoire des Colonies*, XXXVIII (1951), 187–90; Jean Orcibal, *Etat présent des recherches sur la répartitition géographique des "Nouveaux Catholiques" à la fin du XVIIe siècle* (Paris, 1948), 3–4n; Faust, "Beleaguered Society," 361; Janine Garrisson, *L'édit de Nantes et sa Révocation: Histoire d'une intolerance* (Paris, 1985), 172; Robert Richard and Denis Vatinel, "Le consistoire de l'Eglise réformée du Havre au XVIIe siècle: Les pasteurs," *B.S.H.P.F.*, CXXVII (1981), 7–8; Rémy Scheurer, "Passage accueil et intégration des réfugiés huguenots en Suisse" in M. Magdelaine and R. von Thadden, eds. *Le Réfuge huguenot* (Paris, 1985), 48–9; Jean-Pierre Poussou, "Mobilité et migrations," in Dupâquier et al., *Histoire de la population française*, II, 125–30. Not surprisingly, relatively few of those involved in the most important current of French emigration abroad prior to 1685, that of laborers and artisans from southwestern France in the direction of Catalonia, appear to have come from predominantly Protestant parts of this region. J. Nadal and E. Giralt, *La population catalane de 1553 à 1717: L'immigration française et les autres facteurs de son développement* (Paris, 1960), part 2.

TABLE 11. Huguenot Immigration in London

A. Average Annual Baptisms in the Eglise Française, Threadneedle Street					
1651–55	102	1671–75	106	1691–95	271
1656–60	90	1676–80	123	1696–1700	247
1661–65	113	1681–85	215	1701–05	284
1666–70	91	1686–90	292	1706–10	221
B. New Members Received in the Eglise Française, Threadneedle Street					
1680	247	1690	218	1700	408
1681	1182	1691	160	1701	275
1682	691	1692	209	1702	202
1683	339	1693	199	1703	132
1684	208	1694	161	1704	133
1685	283	1695	186	1705	110
1686	607	1696	102		
1687	2497	1697	122		
1688	715	1698	354		
1689	167	1699	468		

SOURCES: Robin D. Gwynn, "The Arrival of Huguenot Refugees in England, 1680-1705," *Proceedings of the Huguenot Society of London*, XXI (1969), 373; idem, "The Distribution of Huguenot Refugees in England, II: London and its Environs," *Proceedings of the Huguenot Society of London*, XXII (1976), 523.

of Sancerre by Henri II de Bourbon, prince of Condé. Although the son and grandson of great Huguenot champions, Condé had been raised a Catholic at the court of Henry IV and was an energetic crusader against any Protestants unfortunate enough to live in territories under his jurisdiction. Following his acquisition of Sancerre, he ordered the local temple closed and sought to have the lion's share of the local tax burden shifted onto the shoulders of the town's Huguenots. The church was only reopened in 1652 in recompense for the loyalty which Sancerre's Protestants demonstrated to the crown during the Fronde, and the number of baptisms celebrated in the subsequent years was less than two-thirds of what it had been prior to 1640.[50] Similarly, Pontorson, on the border of Normandy and Brittany was a Huguenot *place de sûreté* until 1621, when it was bartered to the king by its commander Gabriel de Montgommery for 100,000 *écus* and a new command. Its temple was closed for a period, and when it reopened five years later in nearby Cormeray, the departure of the duke and his retinue had reduced its ranks to less than half its former size.[51] These, however, represent just two cases out of fifty. The

[50] Gueneau, "Protestants du Centre," 415–16. The baptisms attributed to Sancerre between 1641 and 1651 involved inhabitants of the town but were performed at other nearby churches

[51] A. Galland, "L'ancienne Eglise réformée de Pontorson-Cormeray d'après un registre d'état civil inédit," *B.S.H.P.F.*, LVIII (1909), 448–63. Saumur's church experienced the consequences of political events in a more attenuated fashion. A Huguenot *place de sûreté* until 1621, it was shaken in that year by battles between soldiers and its large student population and then saw the disgrace of its Protestant governor, the great Duplessis-Mornay, who was replaced by a Catholic. Its baptismal curve reveals a marked trough during the sub-

distance which the northern Protestants kept from the agitation of their southern co-religionists in the 1620s meant that the overwhelming majority of churches did not suffer the direct impact of these civil wars in the dramatic ways which many more of their southern counterparts did.

Considerably more important for Protestantism's numerical fate in northern France appears to have been that basic fact of urban life and death in the era, the inability of cities to reproduce themselves naturally. As we have already seen, a far higher percentage of northern France's Protestants lived in cities than did the French population as a whole. This meant that the community was particularly vulnerable to the substantial excess of deaths over births that characterized Europe's larger cities.[52] That this was an important factor in shaping Protestantism's numerical evolution is clearly suggested by the fact that the number of Huguenots declined most sharply and most consistently in those cities within which the Protestants formed a large percentage of the population at the beginning of the century and where the normal flow of migration would not have been expected to bring as many Huguenots into the city as lived there already. Conversely, many of the cities whose Reformed churches managed to maintain their size were ones where the Protestants formed a relatively small percentage of the total population, smaller than that found in the broader regions which fed these cities with immigrants.

Alençon provides a tangible example of these processes at work and shows how they could erode with time the membership of a fairly important church. Examination of the place of origin of 104 immigrants to the city who died in the municipal *hôpital* between 1678 and 1688 reveals that, as in most French cities of comparable size, the great majority of these immigrants came from nearby towns and villages; over two-thirds hailed from places within a 25-kilometer radius.[53] Just two small Reformed churches, with perhaps a thousand members between them, were located within this densely populated area that may have contained upwards of 100,000 inhabitants.[54] Consequently, those moving into the

---

sequent years. Louis André, *Les sources de l'histoire de France. XVIIe siècle (1610–1715)*, 8 vols. (Paris, 1913–35), V, 84.

[52] The late Allan Sharlin recently questioned the existence of this so-called "urban graveyard effect," "Natural Decrease in Early Modern Cities: A Reconsideration," *Past & Present*, 78 (1978), 126–38. A spate of rebuttals have convincingly vindicated the traditional wisdom on the basis of family reconstitution evidence. See especially Jean-Pierre Bardet, "Problèmes d'un bilan urbain: comment l'établir en l'absence de recensement. L'exemple de Rouen au XVIIIe siècle," *Bulletin de la Société d'Histoire Moderne* (1981), 3, 21–9; and Alfred Perrenoud, "Croissance ou déclin? Les mécanismes du non-renouvellement des populations urbaines," *Histoire, Economie, Société*, I (1982), 581–601. Bardet caculates that Rouen's eighteenth-century population of 70,000 would have declined to 45,000 in fifty years and 28,000 in a century in the absence of any migration either into or out of the city.

[53] A.C. Alençon, 3 E l. A few localities mentioned in this register could not be located, making it impossible to calculate more precise percentage. Soldiers lodged in the city were excluded from this calculation.

[54] Alençon's *plat pays* fell primarily in two *élections*, those of Le Mans and Alençon itself. The former contained 12.9 *feux* per square kilometer at the end of the seventeenth century, the latter 13.3. Jacques Dupâquier, *Statistiques démographiques du Bassin Parisien, 1636–1720* (Paris, 1977), 31, 656. On the size of the Protestant population of this region, see A.N., TT 230 (17); Mours, *Essai sommaire*, 14–15.

city included relatively few Protestants. Only 17 percent of Alençon's residents married in the Reformed church between 1668 and 1679 were born outside the city, while the comparable figure in the large Catholic parish of Notre Dame was 36 percent. Yet while few newcomers replenished the ranks of the Huguenot community, there is no reason to presume that migration out of the city was any lower among the Protestants than among the Catholics. In fact, it was probably higher since Alençon's was an elite congregation, and merchants and members of the learned professions were precisely the sort of people who were most likely to leave one city for another in this era.[55] As they left, and as the families that remained died out, Alençon's church could not maintain its size. The number of baptisms shows a gradual, accelerating downward trend over the course of the entire period covered by the church's registers.

Not all churches declined in size as steadily and gradually as Alençon's; the graphs in Figure 1 remind us of that. The important fall in the ranks of Metz's church-members, for example, was primarily concentrated in a single, deadly year, 1635–36, when the plague wiped out 20 percent of the congregation at a stroke.[56] And the decade-by-decade index for these churches shows that the overall trend did not begin to head downward until the second half of the century. What appears to have happened is that, during the first four decades of the century, the vigorous expansion of many of northern France's cities and the fact that many of the "rural" Protestants were already small-town craftsmen or merchants of the kind particularly likely to feel the lure of the big city, bred a flow of rural Protestants to these cities significant enough to forestall any decline in the number of Huguenots within them. Then, once urban demographic trends reversed course, the tiny reservoir of rural and small town Protestants upon which the urban congregations could draw cut deeply into their size. Even in the case of Metz, the church's long-term decline must be attributed largely to immigration patterns which brought fewer new Protestants to town than Catholics during the decades after 1635, when the city gradually recovered from the population losses precipitated by the plague and reinforced by the subsequent campaigning of the Thirty Years' War.

The conversion of a certain number of Huguenots to Catholicism formed the fourth cause of the faith's decline. Assessing the importance of conversions in accounting for the thinning Protestant ranks raises an issue with particularly broad implications for the history of the "petit troupeau" in this period, since perhaps the fundamental force shaping its experience was the mounting pressure to convert. From the public disputations of the first part of the century, to the concerted campaign of private proselytization launched around mid-century by the Congregations for the Propagation of the Faith, to the discriminatory measures restricting Huguenot access to many professions enacted during Louis

[55] Bardet, "Problèmes d'un bilan urbain," 23.

[56] The church's burial registers record 1,346 interments between August 1, 1635, and July 31, 1636.

XIV's personal rule, and finally to the pious bribery of the *caisses de conversion* and straightforward terror tactics of the royal dragoons, France's Catholics waged an escalating campaign to save the Huguenots from the errors of their ways. Faced with this pressure, the Protestant pastorate sought to create a strong sense of attachment to the Reformed cause through preaching and catechetical education that justified Reformed doctrine and pointed out the errors of papistry. As recent commentators have realized, the extent to which the Protestants resisted the blandishments of the *convertisseurs* is one measure of the vitality of the faith. The amount of movement back and forth between the two religions also sheds light on the rigidity of confessional boundaries and the extent to which the two denominations had become closed, self-recruiting communities by this period.

Direct evidence about the frequency of conversions is often scattered and uneven, but it can be obtained from a variety of sources, most especially lists of abjurations or of new church-members. These sorts of records tend to indicate that where the Protestants formed a substantial, stable community, conversions were relatively rare. Where, on the contrary, they formed just a small minority, conversions were significantly more numerous. Thus, in Alençon, the records of the civil courts and the Maison des Nouveaux Catholiques reveal 91 abjurations between 1659 and early 1685.[57] Since, over this same period, the Protestant baptismal registers indicate that the local Huguenot community declined by 500 people or more, and since the majority of the Protestant conversions occurred in the years 1680–84 and involved primarily teenagers, such cases would have accounted for just a small fraction of the decline in the number of baptisms celebrated within this community.[58] In Caen, with its still more important Protestant minority, we also find relatively few conversions. Lists of abjurations from two parish churches reveal 47 between 1654 and 1663, some of them involving outsiders to the city, while the records of the Maison des Nouvelles Catholiques indicate a further 24 between 1658 and 1661; against these must be set 48 known conversions from Catholicism to Protestantism between 1669 and 1680.[59] But in Lyon, where the Huguenots formed a far smaller percentage of the total urban population, and where far more of them were recent immigrants to the city, 568 Protestants are known to have converted between 1659

---

[57] B.P.F., fonds Robert, "Abjurations."

[58] On the other hand, the rate of conversion in the last decade prior to 1685 did amount to a major hemorrhage of Protestant strength in this period. Between 1675 and 1684, nearly one Huguenot in ten between the ages of 15 and 24 was won over to Catholicism. In light of this figure, it becomes easy to understand the bitterness and alarm which characterize the discussion of the royal legislation concerning conversion in this era in Elie Benoist's great *Histoire de l'Edit de Nantes*, 5 vols. (Delft, 1693–95), IV, 445–51. Prior to his flight to the Low Countries in 1685, Benoist was pastor in Alençon.

[59] Galland, *Essai sur l'histoire du Protestantisme à Caen*, 166, 190. Here too a significant increase in the number of conversions is visible after 1680. After averaging eight new entrants per year from 1658 through 1673, the Maison des Nouvelles Catholiques received 24 converts in 1682 and 25 in 1683. Records of two parishes reveal another 50 conversions between 1680 and 1682. *Ibid.*, 190–1.

and the summer of 1685—this out of a total Reformed population roughly comparable in size to Alençon's and far smaller than Caen's.[60] Here, as in Alençon, the converts were disproportionately young newcomers to the city or natives who had lost one or both of their parents.[61] Robert Sauzet's outstanding study of Catholic proselytization efforts in the diocese of Nîmes similarly reveals that the smaller the percentage of Huguenots in any given community, the higher the rate of conversion, although in this region where the Protestants were in the majority, more Catholics may actually have embraced Protestantism than the other way around.[62] Thus, while most of the studies done to date of Catholic efforts to convert the Protestants have shown that the Huguenots were highly resistant to Catholic missionary efforts, these studies have examined primarily regions of considerable Protestant strength, i.e., precisely those regions where the harvest of conversions appears to have been smallest. It seems that conversion was more significant where the Protestants were numerically weak and socially isolated, and that in some regions it did cut into Protestant strength more significantly.

It has not been possible to seek evidence about the number of conversions in every region examined here, nor is it clear that abjuration lists or other surviving church documents are abundant enough to provide more than a very partial tally of all of the passages from one religion to another in this period. This is one of the questions that will not be fully understood until painstaking local studies have been executed, tracing large numbers of families and their religious affiliation over several generations. But in light of the evidence just reviewed, it does not seem unreasonable to treat conversion as a residual variable within the context of this study. That is to say, where a decline in Protestant strength cannot be explained by other, more easily discernible factors such as demographic trends in the region as a whole or the direct impact of military or political events, conversion may be accounted a significant cause of decline. If such a procedure is justified, then the rural and small town congregations of western France emerge as a region where conversion appears to have been particularly important in reducing Huguenot numbers. This impression gains added plausibility when it is remarked that the regions from Lower Normandy through Maine and the Perche into Touraine where we have seen that above-average decline was the

---

60 Odile Martin, *La conversion protestante à Lyon (1659–1687)* (Geneva, 1986), 62, 157.

61 *Ibid.*, 157; analysis of all known converts in Alençon using the evidence of the family reconstitution forms.

62 Robert Sauzet, *Contre-Réforme et Réforme Catholique en Bas-Languedoc: Le diocèse de Nîmes au XVIIe siècle* (Paris, 1979), 166, 178–84, 256–8, 279–90, 360–66, esp. p. 286. Further evidence that conversions were proportionately more numerous where Protestantism was weaker may be found in Gregory Hanlon, *L'univers des gens de bien. Culture et comportements des élites urbaines en Agenais-Condomois au XVIIe siècle* (Bordeaux, 1989), 239–41. In the diocese of La Rochelle, the percentage of Protestants won over to the Roman church annually between 1648 and 1679 was 0.2 percent. Louis Perouas, *Le diocèse de la Rochelle de 1648 à 1724: Sociologie et pastorale* (Paris, 1964), p. 305. But this study says nothing about conversions in the opposite direction.

norm were also regions where Protestantism was primarily the faith of small, scattered groups, primarily drawn from the ranks of the local seigneurs or educated townsmen.[63] Even if the lesser nobility did not desert the Protestant cause to the same degree that its greatest aristocratic champions did over the course of the century, regional studies have shown that this was also a group within which attachment to the Protestant cause weakened over time.[64] In the current state of our knowledge, it does not seem possible to weigh conversion's precise importance as a cause of Protestantism's numerical decline relative to the other causes also eroding the strength of the community in these years, but it does seem probable that it was a force of some significance.

Aside from these four forces which combined gradually to erode Protestantism's numerical strength, one possible additional cause must also be mentioned, although additional research will be required before it can be confirmed that it was also of significance. Evidence from Alençon reveals that the Protestants married later than did their Catholic neighbors, perhaps because of the greater difficulties they faced in establishing themselves in an occupation. As Table 12 shows, the gap was one of greater than two years for both men and women in the years immediately prior to the Revocation—a period, admittedly, when the situation was particularly unfavorable for the Huguenots because of the numerous discriminatory measures limiting their access to certain trades. Breakdown of the figures according to status shows that these differences cannot be attributed to the elite character of Alençon's Protestant community, since a comparison confined to those couples in which the man was a merchant, lawyer, or member of another high status group reveals a gap in the average age at first marriage which is even larger.[65] If further local studies confirm the existence of such a difference between the two confessions, then the depressing effect of the "prudential check" on gross Protestant fertility will also have to be added to the list of causes of Protestantism's dwindling place within seventeenth-century France.

ii. The Midi and Center-West

Within the great crescent of Huguenot strength which ran from Poitou to Dauphiné, the Protestants were in a very different situation from their

---

[63] Among the churches in western France, the parish registers of Authon-du-Perche, Crocy, Laigle, Bellême, Laval, and Preuilly-sur-Claise all provide some indication of the occupational status of their members. Merchants predominate in the first and textile workers in the second, but men accorded the title of seigneur bulk the largest in all of the others. A.N., TT 230 (17) offers further evidence of the importance of aristocratic Protestantism in this region.

[64] In the *élection* of Bayeux, 70 noble family heads (13 percent of the regional total) were Protestant in 1597, 61 (10 percent of the regional total) in 1661. Of the noble families of the Beauce won over to Protestantism in the sixteenth century, a quarter of the families that escaped extinction prior to 1685 converted to Catholicism prior to that date. James B. Wood, *The Nobility of the Election of Bayeux, 1463–1666: Continuity through Change* (Princeton, 1980), 161; Jean-Marie Constant, *Nobles et paysans en Beauce aux XVIème et XVIIème siècles* (Lille: Service de Reproduction des Thèses, 1981), 340.

[65] The differences found between the two confessions are all statistically significant to at least a .02 level of confidence, according to the test for the difference of means.

TABLE 12. Age at First Marriage in Alençon

			"Notables" Only	
	Men	Women	Men	Women
Protestants, 1668–85	28.8	26.5	28.7	25.5
Catholics, 1674–84	25.8	24.4	25.3	22.4

SOURCES: B.P.F., Fonds Robert; A.C. Alençon, 12 E 21-8.

co-religionists north and east of the Loire. In many areas, they formed the majority of the population or faced their Catholic neighbors on terms of equality. Prior to the 1620s, their control of many strongholds was confirmed through the secret articles of the Edict of Nantes. Here, what Elisabeth Labrousse has called "des attitudes triomphalistes, assez 'XVIe siècle,'" reigned for much of the century. But the Protestants' militant response to threats, or perceived threats, to their position, combined with the crown's eagerness to reduce the military danger posed by a large number of fortified garrisons in the hands of an organized minority of uncertain loyalty, gave rise in the 1620s to a series of civil wars which saw the full force of the king's armies brought to bear against the leading Protestant citadels. Far more so than in the north, the numerical evolution of the Huguenot population of the Midi and Center-West was shaped by the force of these events, especially in the cities.

Figure 4 and Table 13 set forth the fate of the sample's nine churches of the Midi and Center-West located in cities of 5,000 or more, a group of churches which includes many of the largest and most important congregations in the entire country. As can be seen, deep troughs appear in the 1620s in many of the graphs for which the data is most continuous, and the number of acts never subsequently regains previous levels. La Rochelle, as might be expected, was especially hard hit. This capital of Huguenot resistance housed about 17,000 Protestants in the 1610s, but the terrible siege of 1629 killed close to 10,000 people, and, following the port's fall, Protestant immigrants were forbidden to settle in the city and take their place. Only 47 percent as many baptisms were celebrated in La Rochelle's several Reformed temples in the 1630s as had been in the 1610s, and over the subsequent decades the size of the community continued to shrink. Montauban, whose Protestant community was the country's largest in the 1610s, experienced a somewhat less murderous siege in 1621, but here too the movement of baptisms reveals a deep trough at the time, followed by only partial recovery. Baptisms were just 70 percent as numerous between 1623 and 1632 as in the 1610s, and again the church continued to shrink in size over the subsequent decades, with the plague of 1653–54 standing out as a second particularly important moment in its diminution. In Montpellier, both the siege of 1621 and the killing plague which swept through much of Languedoc in 1629 left deep cuts in the number of baptisms, reducing the total number of baptisms in the 1630s to 65 percent of the level of the 1610s, while Nîmes, although never directly besieged for an extended period of time like the other three

FIGURE 4. The Cities of the Midi and Center-West

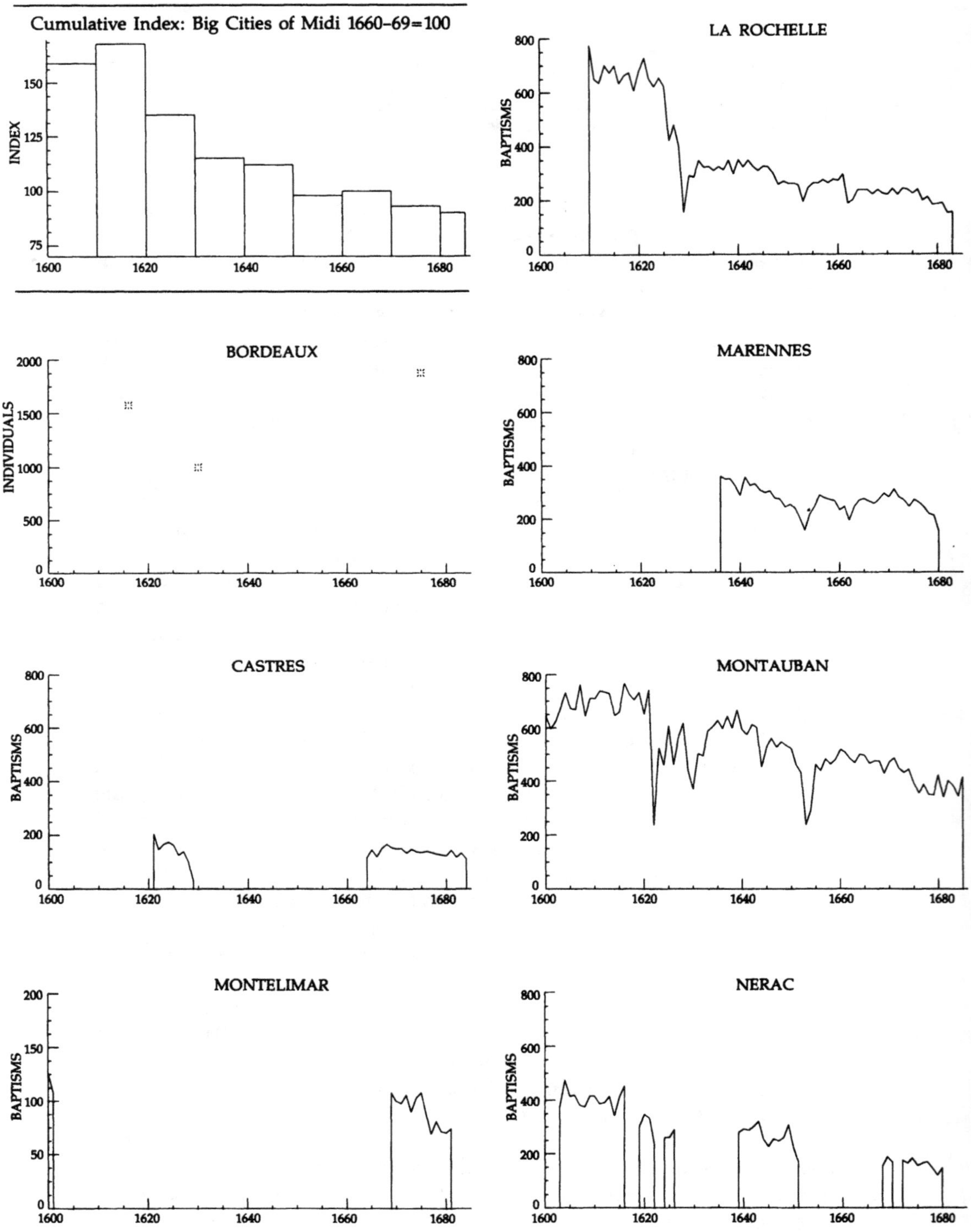

Figure 4. *(continued)*

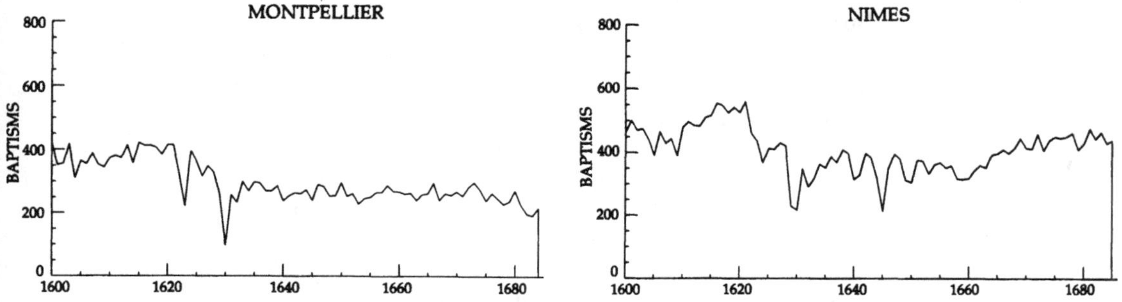

Table 13. The Cities of the Midi and Center-West

	Earliest period for which data available (with dates in question)	1660–70	1670–79	1680–85
Bordeaux	300–400 families (1616)	[72]	75	–
Castres	213 (1620–21)	144	138	127
La Rochelle	671 (1610–19)	234	222	170
Marennes	346 (1636–39)	258	260	–
Montauban	673 (1600–09)	481	412	382
Montélimar	111 (1598–1601)	98	91	70
Montpellier	366 (1600–09)	261	260	222
Nérac	408 (1603–16)	170	161	–
Nîmes	447 (1600–09)	386	436	450

All figures represent the average number of baptisms per year in the period in question unless otherwise indicated. Figures in brackets represent extrapolations.

cities, also clearly felt the impact of the fighting in the region in the 1620s, even before being hit by the plague of 1629. Here baptismal levels in the 1630s were 67 percent of what they had been in the 1610s, but the church's membership would begin to climb again from the 1660s onward, as the city began to experience the dramatic expansion which its enormously successful textile industries would bring it over the late seventeenth and eighteenth centuries.

While the other churches in this category contain gaps in their records which prevent one from following the movement of their Protestant population as continuously as in these leading centers of the cause, several of them also clearly suffered from the events of the 1620s. Much of the dramatic long-term decline in the size of Nérac's church stemmed from this decade, when the city was besieged and subsequently punished for its role in the troubles by having its Chambre des Comptes and Chambre de l'Edit transferred elsewhere.[66] Castres was also besieged in 1621, and

[66] Marc Forissier, *Nérac, ville royale et huguenote* (Nérac, 1941).

the surrounding region was racked by fighting for much of the subsequent decade.[67] Its surviving baptismal records unfortunately begin only in 1620, but the number of acts they record in 1620–21 would never be approached again, while the church's marriage records, which survive from 1609 onward, record just 56 percent as many weddings between 1631 and 1640 as between 1610 and 1619.[68] Of the big city churches in the sample, only three show no trace of having borne the brunt of the events of the 1620s: that of Bordeaux, a small church in an overwhelmingly Catholic city which actually expanded in size over the course of the period, thanks presumably to the play of migration patterns; that of Montélimar, which, like all of Dauphiné, escaped the fighting of the 1620s, and which lost only a tenth of its ranks over the course of the years to 1660–70; and that of Marennes, whose records only begin in 1635 and reveal a pattern of decline over the subsequent five decades. Not only did war and plague cut large swaths through many Huguenot congregations in the 1620s, there is also evidence of mass conversion in certain localities.[69]

Taken together, the big city churches of the Midi and Center-West experienced a greater aggregate decline in the number of baptisms prior to 1660–70 than any other category of churches analyzed here: minus 36 percent over an average period of 54 years.[70] As the decade-to-decade index shows, the pre-1670 decline was concentrated almost exclusively between the 1610s and 1630s. Indeed, the fall in the number of baptisms between these decades was equivalent to the total decrease between 1600–09 and 1660–70. In the decades after 1660–70, some further decline set in, but this decline was less marked than in the northern French churches of the same era. The level of baptisms in the 1680s was 90 percent of the 1660–70 level.

Precisely because the fate of many of these cities was shaped in large measure by what happened to their Huguenot population, the overall population of these cities displayed less of an upward trend than other French cities of comparable size. (See Table 14.) La Rochelle, Montauban,

---

[67] M. Estadieu, *Notes chronologiques et statistiques pour servir à l'histoire de la ville de Castres* (Castres, 1883); idem, *Annales du Pays Castrais* (Castres, 1893); Jules Cambon de Lavalette, *La Chambre de l'Edit de Languedoc* (Paris, 1872). This last court sat for most of its existence at Castres, but between 1623 and 1632 and again between 1671 and 1679 was transferred elsewhere.

[68] A.D. Tarn, E 5198bis-5122. The period 1631–40 has been chosen for this comparison in order to eliminate the exceptional number of marriages celebrated in 1630, in compensation for the numerous households broken or marriages delayed during the preceding years. In the years 1664–73, the level of marriages was still 41 percent below the level of the 1610s. In that same period, the number of baptisms was 33 percent below the level of the years 1620–21.

[69] Catholic documents boast of 300 conversions in and around Montauban, over 800 in Saint-Jean-d'Angély, and 750 in Saint-Antonin between 1622 and 1624. Louis Desgraves, "Un aspect des controverses entre catholiques et protestants, les récits de conversions (1598–1628)," in *La conversion au XVIIe siècle* (n.p., 1983), 98–101.

[70] As a measure of the evolution of this category of churches as a whole, this figure has a standard error of ±1 percent. If Alès, Anduze, and Uzès are classified as well as cities of 5,000+, the category's rate of decline falls to 34 ± 1 percent.

TABLE 14. Importance of the Huguenot Minority within Sample Cities of Known Total Population: Midi and Center-West

Bordeaux			1630					1675
estimated population			42,000					49,000
percent Huguenot			2					4
La Rochelle		1610–19		1631–40		1655–64		1675–84
estimated population		19,500		18,000		18,000		22,500
percent Huguenot		86		45		35		21
Marennes				1636–40			1660–68	
estimated population				8,800			6,900	
percent Huguenot				53			52	
Montauban	1600–09				1650			1677
estimated population	17,000 + small but unknown number Catholics				18,500			16,700
percent Huguenot	90–99?				70			58
Montpellier		1610–19					1661–65	
estimated population		16,300					21,400	
percent Huguenot		60					30	
Nîmes	1600–08			1631–40		1655–64		1675–84
estimated population	13,700			12,300		14,000		18,000
percent Huguenot	83			73		62		62

NOTE: Certain of the urban population estimates offered here must be taken as highly approximate. Montauban's Catholic population in 1650 and 1677 is estimated from baptismal levels concerning those years alone. The Protestant baptisms in Marennes are divided between the city and the surrounding localities on the assumption that their distribution in every period in question was the same as in 1668, when evidence is available about the place of residence of those bringing their children for baptism to the temple. Sources for population data concerning the Catholic fraction of the population: Bordeaux: baptismal figures kindly furnished by Jean-Noël Biraben; La Rochelle: figures estimated from the graph in Louis Perouas, "Sur la démographie rochelaise," *Annales: E.S.C.* (1961), 113; Marennes: A.C. Marennes, état civil, paroisse St-Pierre-de-Salles; Montauban: A.D. Tarn-et-Garonne, 1 GG 1, 2 GG 1; Montpellier: A.C. Montpellier, GG 5–7, 16; Nîmes: baptismal figures kindly furnished by Jean-Noël Biraben. The figures may include some inhabitants living outside the walls of these cities in their surrounding *terroir*.

and Nîmes all needed time to recover from the traumas of the 1620s. The decline in the number of baptisms celebrated in Marennes's Reformed church turns out to have been part of a broader decline in that city's population between 1635 and 1685, one probably linked to the situation of the region's salt trade and the silting up of the nearby port of Brouage. Still, while less expansive than the northern French cities in the sample, these towns did see their aggregate population grow by 14 percent between the earliest and latest dates for which information is available about each of them. The relative decline in the number of Protestants within these cities' walls was thus even greater than its absolute decline. The causes of this at once relative and absolute decline emerge clearly enough from its chronology and pattern. Having seen their ranks reduced sharply by the events of the 1620s, most of these congregations were not able to replenish their numbers even when their cities began to grow again, because migratory patterns brought a higher percentage of Catholics into these cities than had previously lived within them—or, in the case of La Rochelle, because laws forbade Protestants to settle there. Given what is known about the factors encouraging or discouraging large numbers of conversions, this was probably a very minor cause of decline within these bastions of Huguenot strength except during the 1620s.

The Reformed churches located in the smaller towns of the Huguenot crescent form an intermediary category between the big city and the rural churches. Since many were also located in Huguenot *places fortes* caught up in the fighting of the 1620s, they shared much of the fate of those churches located in bigger communities. The overall decline in size which they experienced was nonetheless less dramatic, and it was less thoroughly concentrated between the 1610s and 1630s. At the same time, their evolution displays regional variations similar to those which we shall discover among the rural congregations.

Figure 5 and Table 15 set out the information about the 17 churches in this size and geographic category. Privas experienced particular horrors during the civil wars. Following its capture by the royal troops in 1629, it was allowed to burn to the ground. Then, in 1664, fearing that the city was becoming repopulated by too many Protestants and might again become a thorn in its side, the crown banished all its inhabitants of the R.P.R. Some dared to defy this ban, but the number of Protestant families enumerated by a census of the subsequent year nonetheless suggests that the total number of Huguenots in the city was less than half what it had been at the beginning of the century.[71] The ranks of Millau's Protestants also fell sharply and enduringly in 1629, and one suspects that these years were also a turning point for the church of Sommières, besieged repeatedly during the decade.[72] Many other churches in this category, however, either held their own (Lunel, Alès), declined very gradually over the period (Salies, Embrun), or experienced a particularly sharp drop in the earliest years of the century (Annonay, Barbézieux). Some may have grown at the expense of others, for of the three churches located close to one another in the heart of the Protestant Cévennes—Anduze, Saint-Hippolyte and Saint-Jean-du-Gard—the last two both increased significantly in size while the first shrank markedly.

Overall, these congregations experienced an aggregate decline of 25 percent over an average period of 51 years prior to 1660–70.[73] The fall-off was 35 percent in those eight churches which were located in *places de*

---

[71] Elie Reynier, *Histoire de Privas*, 3 vols. (Aubenas, 1941–46), I, 187; Alain Molinier, *Stagnations et croissance. Le Vivarais aux XVIIe–XVIIIe siècles* (Paris, 1985), 247–50; A. Lloyd Moote, *Louis XIII, the Just* (Berkeley, 1989), 203.

[72] André, *Sources de l'histoire de France*, V, 95, 106, 136.

[73] As a measure of the evolution of this category of churches as a whole, this figure has a standard error of ±3 per cent. The figures remain unchanged with Alès, Anduze, and Uzès removed from this category of churches.

FIGURE 5. The Small Towns of the Midi and Center-West

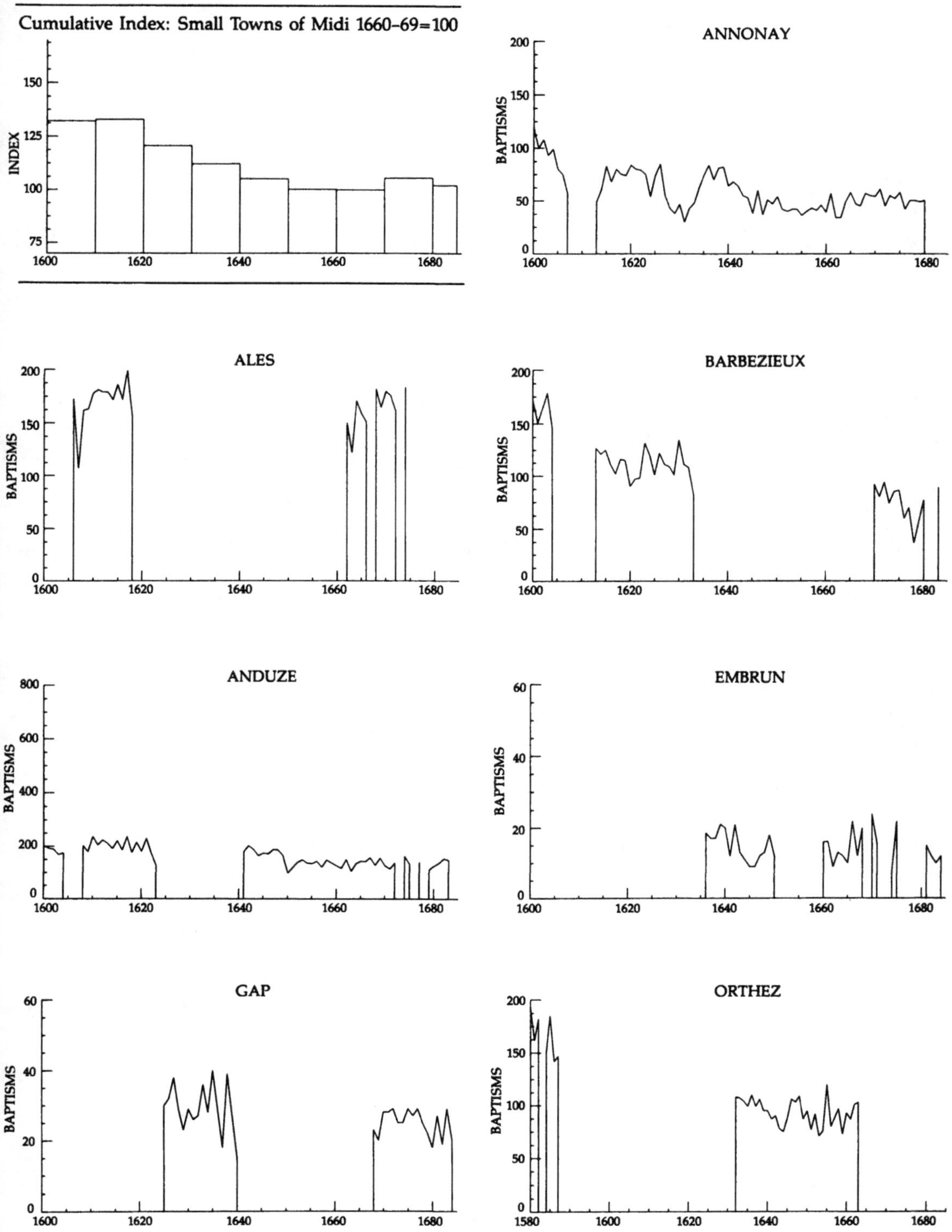

Figure 5. *(continued)*

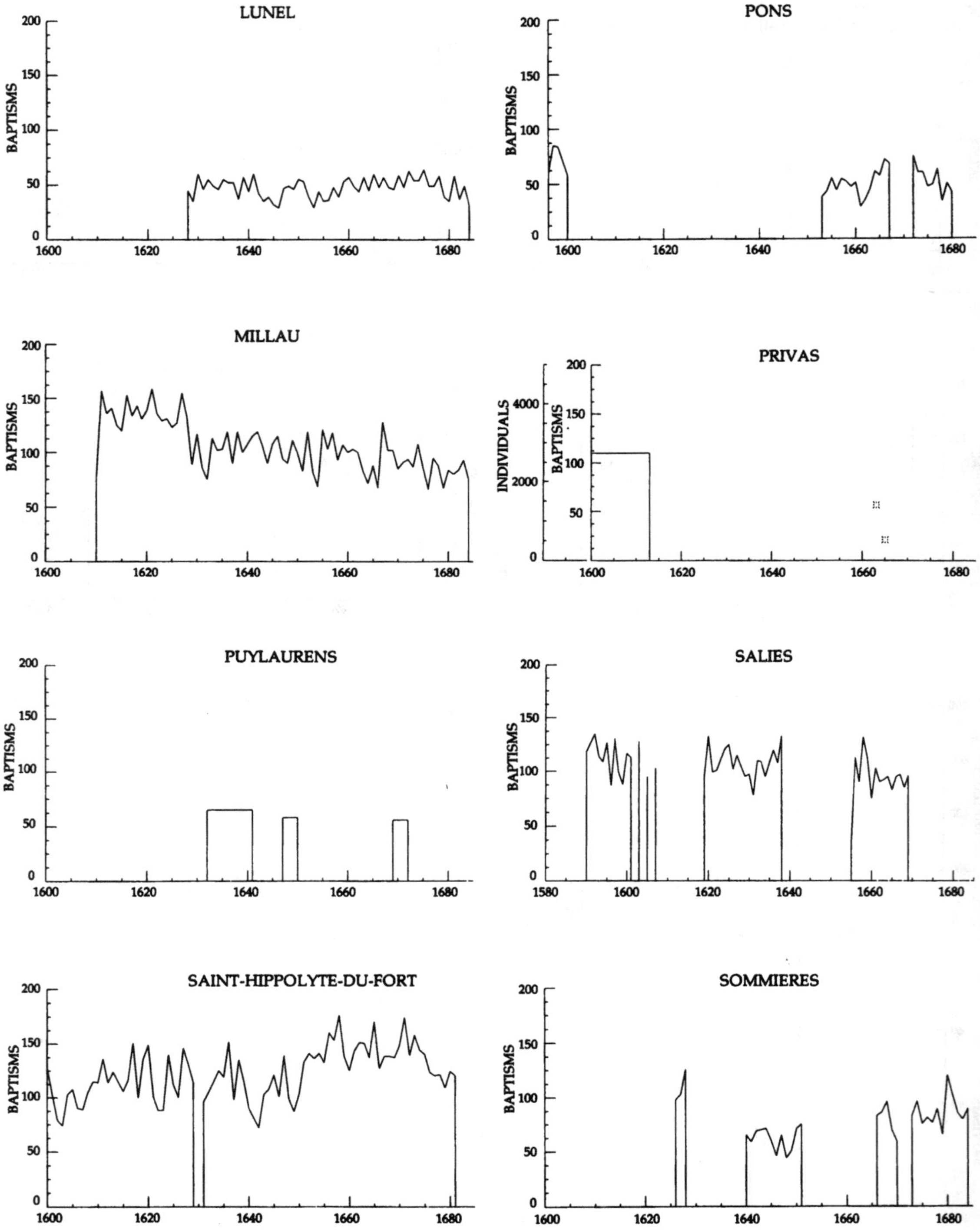

FIGURE 5. *(continued)*

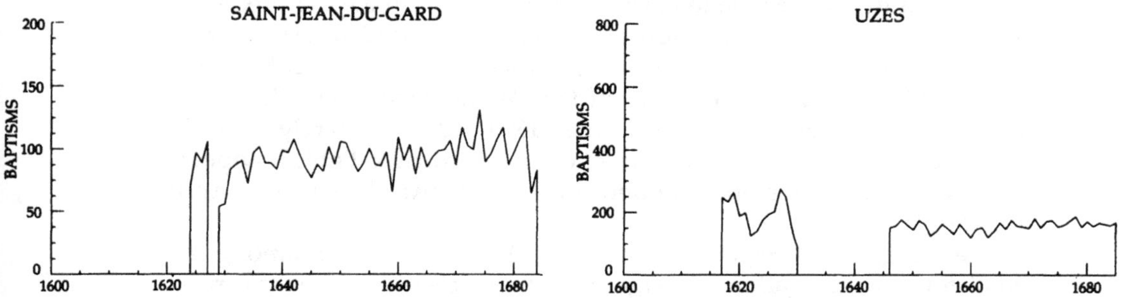

TABLE 15. The Small Towns of the Midi and Center-West

	Earliest period for which data available (with dates in question)	1660–70	1670–79	1680–85
Alès	161 (1606–11)	160	178	–
Anduze	190 (1600–04)	136	133	141
Annonay	94 (1600–07)	48	52	–
Barbézieux	165 (1600–04)	92	72	–
Embrun	19 (1633–39)	14	17	13
Gap	29 (1625–33)	24	27	23
Lunel	53 (1626–29)	52	54	42
Millau	132 (1610–19)	93	87	83
Orthez	[160] (1600–09)	96	–	–
Pons	70 (1596–1600)	52	54	–
Privas	110 (1594–1613)	213 families	–	–
Puylaurens	65 (1632–41)	56	–	47
St-Hippolyte	99 (1600–09)	142	136	–
St-Jean-du-Gard	86 (1624–29)	96	104	95
Salies	111 (1600–07)	91	–	–
Sommières	110 (1626–28)	80	79	96
Uzès	226 (1617–21)	148	167	165

All figures represent the average number of baptisms per year in the period in question unless otherwise indicated. Figures in brackets represent extrapolations.

sûreté or towns otherwise controlled militarily by the Protestants in the first decades of the century, versus 15 percent in the nine communities which did not experience a loss of military privileges over the course of the century.[74] It was also substantially greater in the Vivarais (minus 58 percent for 2 churches), Saintonge (minus 39 percent for 2 churches), and Béarn (minus 31 percent for 2 churches) than in Dauphiné (minus 21 percent for 2 churches) and Bas-Languedoc-Cévennes (minus 12 percent for 7 churches). The decade-to-decade index suggests that two-thirds of this

[74] The eight small towns under Protestant military control around 1610 were Embrun, Gap, Lunel, Orthez, Pons, Privas, Sommières, and Uzès. Haag, X, 257–60, provides a full list of the towns under Huguenot military control.

decline was concentrated between the 1610s and 1630s, with the rest coming gradually over the following twenty years. Unlike the preceding categories examined, this group of churches increased in size ever so slightly in the last decades prior to the Revocation. The level of baptisms in the 1680s was 102 percent of that of 1660–70. Evidence about the movement of the Catholic population between 1600 and 1685 is rarely available for these towns, but from such evidence as has come to light, it appears that their overall population tended slightly downward over these eight decades.[75]

The same sort of regional differences which can be seen among the small town congregations emerge even more clearly within the rural churches of the Huguenot crescent. One region, Dauphiné, witnessed an actual increase in the number of baptisms recorded in its rural churches, amounting to 14 percent between the earliest period for which evidence is available and 1660–70.[76] As can be seen from Table 16 and Figure 6, this stemmed primarily from the substantial increase in the number of baptisms registered in Mens-en-Trièves, but the trend was upward as well in Beaumont-lès-Valence, while four other congregations reveal stability in the number of acts between the earliest date for which their registers are available and 1660–70. Only Orpierre declined in size prior to the 1660s, and even its decrease was modest. Little decline followed in the subsequent decades, for in the 1680s, the level was still 99 percent of what it had been in 1660–70.

If the evidence is insufficient to generalize about trends in the Vivarais or Provence,[77] the abundant data concerning the greatest single region

[75] The fullest evidence exists for Millau, for which Jacques Frayssenge was kind enough to furnish me with annual figures concerning Catholic as well as Protestant baptisms. The city grew very slightly over the course of the period, with the percentage of Protestants declining steadily:

	1610–19	1630–39	1655–64	1675–84
Estimated population	3300 + small number of Catholics	3000	3500	3700
Percentage Huguenot	?	84	72	56

Anduze, Saint-Hippolyte, and Saint-Jean-du-Gard were all virtually entirely Huguenot as late as 1663, so the movement of Protestant baptisms in them can be taken as indicating the movement of their total population between the first years of the century and this date. Together, they display no change. In Orthez, Salies, and Sommières, for which censuses provide an indication of the percentage of Protestants in 1663–65, the number of Protestant baptisms alone in the early years of the century stood at higher levels than the total number of baptisms suggested by these censuses in the 1660s, so these towns clearly all diminished in size. Sauzet, *Contre-Réforme et Réforme Catholique en Bas-Languedoc*, 394–5; A.N., TT 234 (197). Privas also declined in total size. Molinier, *Stagnations et croissance*, 247–50.

[76] Standard error of this figure as an estimate for all churches in this category: ±10.5 percent.

[77] It should be stressed that the single rural and two small town churches of the Vivarais for which evidence survive are all highly atypical of the region as a whole. Both Annonay and Boulieu were located far from the major centers of Protestant strength in this region along the valley of the Ardèche and around Largentière, while Privas's suffering as a result of the civil wars and royal policy was exceptional. Although a sharp drop is visible in the size of all three of these churches, it is probable that most churches located in this region evolved according to a pattern far closer in nature to that which characterized the churches of the nearby Cévennes.

TABLE 16. The Rural Congregations of the Midi and Center-West (Béarn excluded)

	Earliest period for which data available (with dates in question)	1660–70	1670–79	1680–85
Dauphiné				
Beaumont	40 (1613–21)	55	44	55
Loriol	56 (1614–19)	55	54	61
Mens-en-Trièves	42 (1604–07)	71	74	68
Montjoux	8 (1608–16)	8	–	–
Orpierre	47 (1633–39)	[37]	35	–
Pont-en-Royans	31 (1613–19)	30	23	25
Vercheny	12 (1633–39)	[12]	–	12
Provence				
Lourmarin	38 (1619–29)	32	36	33
Vivarais				
Boulieu	11 (1600–09)	3	–	–
Cévennes				
Aulas	88 (1613–17)	79	69	–
Lasalle	52 (1600–08)	64	76	–
Monoblet	44 (1600–09)	32	33	42
St-Etienne-V-F	50 (1600–09)	47	39	47
St-Laurent-Minier	27 (1610–19)	29	35	31
Soudorgues	41 (1619–28)	29	34	30
Sumène	45 (1601–09)	65	54	44
Bas-Languedoc				
Aigues-Vives	23 (1623–33)	27	36	37
Codognan	6 (1600–09)	[8]	9	–
Les Vans	41 (1595–1600)	40	40	36
Marsillargues	55 (1600–09)	47	53	47
Haut-Languedoc–Haute-Guyenne				
Briatexte	15 (1600–12)	10	–	–
Mas-Grenier	22 (1600–09)	8	–	–
Réalville-Albias	49 (1618–21)	56	–	–
Revel	68 (1600–09)	50	43	40
Roquecourbe	50 (1614–19)	33	38	42
Saint-Amans	20 (1603–08)	35	33	–
Vabre	61 (1627–29)	68	64	56
Basse-Guyenne				
Coutras	14 (1600–09)	[10]	–	–
Layrac	36 (1610–19)	11	7	–
Mussidan	23 (1600–09)	12	–	–
Aunis–Saintonge–Angoumois				
Dompierre	11 (1636–39)	19	11	12
La Rochefoucauld	36 (1608–19)	15	–	–
Mortagne	36 (1613–20)	25	–	–
Saint-Jean-d'Angle	51 (1636–39)	30	28	–
Saint-Just	174 (1601–09)	109	91	68
Salles	13 (1602–09)	13	–	–
Poitou				
Chef-Boutonne	43 (1602–09)	28	30	25
La-Mothe-St-Héray	367 (1618–30)	[348]	355	–
Mougon	241 (1600–05)	[167]	171	–
Rochechouart	34 (1600–08)	15	–	–

All figures represent the average number of baptisms per year in the period in question unless otherwise indicated. Figures in brackets represent extrapolations. The churches are arranged by synod.

FIGURE 6. The Rural Congregations of Dauphiné

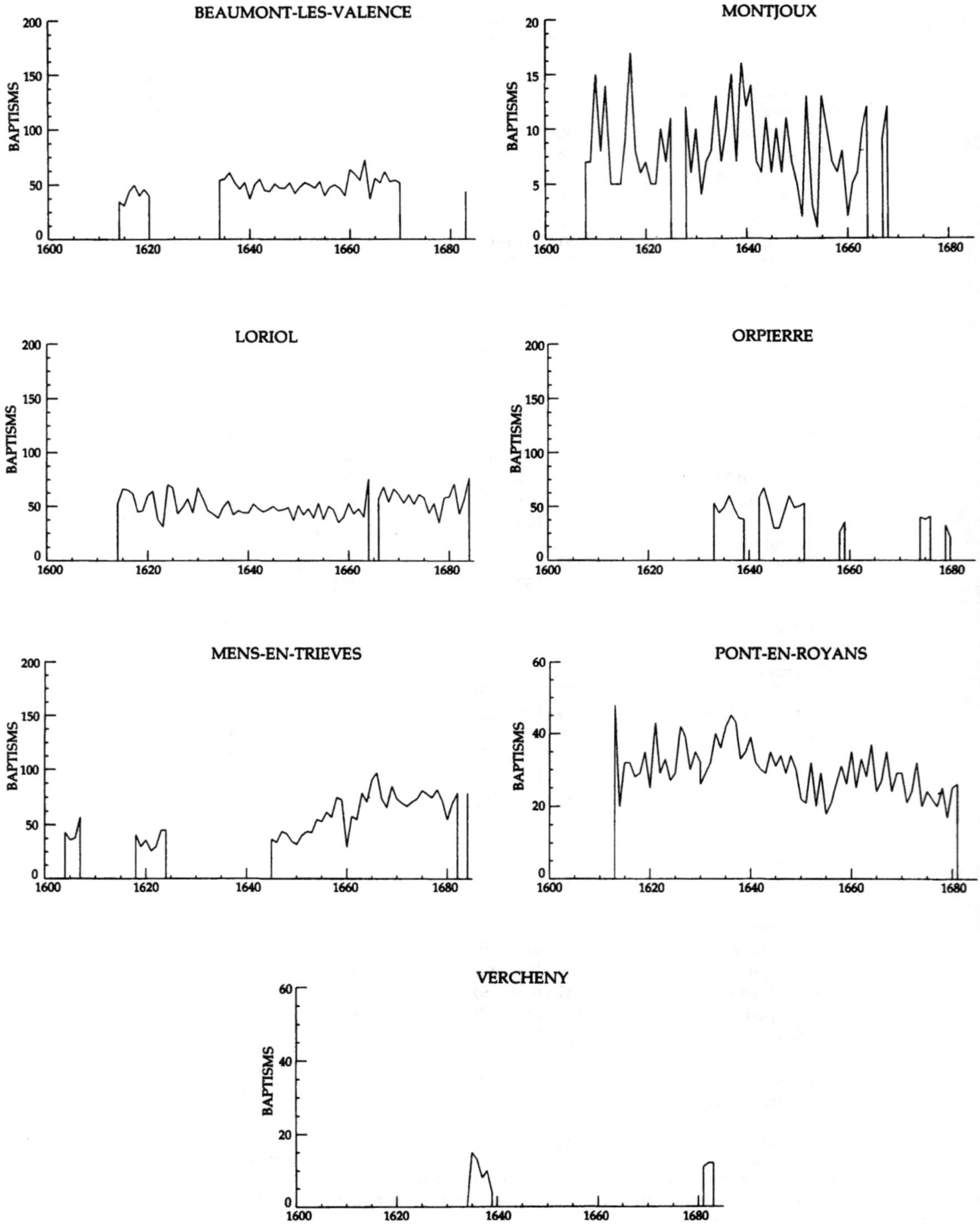

FIGURE 7. The Rural Congregations of the Vivarais and Provence

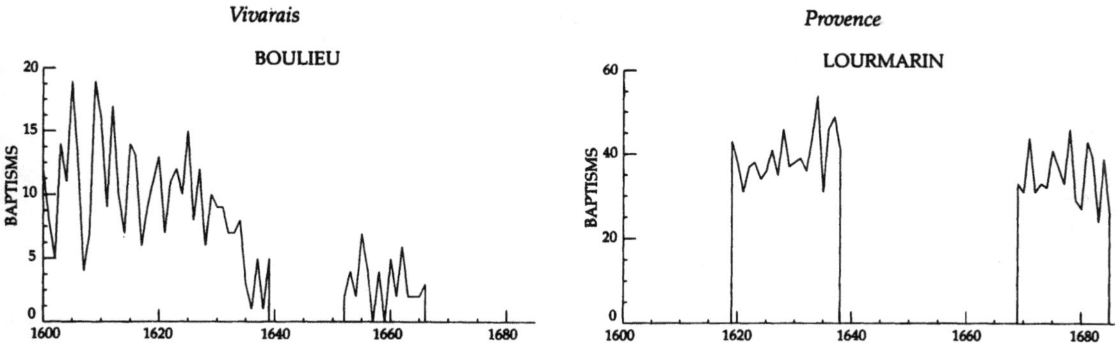

of concentrated Huguenot strength, that stretching from Montpellier and Nîmes up into the Cévennes, show that here the rural Protestant population remained virtually unchanged beween 1600 and 1685. As the history of the small town churches located in this region has already indicated, significant shifts did occur in the distribution of the population between different communities in this region. Monoblet and Soudorgues shrank considerably in size, while Lasalle and Sumène grew. But taken together, the eleven rural churches in the synods of Bas Languedoc and the Cévennes saw the number of baptisms celebrated within them drop by just one percent between the earliest dates in the century for which information is available about each and 1660–70, and by a further one percent between that period and the 1680s.[78]

Continuing westward, the synod of Haut-Languedoc-Haute-Guyenne was a region of transition. Despite some variation among them, the four churches located in the rugged hills above Castres—Briatexte, Roquecourbe, Saint-Amans, and Vabre—displayed an aggregate growth of four percent to 1660–70, even though they were heavily engaged in the fighting of the 1620s. (Roquecourbe's registers note the death of church members in skirmishes as far afield as Montauban and Lombez.) By contrast, the three churches located slightly farther westward in the plain of the Lauragais and the valleys of the Garonne and Aveyron—Revel, Réalville-Albias, and Mas-Grenier—showed an aggregate tendency toward decline. This was especially marked in Mas-Grenier, whose church shrank by more than half over the course of the period to 1660–70. Overall, the seven rural churches of this synod registered a decline of 7 percent to that decade.[79] The downward trend accelerated in the last decades prior to the Revocation, with the level of baptisms in the 1680s falling to 91 percent of that of 1660–70.

---

[78] Standard error for the change to 1660–70 as an estimate for all churches in this category: ±5.5 percent.

[79] Because of the considerable variation within this category of churches, the standard error of this figure as an estimate for the entire category of churches is a high ±12 percent.

FIGURE 8. The Rural Congregations of the Cévennes and Bas Languedoc

Cévennes

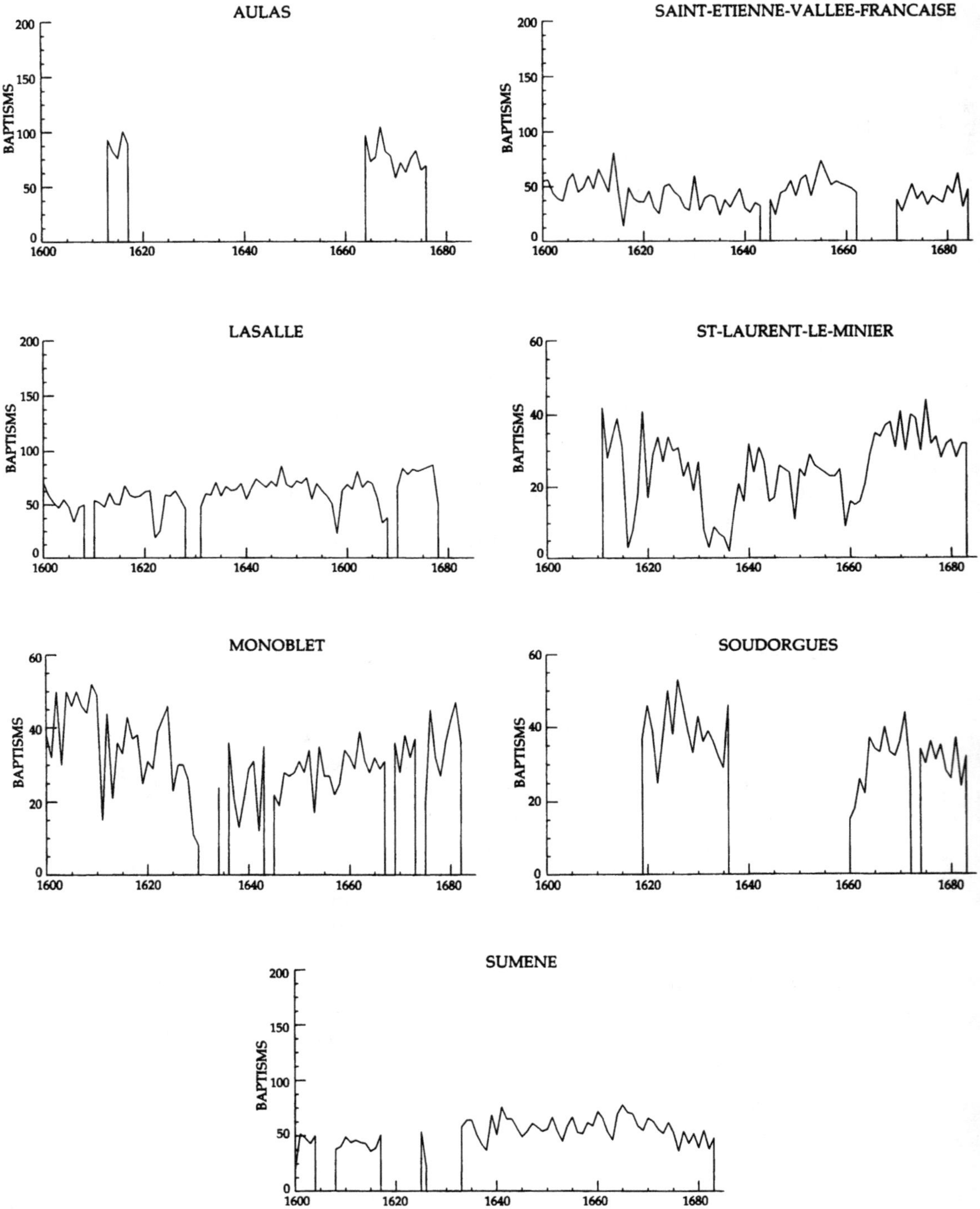

FIGURE 8. ***(continued)***

Bas-Languedoc

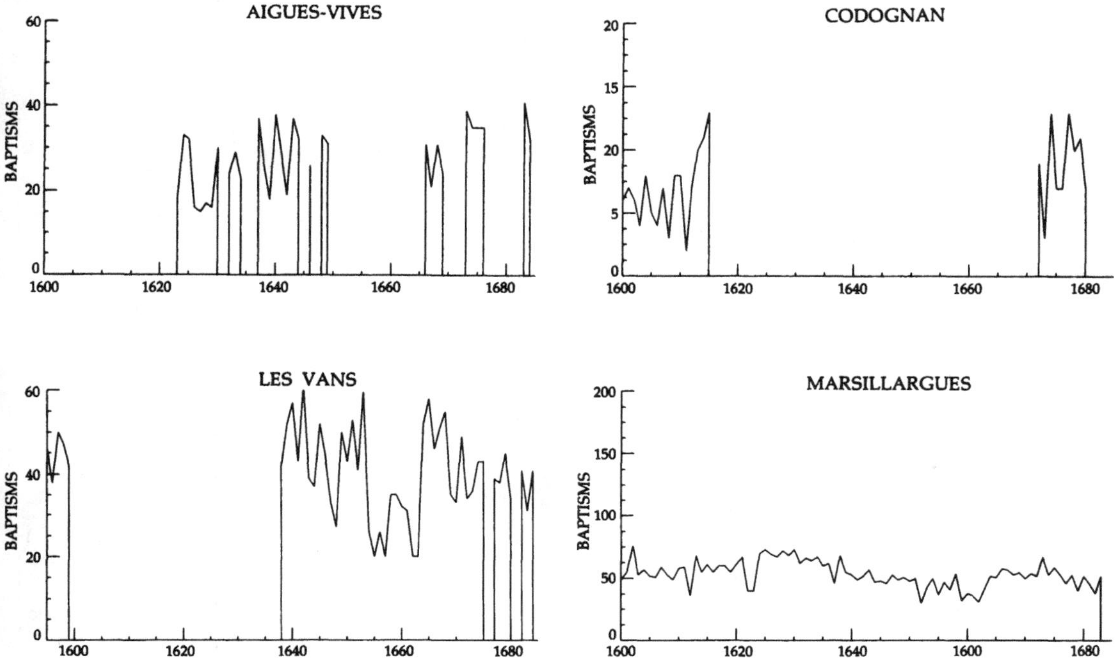

Across the plains and valleys of Aquitaine, Saintonge, and Poitou, the rural churches appear to have had even greater difficulties in retaining the faithful. Just three churches represent the synod of Basse-Guyenne in the sample: Coutras, which remained constant in size between 1600 and 1650, Mussidan, which experienced an extended decline amounting to 47 percent between 1600–09 and 1660–70, and Layrac, which witnessed an even greater extended decline of 69 percent between 1610–19 and 1660–70. The same significant downward trend appears in Mortagne-sur-Gironde in Saintonge, in La Rochefoucauld in the Angoumois, in Rochechouart on the border between the Limousin and Haut-Poitou, in Saint-Just and Saint-Jean-d'Angle in the *marais salants* near Brouage, and in Mougon and Chef-Boutonne in the great region of rural Protestantism around Niort and Saint-Maixent. The only unquestionable exceptions to the general pattern of decline within this region were two small congregations located in the thinly settled plain of Aunis, Salles and Dompierre-Bourgneuf. As for the registers of the large, adjoining Poitevin churches of La-Mothe-Saint-Héray and Exoudun, these pose an archivistic conundrum. Records of these two churches, which consolidated into one when the temple of Exoudun was closed in 1666, were apparently once kept

FIGURE 9. The Rural Congregations of Haut-Languedoc–Haute-Guyenne

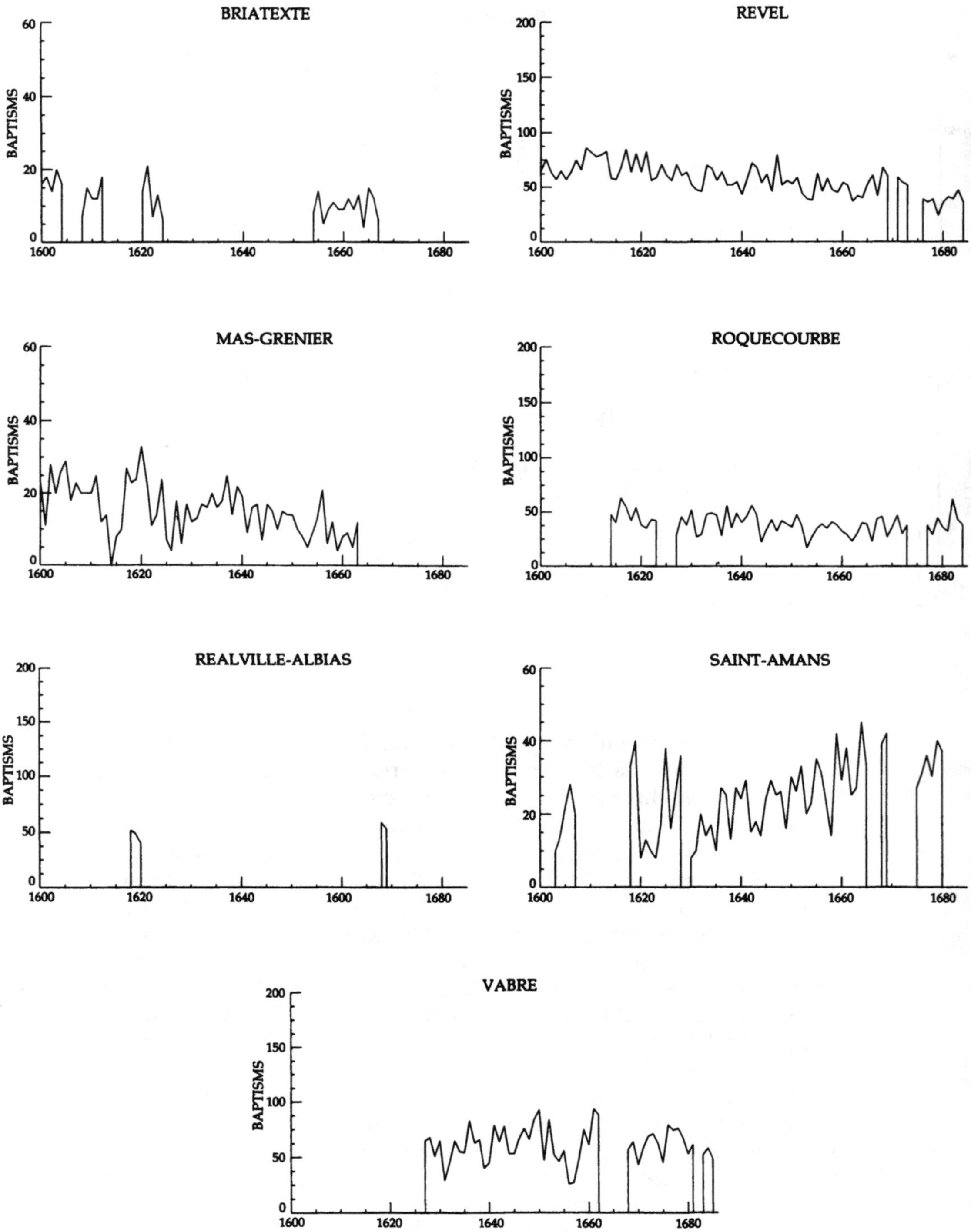

FIGURE 10. The Rural Congregations of Basse-Guyenne, Aunis-Saintonge-Augoumois, and Poitou

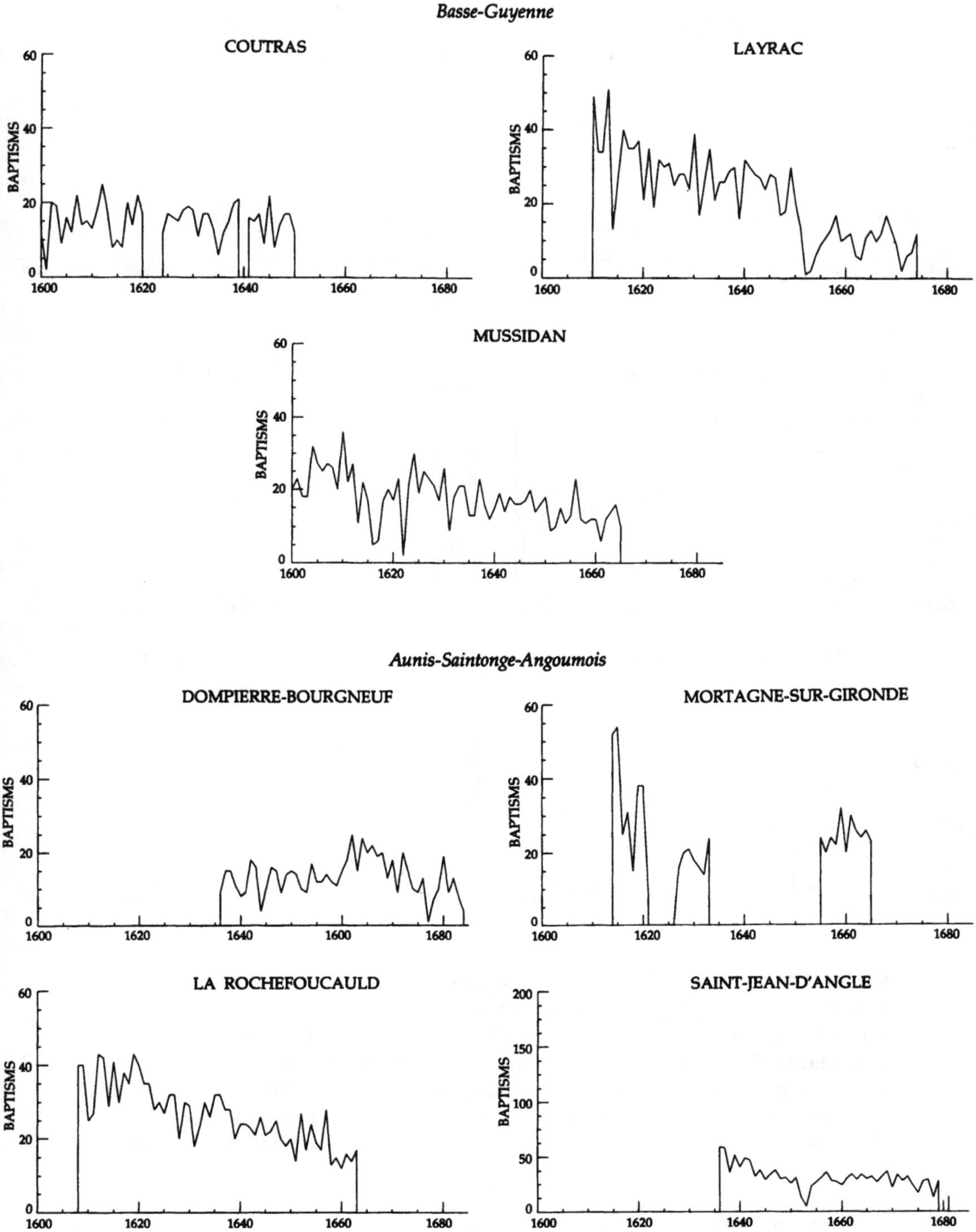

FIGURE 10. *(continued)*

Aunis-Saintonge-Augoumois

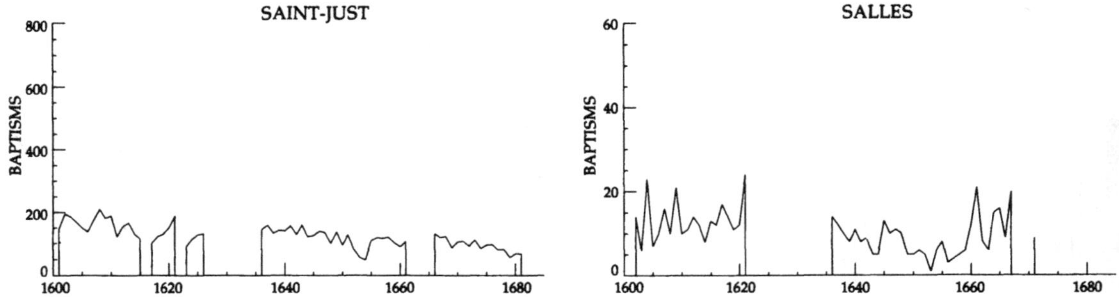

Poitou

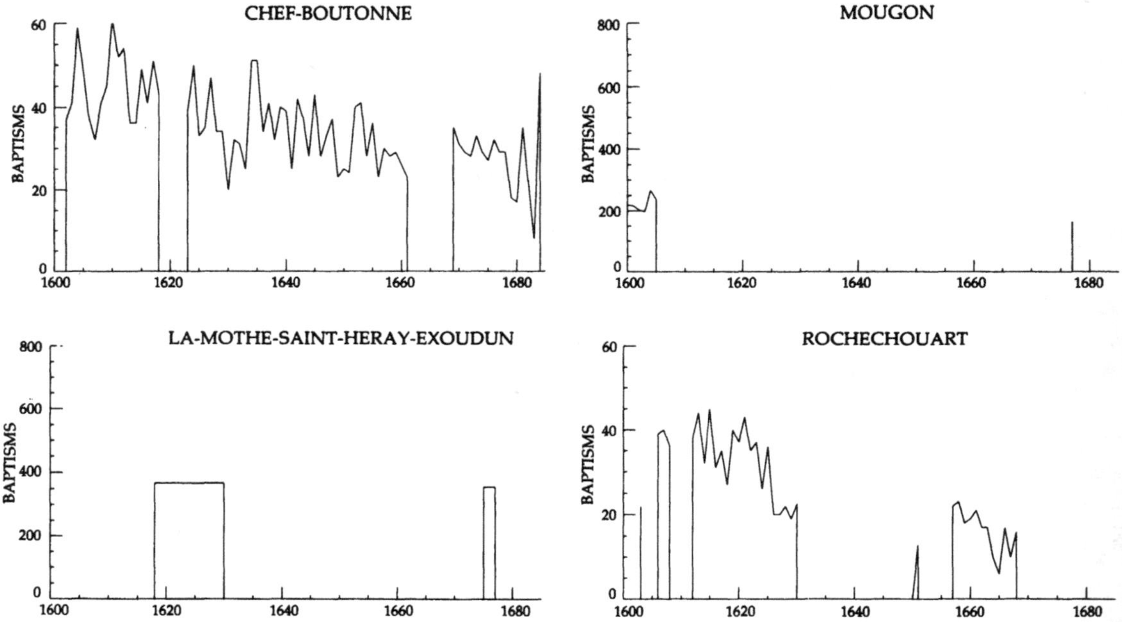

separately.[80] Today, the Archives Départementales des Deux-Sèvres house four registers kept together in a single *liasse* marked "La-Mothe-Saint-Héray-Exoudun." Exasperatingly, none of the three earliest registers bears a title page, nor is the place of residence of those bringing their children to be baptized noted in any of the four registers. Several of them overlap in time, and the acts they contain concern different individuals. If, as seems probable, the earliest registers are those of the two different

[80] See Dez, *Histoire des Protestants du Poitou*, 461–2.

churches of La-Mothe-Saint-Héray and Exoudun, while the last one, from the 1670s, concerns the two churches merged, then the figures presented in Table 16 and the Appendix can be derived from these records—making the obviously somewhat risky assumption that the overall boundaries of the two churches did not change. As can be seen, if these assumptions are correct, these two large churches altered little in size between 1618–30 and 1675–77. Since these two churches were so large, a significant difference in results hangs upon the decision whether to accept this evidence as reliable or not. For that reason, total statistics for the rural churches of the synods of Poitou, Aunis-Saintonge-Angoumois, and Basse-Guyenne combined have been calculated twice, once with the figures for these churches included and once with them excluded. The aggregate decline to 1660–70 works out to 26 percent if they are retained and 37 percent if they are not.[81] Although records for relatively few of these churches survive from the 1670s and 1680s, those which do suggest continued, sharp decline in these decades.

From this review of Protestantism's fate across the Midi, it is clear that the cause experienced far greater decline in its ranks in the Center-West and Aquitaine (although it should be remembered that evidence survives for just a few communities in this latter region) than in Dauphiné and Languedoc. What explains these regional contrasts? Even though preliminary results of Biraben's investigation of the movement of the French population prior to 1670 suggest that Dauphiné and the Mediterranean and Western coasts may have been more buoyant demographically than the interior of Aquitaine,[82] regional variations in the general rate of population growth can provide at best a very partial explanation of the observable phenomena. That greatest heartland of rural Huguenot strength, the Cévennes, seems to have witnessed no population growth at all in this period. Four rural communities located in the most overwhelmingly Protestant part of the region that are represented in the sample, Lasalle, Monoblet, Saint-Etienne-Vallée-Française, and Soudorgues, were all still 95 percent Huguenot or more in the decades just prior to the Revocation.[83] Since the number of baptisms celebrated in their Protestant churches fell slightly over the first six decades of the century, we can conclude that their overall population changed little over this period, just as was the case for the small towns of the region.[84] If the Protestant churches of this area registered less decline than was the norm elsewhere in the Midi, it was thus not because they were located in an area of particular demographic dynamism. On the contrary, this was a region where Protestantism's strength grew relative to Catholicism, even

[81] Standard error of this figure as an estimate for all churches in this category: ±6 percent.

[82] Biraben and Blum, "Population Trends in France, 1500 to 1800," 7–9.

[83] Sauzet, *Contre-Réforme et Réforme Catholique en Bas-Languedoc*, 394–5; Jean-Robert Armogathe, "Missions et conversions dans le diocèse de Mende au dix-septième siècle (1629–1709)", unpub. thèse de l'Ecole Pratique des Hautes Etudes, 1970, 9.

[84] See above, note 75.

as the overall population of the region remained stable.[85] In the *élection* of Niort, in contrast, the number of *feux* is known to have increased by 7.5 percent between 1630 and 1685, while the increase was greater still (13 percent) in the three localities in this administrative unit represented within our sample, Chef-Boutonne, La-Mothe-Saint-Héray, and Mougon.[86] Here, the Huguenots were losing ground even as the overall population grew a bit, indicating a genuine failure to retain the allegiance of the faithful.

Detailed social histories of the Protestant communities of these regions and of the relations between their members and their Catholic neighbors are still in their infancy, but the work done to date already hints that the extent of interaction and intermarriage between members of the two faiths varied considerably from region to region.[87] One can hypothesize that the boundaries between the two faiths may have been far more porous in Aquitaine and the Center-West than in Dauphiné or the Cévennes, and that this encouraged more passage from Protestantism to Catholicism in the former regions than in the latter. It may also be that the degree of indoctrination in the basics of the faith was greater among the rural Protestants of the Cévennes and Dauphiné. Or perhaps the strength of aristocratic power in Poitou and the southwest created a seigneurial Protestantism characterized by less tenacious attachment to the cause on the part of ordinary church members than was the case elsewhere in France. Such an interpretation receives support from a remarkable memoir written by an anonymous Catholic observer in 1618 describing the "Estat de la religion en Poictou." A general indifference to religious matters prevailed among the common people of the province, the memoir suggests. "The *sieurs particuliers* of the villages of the so-called Reformed religion constrain their subjects to go to the *presche*, most of them with the stick and the more moderate among them by preventing anybody from holding any office or tenure under their control or that of the townsmen who own holdings from them." Confessional identity was so weak that "if one asks the mothers to what religion their daughters belong, they think they are responding civilly by saying that they don't belong to any yet and will be of that of their husband."[88]

---

[85] An increase in the percentage of Huguenots is visible in the less exclusively Protestant part of the region around Le Vigan. Sauzet, *Contre-Réforme et Réforme Catholique en Bas-Languedoc*, 284.

[86] Benoist, "Les populations rurales du 'Moyen-Poitou Protestant,'" 495, 905–8.

[87] Gabriel Audisio, "Se marier en Luberon: catholiques et protestants vers 1630," in *Histoire sociale, sensibilités collectives et mentalités. Mélanges R. Mandrou* (Paris, 1985), 243–4.

[88] A.N., TT 262 (8). On the strength of seigneurial institutions in this region of France, see Charles Dugast-Matifeux, ed., *Etat du Poitou sous Louis XIV* (Fontenay-le-Comte, 1865), 93–131 (report of the intendant containing numerous observations about the power and petty tyranny of local noblemen); Pierre Goubert, "Sociétés rurales françaises du 18e siècle: Vingt paysanneries contrastées, quelques problèmes," in his *Clio parmi les hommes* (Paris-The Hague, 1976), 68; Louis Merle, *La métairie et l'évolution agraire de la Gâtine poitevine de la fin du Moyen Age à la Révolution* (Paris, 1958), esp. 63–70; Jacques Peret, *Seigneurs et seigneuries en Gâtine poitevine: Le duché de la Meilleraye, XVIIe–XVIIIe siècles*, Mémoires de la Société des Antiquaires de l'Ouest, 4th ser., XIII (Poitiers, 1976), part II.

Only detailed local studies, especially ones which are explicitly comparative in nature, will unlock the precise keys to the regional differences visible in Protestantism's fate across the Huguenot crescent. The riddle of explaining these differences clearly represents an important and intriguing task for future research.

So far, this survey of Protestantism's evolution in the rural areas of southern France has skirted one region, Béarn. This formerly independent principality united to the crown of France on the accession of Henry of Navarre forms a highly special case and boasts unusual documentation. It was the one region of France where the Reformation was imposed from above by an act of state. Between 1570–71 and 1599, under Jeanne d'Albret and her son Henry of Navarre, the mass was abolished and all parishes were required to conform to a Reformed church order. In 1599, the Edict of Fontainebleau provided Béarn's Catholics with their rough counterpart of the Edict of Nantes, once again permitting worship according to the Roman rite in twelve specified localities across the principality and in those parishes whose patrons had remained faithful to the old church. But functioning parishes often revived only slowly, and it was not until several years after Louis XIII made his *chevauchée de Béarn* in 1620 to oversee the enforcement of subsequent edicts ordering the restitution of all church lands seized at the time of the Reformation, that Catholic worship was restored in every parish.[89] Thereafter, the situation of Béarn's Protestants was comparable to that of the other members of the French Reformed church, with whom the Béarnais had affiliated themselves in 1616 in the vain hope that alliance with the main body of French Protestants might slow the process of Catholic restoration.

Béarn thus represents one of the rare cases in European history of a territory which underwent a generation of enforced Protestantization, then saw a regime of toleration established. Only a fraction of the population became convinced Protestants. In 1665, the royal intendant carried out a religious census that indicated that, out of a total population of 129,457, only 21,804 individuals (4,869 families) were still Protestant.[90] The local synod of the Reformed church protested that this census undercounted the number of its members and produced a document of its own asserting that the proper number of Protestant families was 6,382—or, as-

[89] Béarn's ecclesiastical legislation may be followed on the basis of Pierre Tucoo-Chala, *Histoire du Béarn* (Paris, 1962), 49–68; and Tucoo-Chala and Christian Desplat, *La Principauté de Béarn* (Pau, 1980), 176–7. The slowness with which the old system of parishes actually revived emerges from such Catholic parish registers as that of Nay (A.C. Nay [conserved at A.D. Pyrénées-Atlantiques], GG 1). Although this was one of the twelve specified localities in which Catholic worship was to be restored under the Edict of Fontainebleau, continuous services were only re-established in 1612. For the first decade after that date, the parish register includes many acts involving inhabitants of nearby communities in which Catholic services had clearly not yet been re-established. Only in 1622 does the register cease noting the place of residence of those bringing their children for baptism, a probable indication that the acts henceforward concern this parish alone.

[90] A.N., TT 234 (197). An excellent guide to all of the regional religious censuses dating from the later seventeenth century has been drawn up by René Mieybegué of the A.D. Pyrénées-Atlantiques.

TABLE 17. Average Number of Baptisms per Decade in Six Churches of Béarn

Congregation	1580s	1590s	1600s	1610s	1620s	1630s
Arthez			[49.9]	48.4	23	19.9
Bellocq	76.8	69.1	73.2	67.8	58.6	38
Lagor			45.7	47.6	33.4	30.3
Nay			[40]		23.6	18.1
Orthez	168		[160.1]			103
Salies		113.7	110.9		111.3	106.4
Total			483.8			315.7

suming the same family size, 28,591 individuals.[91] Either way, no more than 17 to 22 percent of the population was still Protestant.[92] A second official census drawn up in 1682 asserts that the number of Protestants had fallen by that date to 19,455 individuals, out of a total population which now numbered 168,093.[93] Again the Reformed church cried undercounting and responded with a document of its own, claiming 6,188 families faithful to the church.[94] Despite the differences between these documents, they agree in suggesting that further decline had occurred in the number of Protestants. On the eve of the Revocation, the Huguenots were thus a weakening minority of less than 20 percent in a region which had once been entirely Protestant by law.

How had the number of the faithful in this region evolved between the Edict of Fontainebleau and the religious censuses of 1665? The baptismal registers of six churches survive which cover part or all of that period. These churches are not representative of the region as a whole, for all were situated in localities in which Protestantism resisted erosion more successfully than elsewhere. (See Table 17.) Still, it does not seem unreasonable to assume that the chronology of the decline registered in these churches between the turn of the century and the 1660s was typical of the region as a whole, even if the extent of that decline was not. As Table 17 makes clear, over four-fifths of the decline in the number of baptisms celebrated in these churches took place over the first three decades of the century, when Catholic services were being reestablished throughout the region. As can be seen from the examples of Arthez, Bellocq, and Lagor, where the registers are continuous for much or all of the period 1600–1630, the years around 1620 witnessed the sharpest fall-off in Prot-

---

91 B. Vaurigaud, "Statistique des églises du Béarn vers le milieu du XVIIe siècle," *B.S.H.P.F.*, V (1857), 1–6. I have eliminated from the total provided by this document the 32 families residing in Saint-Palais, located in Basse-Navarre.

92 As indicated above in Table 2, comparison of the two censuses from the mid-1660s with each other and with the estimates of congregation size which one can derive from the Protestant baptismal registers suggests that the truth lies somewhere between the two estimates.

93 B.N., Ms Fonds Français 8248.

94 A. Cadier, "Les églises réformées du Béarn de 1664 à 1685," *B.S.H.P.F.*, XXX (1881), 111.

TABLE 17. (*Continued*)

Congregation	1640s	1650s	1660s	1670s	Percentage Protestant in 1665 according to census of intendant
Arthez	22		20.2	27.6	34%
Bellocq			[33.3]		79%
Lagor	26.6		23.8		40%
Nay	18.4	16.6	13.1	13.2	35%
Orthez	91.8	86.9	95.8		66%
Salies		111.4	90.5		96%
Total			276.8		

NOTE: Figures in brackets are extrapolations from the nearest available figures. The percentages in the final column refer to all of the communities served by each temple. Since a few of the smaller localities listed in their baptismal register do not appear in the census figures, these percentages contain a margin of error.

estant baptisms, suggesting that Louis XIII's *chevauchée* was the central event for the revival of Catholicism in these communities, not the Edict of Fontainebleau. Further, slow decline occurred between the 1630s and the 1660s.

If the chronological pattern of decline found among these churches is typical of the region as a whole, the following conclusions thus emerge. First of all, comparison between the level of baptisms in these churches around the turn of the century and the total number of baptisms which might be surmised from the combination of the number of Protestant acts and the percentage of Huguenots in these communities around 1665 suggests little growth in the total population of the region between 1600 and 1665. There may even have been some decline. At the time of the Edict of Fontainebleau, Béarn thus certainly housed upwards of 100,000 inhabitants, all of whom, whether they liked it or not, had to be baptized within the Reformed church if they were to receive Christian baptism at all. Once the option of worshipping according to Catholic rites was restored, the majority of the population immediately abandoned the Reformed church. By the 1630s, upwards of three-fifths of Béarn's population was probably back in the Roman fold. Even those families which remained faithful to the Protestant cause then demonstrated less fidelity over subsequent generations than did their co-religionists in most other regions. The number of baptisms declined by a further 12 percent between the 1630s and 1660s. The rival censuses of 1665 and 1682 reveal still further decline of 4–12 percent between those dates. Finally, at the Revocation, fewer refugees in both absolute and proportional terms fled Béarn than any other *province synodal* of the French Reformed church, while fidelity was equally rare among those who remained within the kingdom. In 1787, with the restoration of legal toleration, just 4,784 Protestants remained in Béarn.[95]

[95] Mours, *Les églises réformées en France*, 168–76, esp. 172; Tucoo-Chala, *Histoire du Béarn*, 76.

FIGURE 11. The Rural Congregations of Béarn

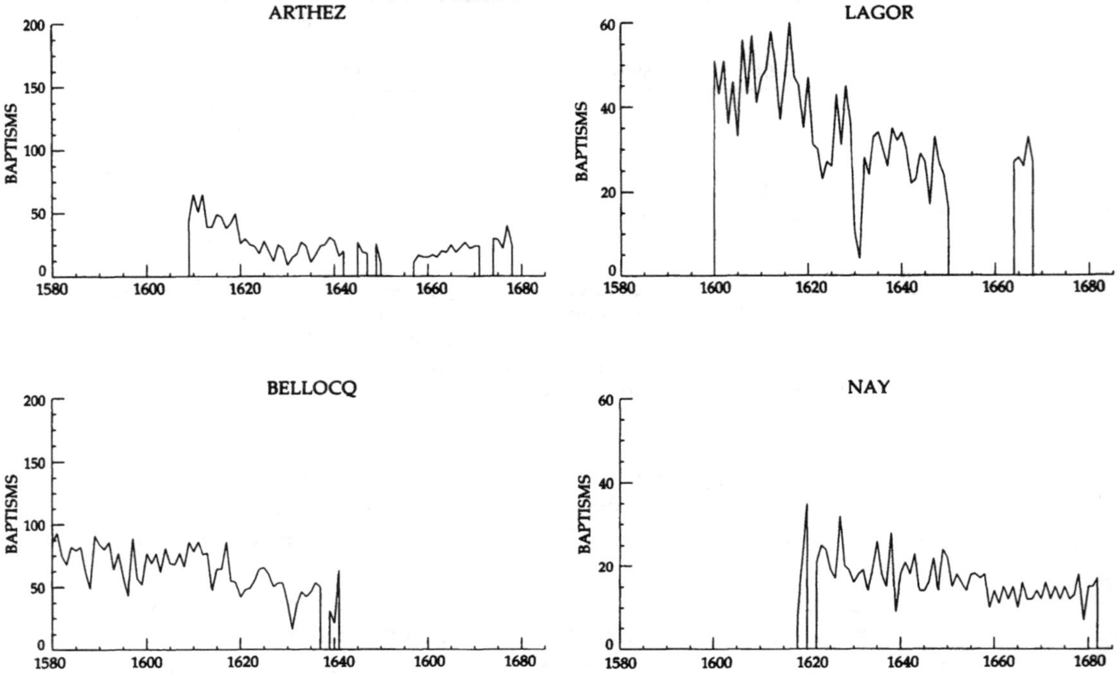

Was the striking failure of Béarn's magisterial reformation to create an enduring Protestant community the result of difficulties encountered by a small, poor state in implementing the process of religious change and recruiting an effective parish clergy committed to the spread of a new understanding of the gospel? Should it be attributed to pre-existing social arrangements or cultural patterns which made the region particularly resistant to efforts from above to implant Protestantism? Or was the extent to which Protestant ideas took hold among the mass of the Béarnais in one generation no different from the degree to which the new faith took root over the same span of time in other regions where the Reformation was imposed from above on a fairly isolated and overwhelmingly rural area? In the absence of any good study of the process whereby the Reformation was implemented in Béarn—and, for that mattter, a dearth of studies of other comparable regions—one can only raise these questions. Clearly, this is another area which beckons further research. Clearly, too, the contrast between the withering away of Protestantism in this region and the greater fidelity found elsewhere in France shows the differences in the tenacity with which subsequent generations clung to a minority religion resulting from personal choice and one born of princely decree.

One final set of statistics remains to be calculated for the rural churches of the Midi. This concerns the aggregate evolution of these 44

FIGURE 12. Cumulative Index, Rural Churches of the Midi and Center-West

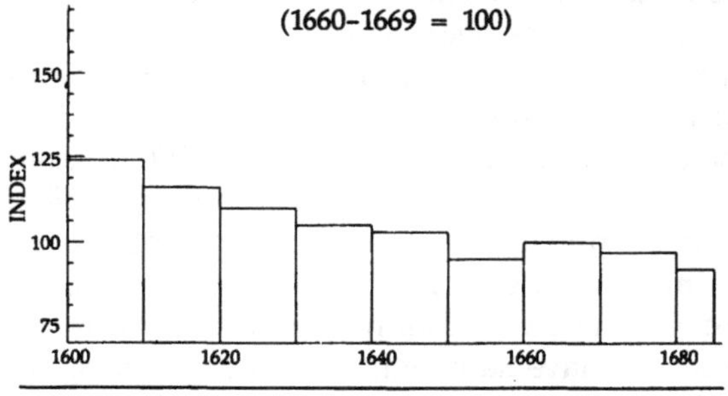

churches. Together (making no attempt to compensate for the uneven survival of records by synod), they registered a decline of 16 percent over an average period of 52 years prior to 1660–70 if La-Mothe-Saint-Héray-Exoudun is included, and 18 percent if it is excluded. The decade-to-decade index (Figure 12) shows a gradual and quite steady decline over the full period 1600–1685, interrupted only by some recovery in the 1660s. The level of baptisms in the 1680s was 92 percent that of 1660–70.

iii. The National Trend

Having surveyed every region and size category of churches, we are now in a position to estimate with some precision the overall movement of the Protestant population from 1600 to 1685. Table 18 takes the revised estimates of the number of Protestants ca. 1660–70 as its starting point and extrapolates backward from the estimates for each category of churches according to the movement of baptisms within that category over the first six decades of the century. As can be seen, such a procedure suggests that approximately 960,000 ± 50,000 Huguenots lived in the

TABLE 18. Estimating France's Total Protestant Population, ca. 1610, Excluding Béarn

Category	A	B	C
N. urban	53,375	133.3 ± 7	71,149 ± 3,736
N. small town	14,000	125.6 ± 7.7	17,578 ± 1,078
N. rural	67,525	127.7 ± 5	86,229 ± 3,376
S. urban	77,900	156.2 ± 3.4	121,716 ± 2,649
S. small town	62,900	130.1 ± 8	81,821 ± 5,032
S. rural	496,200	115.6 ± 5.9	573,393 ± 29,276[a]
		117.9 ± 6	585,142 ± 29,772[b]
TOTAL			951,886–963,635 ± 45,147–45,643

A–Total Protestant population ca. 1660–70 (from Table 2)
B–Ratio of baptisms at earliest available date to baptisms in base period plus standard error
C–Estimated total Protestant population ca. 1610
[a] with La-Mothe-Saint-Héray-Exoudun
[b] without La-Mothe-Saint-Héray-Exoudun

kingdom of France, excluding Béarn, around the end of the reign of Henry IV. When it is recalled that the movement of baptisms exaggerates slightly the extent of decline over these years, it is evident that this figure must be reduced slightly to obtain a truer estimate—perhaps by an additional 10,000 to 50,000 souls, yielding a final estimate of 930,000 ± 70,000. To these must be added the 100,000–125,000 inhabitants of Béarn, the great majority of whom were still at least nominally Reformed. These results, it might be noted, come remarkably close to the estimate of Protestantism's numerical strength set forth by Jean Gontery in a 1610 sermon in the church of Saint-Etienne-du-Mont in Paris, where the Jesuit father is recorded to have said that the Protestants claim to be 900,000 souls in all of France.[96] Another, more commonly repeated estimate of the number of Huguenots in France around the beginning of the seventeenth century appears to be slightly farther off the mark. This is the assertion that 1.25 million Huguenots lived in France in 1598, a figure purported to derive from a census of Protestants carried out by Henry IV at the time of the Edict of Nantes. No reference to this estimate is known prior to 1692, and its authenticity seems questionable.[97]

Figure 13 sets out the decade-to-decade trend. The same sources which speak of a census of Protestants carried out under Henry IV also claim that the ranks of the cause increased by a third over the subsequent years prior to Richelieu's arrival in power, but the data examined here offer no evidence of such growth. Many urban congregations may have registered a modest increase in size, but this was more than counterbalanced by the movement of the rural churches, particularly those in Béarn and the Center-West. The 1620s and 1630s were then the years of the most rapid decline, centered overwhelmingly in the Midi and resulting from the full restoration of Catholicism in Béarn and the disastrous impact of the civil wars and plague upon so many southern centers of Huguenot strength. More gradual decline continued through the 1650s, before the 1660s brought the one decade in which Protestant baptismal levels increased, largely, one supposes, as a result of the country's general recovery from the economic difficulties of the era of the Thirty Years' War and the Fronde. As measures of persecution intensified in the final decades before the Revocation, the ranks of the Huguenots began to thin again, with the decline proving particularly marked in the churches of northern France. From the late 1670s onward, in fact, many of the congregations in northern France displayed a condition of perma-

[96] Pierre de l'Estoile, *Mémoires-Journaux*, 12 vols. (Paris, 1889–95), X, 337–8, quoted in Jacques Pannier, "La Réforme dans le Vermandois: l'Eglise de Saint-Quentin," *B.S.H.P.F.*, XLV (1896), 232. L'Estoile identifies the Jesuit preacher as "Gontier," but no Jesuit of that name appears in Henri Fouqueray's detailed *Histoire de la Compagnie de Jésus en France des origines à la suppression*, 5 vols. (Paris, 1910–25). Gontery, a central figure among the Jesuits in Paris and an active controversialist, appears to be the correct identification.

[97] "Un dénombrement des réformés de France en 1598," *B.S.H.P.F.*, I (1853), 123–4, citing this estimate in Gregorio Leti's 1692 biography of Elizabeth I. This census is also cited in an eighteenth-century copy of the acts of the 1663 provincial synod of Poitou. Nathaniel Weiss, "Statistique du Protestantisme Français en 1598," *ibid.*, XXXVIII (1889), 551.

FIGURE 13. Estimated Total Protestant Population of France and Béarn, 1600–1685, by Decade

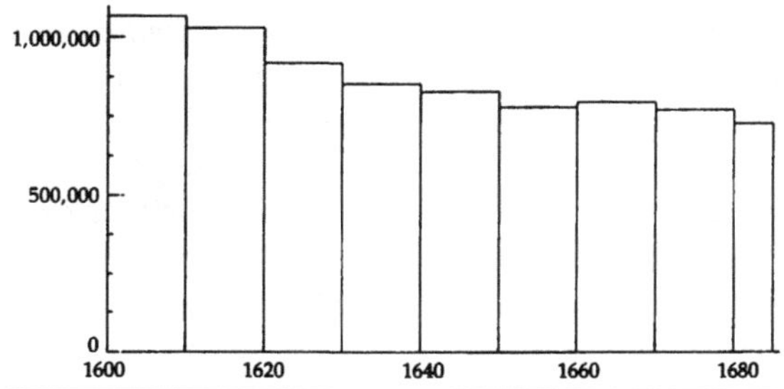

nent demographic crisis, with burials consistently outnumbering baptisms as emigration and conversion both accelerated.[98] But while the minority congregations of the north eroded rapidly in the years of increasing harassment prior to 1685, Huguenot ranks remained firm in many regions of the Midi where the Protestants were most numerous. The overall decline of the faith in these last years was thus far less marked than the experience of its most visible urban congregations might have led observers to believe. The broadest lesson of Figure 13 is thus a surprising one. The number of Huguenots diminished more rapidly in the first half of the seventeenth century than in the decades immediately preceding the Revocation. On the basis of a projection similar to that used to estimate the Protestant population around 1610, one can place the number of Huguenots living in France on the eve of the first great *dragonnades* in 1681 at ca. 730,000.

In conclusion, the ranks of French Protestantism experienced, between the reign of Henry IV and the arrival of the first dragoons in Poitou, an irregular decline that amounted to slightly under a quarter of the faith's initial strength if one excludes the exceptional region of Béarn, and to just under a third of its strength if one includes it. This decline was particularly marked in the cities, especially those with large Huguenot communities at the beginning of the period. Whether in La Rochelle or Montauban, Metz or Caen, Nérac or Alençon, the percentage of the population represented by the Protestants was far smaller on the eve of the Revocation than it had been eight decades previously. While less marked, the decline was real enough in the rural areas and small towns as well, especially those located in the western portions of the kingdom.

---

[98] This phenomenon may be observed in Alençon, Blois, Châtillon-sur-Loire, and Dangeau, although it does not appear in Rouen, Mer, Marchenoir, and Saint-Sylvain. I found no evidence of a similar phenomenon in any community of the Midi, although I did not examine the movement of burials in every community whose registers I utilized. Those in the Midi for which I did explore this question include Chef-Boutonne, Mens-en-Trièves, Gap, Sommières, Anduze, Roquecourbe, and Nérac. Gueneau, "Protestants du Centre," 243–4; Bollon, "Minorité broyée et Malthusianisme," 501.

While the Protestants' failure to maintain their ranks in certain regions points to the force of conversion in reducing their numbers in these areas, the restoration of Catholicism within a Béarn which had been only partially protestantized, the bitter harvest of the revolts of the 1620s, the inability of many of the large urban congregations to reproduce themselves, and the apparent lack of economic and demographic dynamism within such strongholds of rural Protestantism as the Cévennes and the Pays de Caux must all be accounted significant causes of the decline as well. The long, slow erosion of France's Huguenot community between 1600 and 1685 was a complex phenomenon with multiple causes.

PART II
DEMOGRAPHY AND *MENTALITES*

In the effort to know the "chrétien quelconque d'autrefois," historians of Protestantism must be particularly resourceful. The past generation may have seen the aims and methods of religious history renewed by a concern to reconstruct the beliefs and practices of Europe's ordinary inhabitants, but it is no accident that most of the pathbreaking studies in this enterprise have been devoted to Catholic Europe. Catholicism's abundance of voluntary associations, such as confraternities, and of rituals, such as pilgrimages or anniversary masses for the dead, makes it a religion whose ordinary practice is particularly rich in those gestures of commitment which leave traces for future generations of historians. In deemphasizing individual ritual gestures and stressing the inward experience of faith, the Reformers created a religion whose practice is far harder for historians peering back across the centuries to seize.

To be sure, certain documents do enable historians of Protestant societies to gain insight into the religious culture of those who lived within them. In those regions where ecclesiastical visitations were regularly performed, the records of these visits provide glimpses into the assiduity of participation in the sacraments and the educational enterprises of the church, even if the encounter between educated urban divines and uncommunicative villagers suspicious of officious outsiders must be interpreted with caution. Spiritual diaries or memoirs often cast a remarkably sharp light on the lives of those believers committed enough to keep such diaries. Consistory or church court records tell of the behavior of notorious sinners. Still, the limitations of all of these sources are evident.

As the Prologue has already suggested, historical demography can contribute to religious history not simply by illuminating the numerical evolution of a religious group, but also by shedding light on aspects of its behavior that are difficult, if not impossible, to establish in any other fashion. (Part I's discussion of the length of time people waited to have their children baptized has already attempted to illustrate this claim.) Furthermore, the great advantage of the statistics derived from parish register sources is that they shed light on the behavior of the entire community in question, not merely on those who excelled in either piety or detectable misbehavior. Of course, the findings yielded by such methods have their limitations too. While curves and statistics can reveal how widespread certain forms of behavior were and how these changed over time, they cannot tell us the meaning of these practices for those who engaged in them. This can only be learned from literary sources, and thus the demographic data need to be set in as rich a context of ethnographic information as possible. For this reason, the evidence unearthed through demographic investigation is best thought of as complementary to approaches to the historical study of religion drawing on the methods of folklore and historical ethnography, methods whose value has become increasingly evident in recent years.[1] While the ethnographic record can document the existence of certain beliefs and practices and tell us how those who held or performed them interpreted them, it rarely indicates just how widely shared these were or precisely when they appeared or disappeared. This is what demographic sources can clarify.[2]

A. The Seasonality of Marriage

The related issues of birth and marital seasonality offer particularly interesting insights into the attitudes of the first generations of Protestants toward both the old rituals and rhythms of the Catholic church and certain customary beliefs whose origin must be sought outside the theological systems of either church. The alternation between *temps clos* and *temps ouverts*, between periods of feast and periods of fast, was one of the fundamental rhythms of life in pre-Reformation Europe and, later, those parts of the continent which remained faithful to Rome. One aspect of this was the highly seasonal pattern of marriages. Demographic investigation of the seasonality of marriage has shown considerable regional variations in the times when people were most and least likely to wed, with local customs, the calendar of work, and the dates of important local events, notably hiring fairs, all influencing the frequency of marriage in any given month. Throughout Catholic Europe, however, one constant stands out. Very few marriages were celebrated during the months when the church calendar forbade weddings, that is to say, March (Lent) and December (Advent). Figure 14 sets forth this pattern for the Paris Basin between 1670 and 1700.

The Reformation, particularly in its Calvinistic variants, marked a rupture with the old prohibitions against marriage during Lent and Advent. Changes in popular practice quickly followed these theological changes in many parts of Protestant Europe. The March and December dips disappear rapidly from Genevan curves of marriage seasonality in the wake

---

1 As in such works as William A. Christian, Jr., *Local Religion in Sixteenth-Century Spain* (Princeton, 1981) and *Apparitions in Late Medieval Spain* (Princeton, 1981); Philippe Joutard, "Protestantisme populaire et univers magique: le cas cévenol," *Le Monde Alpin et Rhodanien*, V (1977), 145–71; and Lyndal Roper, "'Going to Church and Street': Weddings in Reformation Augsburg," *Past & Present*, 106 (1985), 62–101.

2 Marius Hudry, "Relations sexuelles prénuptiales en Tarentaise et dans le Beaufortin d'après les documents ecclésiastiques," *Le Monde Alpin et Rhodanien*, I (1974), 95-100, offers an excellent example of an ethnographic study which could have been usefully supplemented by demographic investigation. The author assembles a series of fascinating texts describing the local practice of *albergement* (bundling) and denouncing its consequences for the virtue of the region's young women, but he makes no effort to determine if prenuptial conceptions were in fact particularly numerous in this region, as might easily have been done on the basis of its parish registers.

FIGURE 14. **The Seasonal Movement of Marriages in the Paris Basin, 1671–1720**

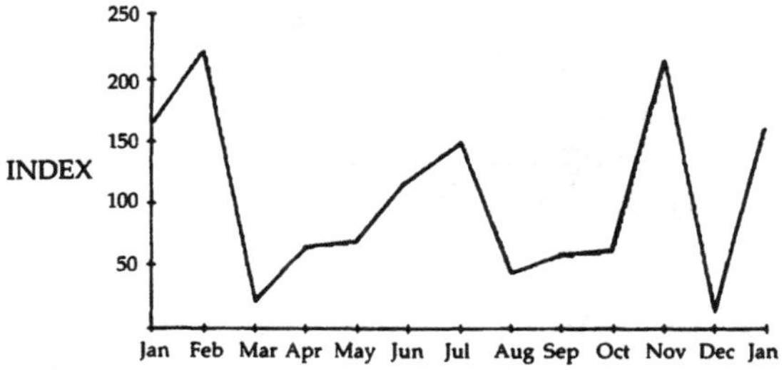

SOURCE: Dupâquier, *Population rurale du Bassin Parisien*, 298.

of the Reformation there.[3] They are similarly absent in Dutch Reformed churches and in Puritan New England in the seventeenth century.[4] But this disappearance of old patterns of seasonality was not universal in those regions which were made Protestant by law. A respect for the old prohibition of marriage during Lent lived on after the Reformation in Scotland, where the break from this custom came only after 1640, as first the Covenanters and then the Cromwellians stepped up the campaign to instill more thoroughly Reformed behavior in the faithful.[5] In England, the old church calendar was never explicitly changed with regard to prohibited periods for marriage, although the ban on marriage during Lent and Advent was challenged by Puritan opinion and was not explicitly reiterated in the Elizabethan Canons or the Book of Common Prayer. The transplanted Englishmen of the colonial Tidewater displayed a pronounced tendency to avoid March marriages, while Wrigley and Schofield's figures for England as a whole show sharp troughs in the number of marriages during Lent and Advent during the later sixteenth and early seventeenth centuries. These, however, subsequently diminished in size to 1800, without the Lenten dip ever disappearing. The precise regional and chronological pattern of the increasing rejection of these prohibitions has not yet been explored in a manner which would

---

3 Alfred Perrenoud, *La population de Genève du XVIe au début du XIXe siècle: étude démographique* (Geneva, 1979), 383–5.

4 G.J. Mentink and A.M. van der Woude, *De demografische entwikkeling te Rotterdam en Cool in de 17e en 18e eeuw* (Rotterdam, 1965), 140; van der Woude, *Het Noorderkwartier*, A.A.G. Bijdragen XVI (Wageningen, 1972), 791; David Cressy, "The Seasonality of Marriage in Old and New England," *Journal of Interdisciplinary History*, XVI (1985), 14–5.

5 Gordon Donaldson, *The Scottish Reformation* (Cambridge, 1960), 180; Walter Roland Foster, *The Church before the Covenants: The Church of Scotland, 1596–1638* (Edinburgh-London, 1975), 73–4; T.C. Smout, *A History of the Scottish People 1560–1830* (London, 1969), 83–6; L.D.S. films 1040102, 1040126 (parish registers of Dunfermline, county Fife; originals in the New Register House, Edinburgh, Old Parochial Registers 424/1–3). Dunfermline's registers reveal the following monthly indices of marriages:

	J	F	M	A	M	J	J	A	S	O	N	D
1562–90	103	142	18	84	108	159	117	94	54	56	144	125
1600–39	104	127	23	75	99	159	125	106	58	66	135	126
1640–79	86	79	62	83	76	154	114	125	47	78	148	146

clarify its causes, but, clearly, it must be linked both to the rise of Puritanism and to the growth of more secular attitudes.[6]

If these comparisons show the interest of seasonal patterns of marriage as an indication of the extent to which Protestant populations in fact broke with traditional Roman practices, what do we find among France's Huguenots? One leading French demographer and historian, citing seventeenth-century evidence from the Sancerrois and Lower Normandy, has argued that the prohibitions against marriage during Lent and Advent were so deeply rooted in the popular mentality that they were even respected by the Protestants, a claim which has subsequently found its way into the textbooks.[7] Yet such fidelity to Catholic custom would seem surprising in a community whose initial members (outside Béarn) had all freely embraced Protestantism and its doctrines. When one looks back to the sixteenth century, besides assembling as much information as possible about the seventeenth, a more complex story emerges. Table 19 sets out the information.

Good registers of marriages which date back to the earliest days of formal Reformed churches in France are rare, but they exist for Anduze, Montpellier, and Metz.[8] These show that the Protestants quickly began to celebrate marriages during the closed periods. Numerous weddings were performed in all three localities during both Lent and Advent, 1562, and the indices of March marriages for these earliest years (where a figure of 100 would be expected if weddings were distributed evenly across the entire year) suggest only the tiniest hint of any tendency to avoid marriage during either Lent or Advent, and that for only one of these churches, that of Metz.[9] The rapid Protestant rejection of traditional Catholic practice concerning the *temps clos* in these communities was part of the joyous, aggressive rejection of Catholic interdictions, now seen as the fraudulent inventions of a venal clerisy, that was so typical of this springtime of the French Reformation. There is little respect for tradition here.

During the subsequent nine decades, from 1570 to 1660, significant regional differences appeared. Between 1572 and 1599, the Protestants of the Cévennes continued to display complete indifference to prohibitions about marriage in Lent or Advent, and their co-religionists in Montpellier

---

[6] E.A. Wrigley and R.S. Schofield, *The Population History of England 1541–1871* (Cambridge, Mass., 1981), 298–300; Cressy, "Seasonality of Marriage," 1–2, 20; J. Wickham Legg, *English Church Life from the Restoration to the Tractarian Movement* (London, 1914), 260–1; Keith Thomas, *Religion and the Decline of Magic* (New York, 1971), 620–1.

[7] François Lebrun, *La vie conjugale sous l'Ancien Régime* (Paris, 1975), 38. See also Cressy, "Seasonality of Marriage," 3; Robert Muchembled, *Société et mentalités dans la France moderne XVIe–XVIIIe siècle* (Paris, 1990), 47.

[8] A few marriages were also recorded by one of Caen's pastors for the period 1560–63. See C.E. Lart, ed. *The Registers of the Protestant Church at Caen (Normandy)* (Vannes, 1907).

[9] The technique for calculating seasonal movements used throughout this study is that outlined in Henry, *Nouveau manuel*, 103–5. Caen's Protestants may have been more hesitant about celebrating marriages during March. Here, just one of 27 recorded weddings for 1560–62 took place in March. Obviously, the number of cases is too small to attach much reliability to these figures.

Table 19. The Seasonal Movement of Marriages

Locality	dates	Jan	Feb	Mar	Apr	May	Jun	Jul	Aug	Sep	Oct	Nov	Dec	n
1562–68														
Anduze	1562–65	93	110	108	141	86	97	86	79	141	108	59	93	164
Metz	1562–68	152	128	83	94	107	106	111	108	71	72	76	92	805
Montpellier	1562–68	96	115	127	130	121	96	81	114	69	80	84	89	798
1572–99														
Anduze	1572–96	100	82	95	111	104	109	89	109	113	92	100	95	950
St-Etienne-V-F	1574–83	161	92	99	119	115	95	107	46	126	92	79	69	154
2 chs. Béarn*	1573–99	195	253	70	66	92	74	42	30	56	44	105	185	592
Metz	1579–99	171	134	24	126	109	91	106	65	72	63	102	141	1893
Montpellier	1580–89	115	143	98	110	92	112	73	82	90	119	60	108	730
* Bellocq, Orthez														
1600–60														
Alençon	1629–59	100	125	137	97	111	109	105	85	88	88	68	88	414
Anduze	1610–59	120	84	108	146	51	117	82	121	93	112	79	86	644
Annonay	1640–59	143	139	116	115	132	87	53	32	126	58	109	95	223
Barbézieux	1600–35	113	196	151	144	116	93	88	59	37	49	66	94	813
2 chs. Béarn*	1620–68	142	128	92	93	87	88	92	85	82	93	101	117	745
Blois	1600–59	110	144	24	116	67	132	167	97	72	76	123	76	387
Castres	1609–59	124	125	138	139	61	122	88	85	70	68	87	96	1574
Châlons s/Mrne	1600–42	129	78	39	120	90	110	126	103	86	106	163	52	366
Loriol	1637–60	69	101	92	178	46	142	84	88	71	126	79	126	308
Marennes	1637–49	123	128	83	91	112	76	114	99	74	82	121	98	736
Marsillargues	1613–54	102	152	109	166	68	155	43	79	87	70	82	95	520
Metz	1600–59	113	159	33	108	106	101	113	107	63	72	93	136	3642
Montpellier	1602–16	94	110	107	156	61	126	72	74	79	95	113	117	906
Mougon	1600–04	158	263	158	100	168	111	71	10	5	15	90	61	231
	1633–59	133	183	55	132	138	114	85	24	26	117	127	74	1478
Nîmes	1625–59	127	125	106	134	61	118	50	71	62	142	105	101	2477
Niort	1622–37	158	151	71	143	94	108	77	54	70	91	59	128	350
Preuilly s/Claise	1600–59	91	133	50	135	50	73	151	131	125	81	83	101	117
Rouen	1631–64	125	157	20	104	127	87	112	75	118	106	104	65	1443
Roquecourbe	1612–59	118	168	128	112	38	142	89	86	40	38	102	144	369
2 chs. Perche#	1600–60	72	119	40	121	125	116	76	109	100	101	112	113	293
Revel	1600–59	111	99	115	143	75	125	122	65	77	89	91	91	820
Tours	1633–49	162	194	46	95	123	103	100	46	103	62	72	100	153
Vabre	1625–49	105	115	122	133	56	115	105	73	61	84	122	112	338
Wassy	1627–59	196	101	116	107	69	95	92	69	107	81	72	92	102
* Lagor, Salies														
# Authon-du-Perche, Montgoubert														
1660–84														
Alençon	1660–83	114	102	140	64	150	123	114	62	96	88	75	72	228
Annonay	1660–79	79	141	98	126	128	82	55	110	101	61	120	104	198
Blois	1660–78	185	166	34	87	151	87	118	118	104	17	104	34	70
Castres	1660–84	95	131	105	164	50	117	111	83	85	97	79	87	571
6 chs. Gard*	1668–84	111	120	99	181	31	109	70	72	81	149	102	78	571
Loriol	1661–83	101	73	53	141	75	100	93	88	82	119	123	150	267
Marennes	1669–80	76	155	47	82	106	108	135	110	91	100	116	78	576
Marsillargues	1668–83	104	74	147	158	61	146	31	37	89	98	114	141	192
Montélimar	1660–81	127	170	145	102	99	84	81	67	77	74	91	88	334
Montpellier	1668–80	107	129	97	158	68	114	69	88	80	74	122	100	780
Nérac	1668–80	117	151	56	163	32	150	36	65	88	93	100	157	292
Nîmes	1660–84	102	121	120	153	40	114	64	62	62	133	123	108	2191
Niort	1670–80	175	199	13	86	98	128	120	32	38	169	150	0	551
2 chs. Provence#	1669–84	101	110	151	167	117	150	67	50	104	67	69	50	211
Revel	1660–84	121	119	103	175	36	100	133	127	25	121	75	66	195
Roquecourbe	1660–84	90	126	77	112	26	146	122	96	106	70	119	115	184
Rouen	1665–84	114	126	22	85	129	94	138	76	92	116	117	91	740
Saint-Just	1669–83	110	152	26	98	153	107	136	84	116	75	107	40	408
Tours	1670–78	181	174	68	140	125	59	113	68	47	79	70	79	104
Wassy	1660–84	75	146	66	94	124	189	91	91	34	33	129	132	142
* Alès, Anduze, Lasalle, Monoblet, Sommières, Soudorgues														
# Lourmarin, Manosque														

and Béarn respected them scarcely more.[10] In Metz, however, a clear and very marked tendency to avoid marrying in Lent, although not in Advent, re-appeared from 1579 onward; indeed, the fall in the number of March marriages visible in this church between 1579 and 1599 was every bit as pronounced as in Catholic parishes of the era, and from the time of the League through the 1630s, its marriage registers even noted the date of Easter and the resumption of weddings in its aftermath. During the first six decades of the seventeenth century, pronounced respect for the Lenten interdict can also be clearly observed among the Protestants of Châlons-sur-Marne, Rouen, the Perche, Blois, Tours, Preuilly-sur-Claise, and, after 1630, Mougon. By contrast, throughout the regions of Huguenot strength from the Vivarais across Languedoc to Béarn – as well as in Barbézieux, Alençon, and Wassy – no attention whatsoever continued to be paid to the *temps clos*. Between these two extremes, a modest tendency to avoid March marriages can be observed in Loriol, Marennes, and Niort. Only in Rouen and Châlons-sur-Marne were the Advent restrictions much observed.

From the chronology just revealed, it seems clear that, where French Protestants displayed signs of respect for the Catholic prohibitions against marriage during Lent and Advent in the seventeenth century, this was rarely if ever the product of uninterrupted fidelity to deeply rooted traditions. Instead, it appears to have been a mark of political insecurity and the desire not to offend Catholic sensibilities. Part I has already alluded to the considerable differences which distinguished the behavior of those Protestants who lived in regions where the faith was numerous and powerful from that of those who had been made acutely aware of their vulnerability by the events of the recurring civil wars, most especially by the Saint Bartholomew's Massacre.[11] In comparison with certain other aspects of Huguenot behavior, the Protestants' disregard of traditional interdictions against marriage during Lent or Advent does not appear to have been especially shocking to their Catholic neighbors. Unlike conflicts over the burial place of recent converts or the Protestant refusal to pay the respect which the Catholics considered appropriate

---

[10] It must be admitted that the case of Béarn poses some difficult problems of interpretation. The number of baptisms celebrated in March there fell well below the level one would expect if marriages were distributed evenly across the year, but the two communities in the sample for which evidence is available for the sixteenth century were characterized by a highly seasonal marriage pattern, in which over half of all weddings took place in winter from December to February. The number of weddings celebrated in April was also well below what one would expect if marriages were distributed evenly across the year. It is consequently hard to know whether the March dip was simply a part of broader seasonal rhythms which governed life in this part of the world or was linked to Lent in some way. It was, in any case, not very pronounced.

[11] See pp. 29–30, 50–1. For the very different attitudes governing Protestant behavior in different parts of the country, see also Labrousse, "La conversion d'un huguenot au catholicisme en 1665," *Revue d'Histoire de l'Eglise de France*, LXIV (1978), 57; Labrousse, Philippe Joutard, Janine Estèbe, and Jean Lecuir, *La Saint-Barthélemy, ou les résonances d'un massacre* (Neuchatel, 1976), 83–6; Philip Benedict, *Rouen during the Wars of Religion* (Cambridge, 1981), 147–50, 242; Sauzet, *Contre-Réforme et Réforme Catholique en Bas-Languedoc*, 190–201, 305–24.

when encountering a procession in the street, the celebration of weddings during Lent was not a common cause of the anti-Huguenot *émotions* which punctuated the seventeenth century with some frequency, nor do Catholic peasants appear to have been particularly offended by remarks made in conversation that Lent was merely a human invention.[12] Nonetheless, marrying during Lent did violate Catholic sensibilities, and the Huguenots surely wished to avoid this in those regions where they felt least secure. The geographic pattern of respect for Catholic prohibitions regarding Lent displays a clear correspondence with the regions where the Protestants were numerically most isolated and politically most vulnerable. But this distinction between those churches whose members displayed a tendency to avoid marriage in March and those whose members paid no attention to Lent is not simply the distinction between the churches of northern France and those of the Huguenot crescent. It is noteworthy that the Protestants of Wassy and Alençon dared to disregard the Lenten interdicts—a sign, I would hypothesize, that they felt safer about their local political situation than most of their co-religionists of northern France. Equally noteworthy is the appearance of respect for these interdicts in the churches of Poitou and Saintonge after the revolts of the 1620s and their repression.

In 1662, a decision of the Conseil d'Etat made the prohibitions of the Roman church binding on the crown's Protestant subjects as well.[13] Now the Huguenots were legally required to abstain from marrying during Lent and Advent or to obtain a license if they wished to do so. Combined with the general intensification of persecution during the years of Louis XIV's personal reign, this *arrêt* furthered the Huguenot tendency to respect the Catholic interdicts, but even it failed to generate universal compliance with these rules. Once again the pattern of compliance or non-compliance suggests that this was closely linked to each church's local political situation.

In the provinces of the Center-West, the authorities were particularly vigilant about enforcing measures directed at the Huguenot population.[14] Here—in La Rochelle, Niort, Saint-Just, and Marennes—March and December marriages fell off dramatically.[15] A greater, although by no means universal, respect for the Catholic prohibitions may also be seen in Loriol and Nérac. But the crown's writ still ran considerably

[12] Benoist, *Histoire de l'Edit de Nantes*, recounts numerous episodes of anti-Huguenot violence in the seventeenth century. None of these appears to have been provoked by marriages held during prohibited periods. See also *Plaintes des Eglises réformées de France, sur les violences et injustices qui leur sont faites en plusieurs endrois du Royaume* (n.p., 1597); Pierre Blet, *Le clergé de France et la monarchie: Etude sur les Assemblées Générales du Clergé de 1615 à 1666*, 2 vols. (Rome, 1959), II, 342–88; Marc Venard, "Le comportement du peuple provençal face au fait protestant au XVIe siècle," in *Cinq siècles de Protestantisme à Marseille et en Provence* (Marseille, 1978), 33.

[13] Benoist, *Histoire de l'Edit de Nantes*, III, 479.

[14] *Ibid.*, III, 624 and *passim*; Faust, "Beleaguered Society," 14 and *passim*.

[15] For La Rochelle, see Faust, "Beleaguered Society," 189. As the author does not provide annual index values, I have not included this case in Table 19.

weaker in Languedoc. From Castres and Revel to Montpellier and the Cévennes, the number of Protestant marriages celebrated during March was slightly lower than in the preceding or following months after 1662, but remained considerable. In Marsillargues, proportionately more marriages were celebrated during March than previously, while Lourmarin, Manosque, Montélimar, and Nîmes were other communities in which the Protestants consistently defied this legislation with apparent impunity. Quite curiously, the frequency of March marriages by Protestants also increased in Blois, Tours, and Alençon. When Elie Benoist wrote that the "Reformez" paid no attention to the 1662 edict, he was reporting accurately the experience of his own church, but his statement cannot be generalized to all of the kingdom's churches.[16] In most northern churches, the drop-off in marriages during March was quite pronounced. But the regulations concerning Advent were far less widely respected here, as was the case throughout the century. It would appear that marriage during Advent was not as offensive to Catholic sensibilities as marriage during Lent, and that the legal prohibition of Advent marriages after 1662 was only enforced in the Center-West.

In sum, in the first flush of the Reformation's implantation in France, the country's Huguenots violated canon law interdictions against March and December marriages with what one presumes to have been calculated insouciance. Following the Saint Bartholomew's Massacre, those living in regions where the faith was least secure recognized that discretion dictated that they ought to respect at least the Lenten interdict, and over the subsequent century more and more communities bowed to this rule, first as their political situation weakened, then as the legal obligation to do so was imposed. Still, even on the eve of the Revocation, the Protestants of large parts of the country continued to feel secure in defying the law on this score.

The examination of the seasonal movement of marriages contains other lessons as well. One of the most striking findings to emerge from the investigation of marriage seasonality in other Protestant countries is that, even where the pattern of marriage tied to the Catholic church calendar disappeared, the triumph of the Reformation did not necessarily involve the rationalization of attitudes toward the seasons that might be expected as a consequence. In many Calvinist regions, other beliefs about the appropriateness or inappropriateness of certain times for marriage took hold instead. Figures from the Low Countries show a pronounced tendency for marriages to cluster in May between 1670 and 1800.[17] For Geneva and the nearby Pays de Vaud, Perrenoud has docu-

---

[16] Benoist, *Histoire de l'Edit de Nantes*, III, 623–4: "Comme il [the arrêt of 1662] assujettissoit les Reformez aux loix canoniques, pour lesquelles ils n'ont jamais eu la moindre veneration, ils n'y defererent point; et ils continuerent par tout à benir les mariages en toute saison."

[17] Mentink and ven der Woude, *Rotterdam*, 140; van der Woude, *Noorderkwartier*, 791; A.J. Schuurman, "De bevolking van Duiven, 1665–1795: Een historisch-demografische studie," *A.A.G. Bijdragen*, XXII (1979), 154. These authors provide no full explanation of this phenomenon.

mented the striking advance of a converse tendency to avoid marrying in May. This *creux de Mai* first appears in Genevan statistics in the 1570s and becomes marked from the turn of the century onward, enduring into the nineteenth century. In the surrounding countryside and in the city of Lausanne, it is already pronounced in the later sixteenth century, when parish registers first become available.[18]

The belief reflected in these Swiss figures, namely that May was an unlucky time for marriages, is well known to demographers and folklorists of France as well. Folklorists have collected numerous proverbs to the effect that May marriages are doomed to be short-lived or to yield sickly or deficient children, if any children at all. Demographers have shown that a tendency to avoid marrying in May spread gradually over the course of the nineteenth century, moving outward from two centers: the Mediterranean coast and the lower Loire valley and nearby Upper Poitou. The *creux de Mai* does not appear, however, in most statistics on the seasonality of marriage from the last century of the Ancien Régime.[19]

After reviewing the various explanations which have been proposed to account for this phenomenon, Perrenoud argued that the idea that May was an unlucky time to marry was a widespread and deeply rooted popular belief—very possibly linked to the larger cycle of May *reinages* and courting festivities—which came under attack during the Counter-Reformation as the church sought to enforce its own calendar of prohibitions at the expense of all "pagan" and "superstitious" rivals. A provincial council held in Bordeaux in 1624 ordered all clerics in that archdiocese "to uproot from people's minds the insane and superstitious notion some have not to wish to marry in the month of May, as if the month augured badly for marital fidelity and the prosperity of the marriage." Only where or when the control of Rome had been rejected, Perrenoud suggests, whether at the Reformation or with the "dechristianization" of the nineteenth century, could this belief flower. Far from being uncompromisingly hostile to all superstition, then, Calvinism may actually have provided more fertile ground than Counter-Reformation Catholicism for the development of certain beliefs about lucky and unlucky times.[20]

---

[18] Perrenoud, *Population de Genève*, 383–9; *idem*, "Calendrier du mariage et coutume populaire: Le creux de Mai en Suisse romande," *Population*, XXXVIII (1983), 925–40.

[19] Arnold Van Gennep, *Manuel de folklore français contemporain*, 5 vols. (Paris, 1937–47), I, 379–80; Jean Bourgeois, "Le mariage, coûtume saisonnière: contribution à une étude sociologique de la nuptialité en France," *Population*, I (1946), 623–42; Jacques Houdaille, "Un indicateur de pratique religieuse: la célébration saisonnière des mariages avant, pendant et après la Révolution française (1740–1829)," *Population*, XXXIII (1978), 367–79; Nicole Belmont, "Le joli mois de mai," *L'Histoire* (May, 1978), 16–25; Perrenoud, "Calendrier du mariage et coûtume populaire," 925–7. Of the many monographs and articles devoted to the historical demography of individual Old Regime communities or regions, I have encountered only one in which the examination of the seasonal movement of marriages reveals an eighteenth-century *creux de Mai*: Jean-Pierre Poussou, *Bordeaux et le Sud-Ouest au XVIIIe siècle: Croissance économique et attraction urbaine* (Paris, 1983), 613 (concerning Sainte-Foy-Tarentaise in Savoy).

[20] Perrenoud, "Calendrier du mariage et coûtume populaire," *passim*, esp. 926–7. In a

As Table 19 makes clear, the Huguenots of much of southern France came to share the aversion to May marriages. A clear *creux de Mai* is visible in communities from Dauphiné across Languedoc to the Agenais in the seventeenth century, appearing in Loriol, the Cévennes, Marsillargues, Montpellier, Castres, Vabre, Roquecourbe, Revel, and Nérac. This phenomenon was confined to this region. The *creux de Mai* does not appear in Annonay, Provence, Béarn, or the Center-West, nor does it make anything other than a single appearance in northern France (Blois 1600–1659), an appearance that is in all probability a statistical fluke.

The records of Anduze and Montpellier, which extend back into the sixteenth century, permit us to establish some chronological boundaries to this tendency to avoid marriage during May. (See Table 20.) In both communities, the May dip emerges clearly only from the first decades of the seventeenth century onward, although a faint trace of such a pattern may be observed in Montpellier in the 1580s and Anduze in the 1590s. The *creux de Mai* thus represents here, as in Geneva, not the survival of pre-Reformation beliefs, but a new pattern of behavior that only took hold in these two communities around the turn of the century.

As Table 20 also indicates, shunning May marriages was by no means an exclusively Protestant phenomenon in the seventeenth-century Midi. If French demographers of the Ancien Régime have not previously insisted much on the *creux de Mai*, this seems to be simply because so few parish register studies have been devoted to southern France for the period prior to the eighteenth century. The recent *Histoire de la population française* includes aggregated figures by region combining data about marriage seasonality for three decades between 1580 and 1689 that shows a tendency to avoid May marriages in the Midi and Rhône regions.[21] Soundings in early parish registers across Languedoc and Aquitaine reveal that the aversion to marrying in May was marked among the Catholics of Nîmes, Montpellier, Lunel, Nérac, Castelnaudary, Bordeaux, and two villages of the modern department of the Aude – in other words, in both city and countryside and in regions that remained almost entirely faithful to Rome as well as those where the Catholics lived side by side with an important Protestant population.[22] Comparison of Catholic and

still unpublished paper, "The Sacred and Conjugal Sexuality in Sixteenth-Century Lyon," Natalie Zemon Davis links the avoidance of marriage during May to traditional beliefs that women's sexual appetite was at its height in that month. "Marrying under the sign of such disturbing sexuality," she argues, "bode ill." I would like to thank Professor Davis for showing me this paper prior to publication.

[21] Dupâquier et al., *Histoire de la population française*, II, 297–9.

[22] Seasonal Movement of Marriages: Catholic Communities of the Midi

		J	F	M	A	M	J	J	A	S	O	N	D	n
2 parishes of Aude*	1608–89	78	272	23	81	36	202	141	59	72	72	168	19	361
Bordeaux	1660–80	132	254	23	107	33	119	101	79	115	60	181	6	–
Castelnaudary	1630–70	117	252	30	143	22	204	105	54	80	48	154	12	1189
Lunel	1610–67	140	203	36	180	59	142	62	73	64	89	142	23	420
Nérac	1624–82	129	186	35	109	71	124	99	69	131	57	212	0	167

* Barbaira, Bellegarde-du-Razes

SOURCES: L.D.S. films 1179035 and 1179046 (A.D. Aude 1 E 27 and 1 E 32); M. Sudre, "Aspects

Table 20. The Appearance and Evolution of the Creux de Mai

ANDUZE Protestants				CASTRES Protestants			
Years	Apr	May	Jun	Years	Apr	May	Jun
1562–79	114	99	97				
1580–96	117	103	113				
1610–23	153	59	130	1609–29	132	74	126
1642–59	138	43	105	1630–59	149	46	117
1660–83	205	30	81	1660–84	164	50	117
MONTPELLIER							
Protestants				Catholics			
Years	Apr	May	Jun	Years	Apr	May	Jun
1562–68	130	121	96				
1580–89	110	92	112				
1602–16	156	61	126				
				1623–28	97	90	144
				1631–49	153	71	140
				1650–69	126	55	135
1668–80	158	68	114	1670–84	138	79	139
NIMES							
Protestants				Catholics			
Years	Apr	May	Jun	Years	Apr	May	Jun
				1608–20	178	100	133
1625–39	115	73	110	1630–39	134	70	125
1640–59	155	47	127	1640–59	175	58	150
1660–84	153	40	114	1660–84	135	66	117
				1690–99	120	90	91

Protestant behavior within two confessionally divided cities, Nîmes and Montpellier, suggests that the practice may have taken hold slightly earlier among the Huguenots in Montpellier than among their Catholic neighbors and that in both cities it may have begun to weaken slightly earlier among the Catholics than among the Protestants. Still, what is most striking is the parallelism between the behavior of the two groups.[23] The belief in the unluckiness of May marriages was clearly shared by Catholic and Protestant alike in important parts of France in the seventeenth century. Then, the belief weakened. By the 1690s, the

démographiques de la paroisse Saint-Michel de Bordeaux (1660–1680)," *Annales de Démographie Historique*, 1974, 239; L.D.S. films 1217818–9 (A.C. Castelnaudary, GG 4, 7, 10, 12, 16, 22, 25, 30, 33, 37), 1179307, 730822 (A.D. Lot-et-Garonne, 4 E 199/18–19). May marriages were also avoided in Lyon in the 1570s and in the Morvan in the seventeenth century. Davis, "Sacred and Conjugal Sexuality," 9; Jacques Houdaille, "Quatre villages du Morvan 1610–1870," *Population*, XLII (1987), 664.

[23] In interpreting the evidence in Table 20, it should be recalled that the 1620s were troubled years in Montpellier and that figures from this decade may reflect atypical patterns. Unfortunately, in the regions for which I have explored this issue, Catholic marriage registers exist for only a few, scattered years prior to 1600 and are too spotty to enable one to reconstruct the chronology and geography of this practice's spread.

creux de Mai had disappeared from the seasonal movement of marriages in Nîmes; it is scarcely visible in Bordeaux in 1711–15.[24]

What we are dealing with here is thus a popular belief, embraced by Catholics and Protestants alike, which waxed and waned at several different moments in French history. Is its eighteenth-century declension to be attributed to a successful assault by reforming Catholicism on "superstition" and rival calendrical systems? One can wonder, since—the Bordeaux example to the contrary notwithstanding—concern with this issue was decidedly muted in synodal statutes from the Midi.[25] The practice may have come and gone for very different reasons, perhaps following a process of spreading enthusiasm sparked by reported events which appeared to confirm the belief, and subsequent disenchantment as such events became rarer, similar to the process governing the cycles in the popularity of healing shrines.[26] Reconstructing the full story of the rise and fall of the *creux de Mai* is another task that requires still more extensive investigation than it has been possible to carry out here.[27] The information assembled in this study nonetheless underscores several larger points of importance. First, the two confessions clearly did not form self-enclosed worlds of belief and practice in seventeenth-century France. New cultural or folkloric elements which arose independently of either theological system could become shared by the faithful of both. Second, it has become increasingly evident in recent years that the image of *méridional* Calvinism as so complete and powerful a system of religious culture that it effaced all competing folk beliefs or cultural practices—a picture encapsulated in the image of *cévenol* women singing psalms to their babies as lullabies—is overdrawn. Reformed synodal records from

---

[24] Poussou, *Bordeaux et le Sud-Ouest au XVIIIe siècle*, 603.

[25] I have examined the following synodal decrees for southern France: *Ordonnances et constitutions synodales decrets et reglemens, donnés au Dioceze de Bordeaux par feux Nosseigneurs le Cardinal de Sourdis, Henry Descoubleau de Sourdis, Henry de Bethune, Archeveques de Bordeaux. Reveus, confirmés et augmentés par Monseigneur Louis d'Anglure de Bourlemont, Archeveque de Bordeaux, Primat d'Aquitaine* (Bordeaux, 1686); *Statuts synodaux du dioces d'Alby, publiez au synode tenu le XXVI May MDCXCV* (Paris, 1695); Simon de Peyronet, *Jus sacrum ecclesiae tolosanae* (Toulouse, 1669); *Statuts et reglemens synodaux du diocèse d'Agen. Leus et publiez depuis l'année 1666 renouvelez et confirmez dans le Synode tenu à Agen les 11 et 12 du mois d'Avril 1673* (Agen, 1673); *Statuts synodaux du diocese d'Alet. Faits depuis l'année 1640 jusqu'en 1674* (Paris, 1675); *Ordonnances synodales pour le diocese d'Uzes avec le prosne et autres formulaires necessaires pour l'administration des sacrements* (Nîmes, 1635; another ed. Montpellier, 1654); *Ordonnances synodales du dioceze de Rodez* (Rodez, 1674). Only the synodal statutes of Agen refer to the issue, urging parish curés to seek to abolish "distinctions de mois et de jours heureux ou mal-heureux pour le mariage" as part of a far broader assault on superstitions. Among the many synodal references to superstition assembled by Jean-Baptiste Thiers in his *Traité des superstitions* (2nd. ed. Paris, 1697–1704), denunciation of the belief in lucky or unlucky days or months for marriage appears in the statutes of the diocese of Sens for 1658, of Évreux for 1664, and of Grenoble for 1690. Thiers's own discussion of superstitions regarding time (Part 1, Book 4, ch. 3) makes no reference to the belief that May was an unlucky time for marriage.

[26] William A. Christian, Jr., *Person and God in a Spanish Valley* (2nd ed., Princeton, 1989), 50–78, esp. 64–5.

[27] Ideally, such an investigation would trace as precisely as possible both the geographic and chronological contours of this phenomenon over time and the sociology of those who either embraced or defied it.

later seventeenth-century Dauphiné reveal the continued strength of practices which made May a month of maypoles, "desbauches et insolences," charivaris, and "ranconnements de mariages." A community of Huguenot refugees in Hesse has preserved to the present day May customs that were once traditional in the uplands of Dauphiné from which the founders of this community emigrated, but have now disappeared from Dauphiné itself.[28] Anduze's consistory records reveal the survival of magical practices and conjuring well into the second half of the seventeenth century, and nineteenth-century folklorists found that *cévenol* Protestants continued to seek remedies against the evil eye then.[29] The spread of the *creux de Mai* throughout Huguenot communities of the Midi provides still more evidence of this coexistence of Calvinism and "popular culture."

B. Lent and Conceptions

In addition to the sharp drop in the number of marriages during March and December, the seasonality of demographic events followed the Roman church calendar in a second way, too, in traditional Catholic Europe. A small but clear dip in conceptions is visible during Lent in virtually all the Catholic regions for which the seasonal movement of conceptions has been calculated from a number of cases sufficient to yield reliable results.

Where the decline in marriages during Lent and Advent clearly resulted from the provisions of canon law, the cause of this March dip in conceptions has been the subject of extended debate. Initially, modern demographers tended to attribute the fall in conceptions during March to church teachings which discouraged sexual intercourse during Lent. In the early Middle Ages, it was strictly forbidden to make love during Lent. By the close of the Middle Ages, this *necessitas obedientiae* had become a *consilium reverentiae*, but it was still recommended as such by preachers and catechists during the sixteenth and seventeenth centuries.[30] If fewer children were conceived during March, this was because at least a fraction of the Catholic faithful followed these precepts.

But not all historians have been willing to ascribe the fall in conceptions to greater continence during Lent on the part of the Catholic

---

[28] Pierre Bolle, *Le protestant dauphinois et la république des synodes à la veille de la Révocation* (Lyon, 1985), 171; Jean Imbert, "La Mayence dauphinoise en pays Hessois," *Le Monde Alpin et Rhodanien*, I (1974), 185–7.

[29] A.C. Anduze (at A.D. Gard), GG 45, fos. 116, 315; Joutard, "Protestantisme populaire et univers magique," 151–5. The Anduze consistory records also testify to the survival of a vigorous and rowdy *abbé de jeunesse* still able in the 1660s to extract its traditional levy upon newly married couples despite repeated attempts to end this practice on the part of both the consistory and the *consulat*.

[30] Etienne Hélin, "Opinions de quelques casuistes de la Contre-Réforme sur l'avortement, la contraception et la continence dans le mariage" in Hélène Bergues et al., *La prévention des naissances dans la famille: Ses origines dans les temps modernes* (Paris, 1960), 247–9; Davis, "Sacred and Conjugal Sexuality," 3–4.

faithful. In an article published in 1974, François Lebrun expressed the most serious doubts.[31] Abstinence from sex during Lent, he noted, was urged neither in the numerous seventeenth-century sets of synodal statutes nor in such influential devotional handbooks of the era as Saint François de Sales's *Introduction à la vie dévote.* Once Jansenism developed, it was awkward for non-Jansenist priests to counsel parishioners to refrain from intercourse during Lent, since one of the rigorist positions of Jansenism which main-line churchmen denounced as erroneous was a revival of the older claim that abstinence was positively required during this period. Furthermore, Lebrun investigated the movement of conceptions in one rural parish whose priest was a committed Jansenist and found no increase in the respect for continence during Lent as a result of this priest's tenure, but rather a decline. Lebrun's arguments were not entirely convincing. His calculation of seasonal fluctuations in the Jansenist parish rested on too few cases to be statistically significant, and he himself cited seventeenth-century texts which instructed priests to exhort their parishioners to continence during times of fast. Furthermore, he offered no alternative explanation that would explain the March dip in conceptions. Nonetheless, his article opened up once again a question that had appeared to be closed.

The most spectacular discovery concerning the March dip in conceptions was recently made by Jean-Pierre Bardet. In his study of Rouen's population, he found that fewer conceptions occurred during Lent not only within the population at large, but also within two sub-populations whom one would hardly expect to show much respect for Catholicism's teachings about sexual continence in Lent: the Protestants, and the mothers of illegitimate children. Only common conditions imposed on all of these groups could account for this pattern, he reasoned. The dip must have resulted from temporary sterility provoked by the changes in diet associated with Lent, an explanation proposed by Jacques Dupâquier as well.[32] Since butchers' shops were closed by law during Lent, no towndweller could avoid the church's ban on eating meat and butter. Of course, it might be wondered if the ordinary Ancien Régime Frenchwoman's diet included enough meat and butter for immediate physiological consequences to follow from being unable to eat these. Still, if the Bardet-Dupâquier interpretation is correct, the March dip in conceptions reflects not voluntary but imposed asceticism. Rabelais would certainly have been pleased to learn of this difference of opinion among modern schoolmen, since the terms of the debate are precisely those which set Pantagruel and Friar John to arguing: do seasonal movements in the number of conceptions around Lent result from changes in diet or in actual sexual behavior?

---

[31] Lebrun, "Démographie et mentalités: Le mouvement des conceptions sous l'Ancien Régime," *Annales de Démographie Historique* (1974), 45–50. See also Pierre Chaunu, *La civilisation de l'Europe des Lumières* (Paris, 1971), 132.

[32] Bardet, *Rouen,* I, 311–16; Dupâquier, *Population rurale du Bassin Parisien,* 325–9, 380–1.

FIGURE 15. **The Seasonal Movement of Births and Baptisms, Anduze**

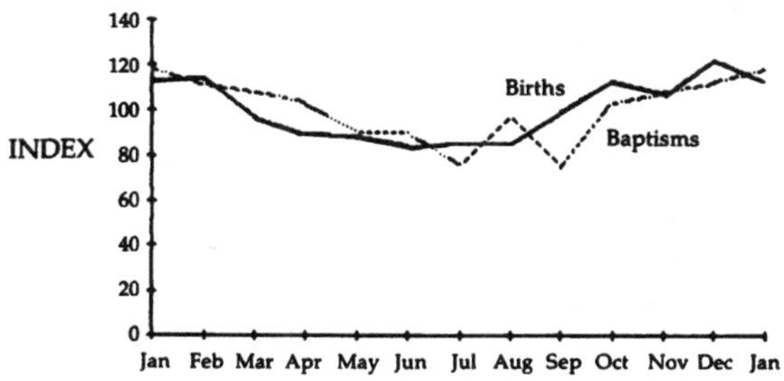

Care must be exercised in calculating the seasonal movement of conceptions among the Huguenots. While the standard method for determining this, extrapolating backward nine months from the seasonal movement of baptisms, is acceptable in studies involving communities where the delay between births and baptisms was brief, such techniques can lead to misleading conclusions for communities where parents commonly waited weeks or even months before having their infants christened. Figure 15, which compares the movement of births and baptisms in Anduze around mid-century, reveals that in certain periods of the year, most notably July and September, Anduze's inhabitants waited longer before having their children baptized than in others. Consequently, the seasonal movement of baptisms fails to convey accurately the seasonal movement of births. For most Huguenot congregations, one must patiently note down the precise date of birth for each child to determine the seasonal pattern of conceptions.

This has been done for two communities whose registers regularly note the date of birth as well as of baptism, Anduze and Annonay. The movement of baptisms has also been utilized for four congregations located in parts of France where the typical delay between birth and baptism does not appear to have been long, Niort, Tours, Alençon, and Rouen.[33] The results are set forth in Table 21. To these cases could be added that of the Brie, studied by Eva Telkès, who found no decline in March conceptions there.[34]

The results of this exercise just add to the uncertainties involved in seeking to make sense of the March dip in conceptions. As can be seen, the same March dip found in Rouen appears in Alençon and Tours. But in Niort, Anduze, and Annonay, as in the Brie, no decline emerges.

If the legal closing of butchers' shops were the key to the March dip in conceptions, then we would expect to find such a dip everywhere

[33] The figures for Tours are taken from Maillard, "Religion et démographie," 549.

[34] Telkès, "Les Protestants en Brie au 17ème siècle: Approche démographique et socio-économique" (unpubl. *mémoire de maitrise*, Université de Paris, 1971), unpaginated. Telkès does not provide the precise monthly figures.

TABLE 21. The Seasonal Movement of Conceptions

		Month of birth or baptism:											
		O	N	D	J	F	M	A	M	J	J	A	S
		Month of conception:											
Community and dates	# of cases	J	F	M	A	M	J	J	A	S	O	N	D
Rouen, 1630–84	–	109	112	98	107	102	110	104	91	85	89	96	97
Alençon, 1620–80	2666	94	101	93	105	118	118	115	95	91	84	87	99
Niort, 1623–36,'70–80	3881	103	95	111	120	128	109	95	92	67	76	93	113
Anduze, 1609–83	6385	113	107	123	113	114	97	90	89	84	86	86	100
Annonay, 1600–64	3368	113	102	106	116	117	106	91	90	85	87	94	93
Tours, 1632–84	–	110	125	85	101	100	103	99	103	87	81	100	106

among the Huguenots except where they controlled local government or felt that they could defy the regulations banning the sale of meat during Lent. Edicts forbidding meat from being sold or served publicly during Lent were promulgated by the crown in 1549 and 1563, as Protestantism grew in strength in France. They were reiterated locally in certain areas in the seventeenth century after violators were found infringing them, or as part of broader anti-Huguenot campaigns.[35] It is clear, however, that the Huguenots could ignore them with impunity in certain regions of seventeenth-century France. A Dutch traveler noted with some pleasure that a Protestant innkeeper served him meat on a Friday in Pons in 1635, while according to Elie Benoist, it was common for all the rules concerning Catholic fast days to be ignored in those regions where the Huguenots formed a majority of the population and dominated the *consulat*.[36] In light of this, it is not surprising to find no March dip in a Huguenot town such as Anduze or even in Annonay, where the Protestants formed roughly half of the population. But the absence of such a dip in Niort admits of no such explanation, since the Huguenots were in the minority here and the authorities in Poitou seem generally to have been vigilant in their enforcement of the laws concerning Protestant behavior. Indeed, according to a complaint of the 1601 provincial synod of Poitou, officials in nearby Saint-Maixent even conducted house-to-house searches on fast days to ensure that the Protestants were not eating meat.[37]

If forced to explain the evidence which has come to light with regard to this question to date, one might argue that the decline in March conceptions within France's Catholic population resulted from the combination of abstinence from sex and dietary changes during Lent, and that

[35] Nicolas Delamare, *Traité de la police* (Paris, 1722), I, 388; Jacques Decanter, "La vie municipale à Rochechouart de 1639 à 1643," *Bulletin de la Société Archéologique et Historique du Limousin*, LXXXXV (1968), 180.

[36] Hans Bots, "Voyages faits par de jeunes hollandais en France. Deux voyages types: Gysbert de With et Nicolas Heinsius," in *La découverte de la France au XVIIe siècle* (Paris, 1980), 475; Benoist, *Histoire de l'Edit de Nantes*, III, 23–4, 40.

[37] B.P.F., MS 579 (1), fol. 31.

those Protestant communities sharing a similar decline were particularly prosperous urban ones within which the legal closure of butchers' shops would have altered members' diets sufficiently to provoke a visible drop in the number of conceptions. But it must be admitted that this explanation is highly speculative. The mysteries of this particular *creux de Mars* continue to defy simple explanation. We have not progressed much beyond Rabelais.

C. "Paillardise"

A final area where demographic statistics can illuminate the degree of respect accorded moral norms espoused by the churches lies in the area of sexual morality, as revealed by statistics of illegitimate births and premarital conceptions. Few scholars today would pose the question in precisely the same terms as Locke: "Were the Reformed better than the Papists?" Nor is it possible, after the many recent studies devoted to the history of courtship practices and of bastardy, to view the strength of commitment to religious teachings as the only force controlling levels of illicit sexual activity in early modern Europe. Local customs governing courtship and the degree of sexual intimacy permitted fiancées varied widely from region to region, and these produced significant regional variations in the rates of illegitimate births and prenuptial conceptions. Within the Paris Basin, for instance, illegitimacy rates seem to have been consistently higher in Normandy than anywhere else, and pregnancy out of wedlock does not seem to have brought the shame upon the young couple that it did in the Ile-de-France.[38] Economic conditions also exerted their influence. Illegitimacy rose in periods of economic difficulty, while Segalen hypothesizes that the amount of freedom given young people during courtship was linked to the local distribution of economic power. In regions characterized by considerable economic inequality and sharp class lines, free contact between all of the young people of the village posed a threat to maintaining the social order, and customs were more restrictive than in areas where wealth and property were more equally distributed.[39] For all the importance of these forces, however, the influence which the religious climate exercised on sexual behavior remained considerable. Perhaps the most striking evidence of this is the astoundingly low levels of illegitimacy and of prenuptial conceptions

---

[38] Dupâquier, *Population rurale du Bassin Parisien*, 367–70. See also the important collection of essays edited by Peter Laslett, Karla Oosterveen, and Richard M. Smith, *Bastardy and its Comparative History: Studies in the History of Illegitimacy and Marital Nonconformism in Britain, France, Germany, Sweden, North America, Jamaica and Japan* (Cambridge, Mass., 1980).

[39] Martine Segalen, *Love and Power in the Peasant Family*, tr. Sarah Matthews (Chicago, 1983), 21–4; David Levine and Keith Wrightson, "The Social Context of Illegitimacy in Early Modern England" in Laslett et al., *Bastardy and its Comparative History*, 158–75. The link which these last authors identify between peaks of illegitimacy and periods of economic crisis is corroborated as well by French figures for the later years of Louis XIV's reign. Molinier, *Stagnations et croissance*, 369–70; Kathryn Norberg, *Rich and Poor in Grenoble 1600–1814* (Berkeley, 1985), 95–7.

TABLE 22. Illegitimacy Rates: Illegitimate Births as Percentage of All Baptisms

Protestants		Catholics	
Alençon (1620–85)	0.03%	Bayeux (17th century)	1.2%
		Tourouvre au Perche (1640–1729)	0.8%
Anduze (1642–64)	0.6%	Sérignan (1650–80)	0.9%
La Rochelle (1625–83)	0.5%		
Layrac (1610–74)	0.5%	Layrac (17th c.)	1%
Meaux & Chalandos (17th c.)	0.02%	Coulommiers (1670–1790)	0.3%
		Argenteuil (1670–95)	0.3%
Montjoux	0.9%		
Puylaurens (1630–50)	1.2%		
Rouen (1631–85)	0.8%	Rouen (1670–89)	3.5%

SOURCES: Alençon: B.P.F., Fonds Robert; Bayeux, Tourouvre, Coulommiers, and Argenteuil: Dupâquier, *Population rurale du Bassin Parisien*, 369–70; Anduze: L.D.S. films 670776–7; Sérignan: Alain Molinier, "Une paroisse du Bas Languedoc: Sérignan, 1650–1792," *Mémoires de la Société Archéologique de Montpellier*, XII (1968), 164; La Rochelle: Faust, "Beleaguered Society," 192; Layrac: Gregory Hanlon, "Confession and Community in 17th Century France: Catholics and Protestants in Aquitaine" (unpublished manuscript), 178 (the Catholic figure for this community is given as being "in the vicinity of one per cent"); Meaux and Chalandos: Telkès, "Protestants en Brie," n.p.; Montjoux: Jean Sambuc, "Le registre des protestants de Montjoux (Drôme) 1608–1669 suivi d'une étude sur la famille des seigneurs dudit lieu," *B.S.H.P.F.*, CXV (1969), 92; Puylaurens: G.E. de Falguerolles, "Les paroissiens de l'Eglise réformée à Puylaurens (1630–1650)," *B.S.H.P.F.*, CXI (1965), 94; Rouen: Bardet, *Rouen*, II, 176.

found in Geneva in the generation immediately following the Reformation. An illegitimacy rate of 0.14 percent and prenuptial conceptions of just one percent are striking confirmation of the reformation of manners in this city which so enchanted godly visitors.[40] It is obvious that figures on illicit sexual activity can tell us something about the actual prevalence of that great concern of Calvinist consistories and Catholic confessors alike, "paillardise."

Tables 22 and 23 set forth information about extramarital sexual conduct within several Huguenot congregations in the seventeenth century. Where figures are available about the Catholic population of the same or nearby communities, these have been provided as well in order to permit comparisons between the two faiths that are affected as little as possible by variations in regional customs.

What emerges from these figures is the remarkable infrequency with which babies were conceived out of wedlock. None of the communities for which information is available here reveals rates of either illegitimate births or premarital conceptions quite as low as late sixteenth-century Geneva—not even Meaux and Chalandos in the virtuous Brie. Nonetheless, all witnessed relatively few such events. Furthermore, wherever comparisons are possible with nearby Catholic populations, the Protes-

[40] Monter, "Historical Demography and Religious History," 414–6.

TABLE 23. Premarital Conceptions: Children Born Within Seven Months of Their Parents' Marriage as Percentage of All First Births

Protestants		Catholics	
Alençon (1640–84)	5%	Bayeux (1640–1700)	8%
"notables"	4%		
non-"notables"	11%		
Anduze (1654–65)	4%	Sérignan (1650–80)	11%
Annonay (1640–70)	3%	Bourg-St-Andéol (1662–1715)	15%
La Rochelle (1630–83)	4%		
Meaux & Chalandos (17th c.)	2%	Coulommiers (1670–1790)	4%
		Argenteuil (1670–95)	7%
Rouen (17th c.)	6%	Rouen (17th c.)	10%

SOURCES: Alençon (n = 129): B.P.F., Fonds Robert; Bayeux, Coulommiers, and Argenteuil: Dupâquier, *Population rurale du Bassin Parisien*, 369–70; Anduze (n = 77): L.D.S. films 670776–7; Sérignan: Molinier, "Une paroisse du Bas Languedoc," 164; Annonay (n = 222): L.D.S. films 1069212–3; Bourg-Saint-Andéol (n = 33): Molinier, *Stagnations et croissance*, 362; La Rochelle (n = 1657): Faust, "Beleaguered Society," 192; Meaux and Chalandos (n = 230): Telkès, "Protestants en Brie," n.p.; Rouen: Bardet, *Rouen*, I, 325 (the caption on this table is in error).

tant rates turn out to have been lower. As yet unpublished work on Layrac by Gregory Hanlon has shown that such inter-confessional comparisons of illegitimacy rates must be interpreted with caution. While Protestant women in Layrac bore fewer illegitimate children than their Catholic counterparts, the town's consistory records contain several cases of men denounced for fornication which are not echoed by entries in the baptismal registers recording the christening of their offspring. This was a region where the Protestants tended to be the more prosperous residents of the chief settlement of the community and the Catholics the less wealthy inhabitants of the surrounding hamlets, and it was common across France at this time for illegitimate births to be the product of relationships between higher-status men and lower-status women, especially servants. The higher rates of illegitimacy recorded in the Catholic parish registers of the region thus may stem in part from the offspring of such mixed couplings.[41] More generally, as the figures for Alençon remind us, the children of wealthier families seem to have cleaved more tightly to prescribed standards of sexual behavior than did those of artisan or laborer stock, and part of the observable difference between the Catholic and Protestant figures stems in other cases as well from the frequent position of the Protestants as something of a local economic elite.[42] But this explanation can hardly account for the low rates of prenuptial conceptions found in either Anduze, where virtually the entire population of the town was Protestant, or Meaux, where the Huguenot

[41] Gregory Hanlon, "Confession and Community in 17th Century France: Catholics and Protestants in Aquitaine," 178–9. I would like to thank Professor Hanlon for allowing me to quote from the manuscript version of this important forthcoming book.

[42] This was especially true in Alençon, La Rochelle, and, to a lesser degree, Rouen.

community was composed primarily of *vignerons* and other agricultural workers.[43] While it was a staple of Huguenot sermons to deplore the sinfulness of the *troupeau* and to attribute any misfortunes which befell the community to the increasing wickedness of its members, the evidence regarding Protestant sexual behavior suggests that, within a country and an era generally characterized by remarkably low rates of illegitimate births and premarital conceptions, the Huguenots cleaved a bit more tightly yet than their Catholic neighbors to ruling standards of sexual morality.

Is this to be attributed to the tight consistorial surveillance to which they were subjected? Obtaining a precise idea of just how closely the ministers and elders watched the behavior of church members is extremely difficult. The national synod of 1579 decreed that "all offenses which are duly admitted and for which amends have been made will be removed from the Consistory Books, except those accompanied by disobedience which have been punished by suspension from the Lord's Supper or Excommunication."[44] A brief examination of several surviving seventeenth-century consistorial registers suggests that this rule was not always followed to the letter.[45] In certain years prior to 1661, for example, Anduze's records note cases which came before the consistory which did not result in suspension from communion.[46] Nonetheless, the majority of consistorial registers from this period appear to record primarily administrative matters concerning the running of the church, decisions about the distribution of charity, and general warnings issued to the congregation about misbehavior—not investigations of reported individual misdemeanors—without it being clear how fully this represents the entire scope of the consistory's activities. From the Anduze records, it appears that the intensity of disciplinary surveillance did not come close to approaching the sort of institutionalized spying found in the most rigorously controlled Reformed communities. In nearly all the cases of suspected sexual immorality that were taken up by Anduze's consistory, the evidence of wrongdoing would have been known to much of the com-

[43] Telkès, "Protestants en Brie," unpaginated.

[44] Aymon, *Tous les Synodes Nationales*, 141.

[45] I examined the registers of Anduze, 1659–73 (A.C. Anduze at A.D. Gard, GG 45); Niort, 1629–84 (Bibliothèque Municipale de Poitiers, MS dom Fontenau, XXXVII, fos. 2–137); and Blois, 1665–77 (Paul de Félice, *La Réforme dans le Blaisois: Documents inédits* [Orleans, 1885; repr. ed. Marseille, 1979]). For other studies which make use of seventeenth-century consistory records, see Hanlon, "Confession and Community"; Solange Bertheau, "Le consistoire dans les Eglises réformées du Moyen-Poitou au XVIIe siècle," *B.S.H.P.F.*, CXVI (1970), 527–8; Alfred Leroux, "L'Eglise réformée de Bordeaux de 1660 à 1670 (d'après le cinquième registre du Consistoire)," *B.S.H.P.F.*, LXIX (1920), 177–208; J.-P. Hugues, *Histoire de l'Eglise réformée d'Anduze* (Montpellier, 1864), 556ff.

[46] After 1661, a new secretary took over. Subsequently, the register not only records no such cases of disciplinary matters which did not lead to suspension from communion; the number of cases noted which did result in this penalty also drops off sharply. Continuing references to people readmitted to the peace of the church suggest that suspensions from communion nonetheless continued to be handed out. Hanlon also reports loquacious consistory records for Layrac prior to 1630, "when a cloak of silence falls over the proceedings of the consistory."

munity; either the woman in question was pregnant, a man was maintaining a "femme mal vivante" in his house, or a group of young men had attempted to drag a young woman from her house "aux fins de malverser avec elle."[47] Once again, however, the secretary of the consistory may have seen fit to put down in writing only those cases which had already created a degree of community scandal. There may also have been a further level of consistorial investigation of private sins that has been forever lost from view. If the cases recorded in Anduze's consistorial register can be taken to speak for the level of consistorial surveillance throughout France, then the low rates of illegitimate births and premarital conceptions found in the seventeenth-century Huguenot churches must be attributed at least as much to the church members' internalization of values condemning illicit sex, or to the fear of community shame, as to the external pressure of ecclesiastical discipline. Far more research in the consistory records will be needed, however, before any confident statements can be made about this.

[47] I had hoped to be able to see just how effective consistorial surveillance was by examining whether or not those couples who could be determined through family reconstitution techniques to have engaged in premarital intercourse drew the attention of the consistory. Unfortunately, none of the cases where children were born to couples in Anduze within seven months of their marriage occurred during the years when the register I examined provides details about disciplinary cases.

CONCLUSION

Within the historiography of seventeenth-century French Protestantism, itself dominated by historians of Huguenot stock, the chief interpretive debate of the past generation has concerned the vitality of the community in the generations preceding the Revocation of the Edict of Nantes. The debate began when the leading historian of the subject, Emile G. Léonard, broke polemically with the previously reigning *topos* of an innocent and defenseless community unjustly persecuted, in his 1961 *Histoire générale du Protestantisme.* Léonard suggested instead that the Reformed community bore a degree of responsibility for its ultimate fate in the France of Louis XIV, to the extent that it had allowed itself to be weakened internally over the course of the century by too many compromises with the monarchy and *le monde.*[1] This diagnosis appealed to the prophetic streak so pronounced in Pierre Chaunu, who, in a long review essay, extracted from Léonard's work the lesson that the community was "spiritually sick" until it was saved *in extremis* by "the beneficial . . . revival of persecution."[2] Most recent work has tended to reject this picture of the Huguenot community in the seventeenth century as unduly pessimistic, but few among the *petit troupeau* of historians who have written about this group have been able to ignore Léonard's ideas.[3]

For historians approaching the history of French Protestantism less out of a desire to come to grips with the strengths and weaknesses of their own tradition than out of a broader interest in the nature of religious life in the post-Reformation era, a different range of questions may seem better suited to illuminating the history of this religious minority. Once a stable situation of religious toleration was established in France, how much movement was there back and forth from one confession to the other? A generation after the initial establishment of Reformed churches in France, how thoroughly had their members internalized the practices and values incarnated in the official theology of the religion? How great

---

[1] Léonard, *Histoire général du Protestantisme*, 3 vols. (Paris, 1961–64), II, 331–50.

[2] Pierre Chaunu, "Les crises du XVIIe siècle de l'Europe réformée," *Revue Historique*, CCXXIII (1965), 36, 59.

[3] See, for instance, Garrisson, *L'édit de Nantes et sa Révocation*; Solange Deyon, *Du loyalisme au refus: Les Protestants français et leur Député Général entre la Fronde et la Révocation* (Lille, 1976); Pierre Bolle et al., *Le Protestantisme en Dauphiné au XVIIe siècle* (n.p., 1983); Elisabeth Labrousse, *"Une foi, une loi, un roi?" La Révocation de l'Edit de Nantes* (Geneva, 1985). Cf. Philippe Joutard, "The Revocation of the Edict of Nantes: End or Renewal of French Protestantism?" in Menna Prestwich, ed., *International Calvinism 1541–1715* (Cambridge, 1985), 339–68, esp. 367.

were the differences between those regions where the new faith was imposed from above by an act of state and those where it was voluntarily embraced by its adherents? And to what extent did Protestantism and Catholicism form rival, self-enclosed worlds of belief and practice in this bi-confessional polity? Questions such as these, it might be suggested, offer the promise not only of illuminating the Huguenot experience, but also of breaking the history of this relatively small religious minority out of the ghetto to which it still is too often confined, so that it may become more fully integrated into the broader social history of post-Reformation European Protestantism and of what German historians call the "confessionalization process."

The information assembled in this study can be seen to speak to both of these *problématiques.* The evidence of Part I suggests that, forty years after the initial establishment of Reformed churches, the level of popular attachment to these institutions varied greatly between the one part of France where the religion was imposed from above as an act of state, Béarn, and the rest of the country. In the former region, roughly three-fifths of the population reverted to Roman Catholicism as soon as it was possible to do so, and the ranks of the Protestants continued to dwindle significantly even after this date. Elsewhere in France, the number of Protestants also declined nearly uninterruptedly between the first decade of the seventeenth century and 1685, but the overall drop-off was only in the vicinity of twenty-five percent over these eight decades. The decline had multiple causes: a net outflow of converts toward Catholicism, the loss of lives and adherents which accompanied the revolts of the 1620s, the gradual erosion of Protestant strength in many cities due to immigration from a more heavily Catholic rural hinterland, the lack of demographic dynamism in such heartlands of Protestant strength as the Cévennes, and some emigration, accelerating to major proportions only after 1681.

In certain regions, to be sure, the decline in Protestant strength dramatically altered the balance of local power. Such erstwhile Huguenot capitals as La Rochelle and Montpellier came to house a majority of Catholics by the second half of the century. Exclusively Huguenot Montauban saw a significant Catholic element arise within its walls, and the substantial communities of such northern cities as Caen, Alençon, and Metz all shrank markedly in size. Without such changes in these cities' confessional makeup, such royal actions as that of placing Montauban's *consulat* entirely in Catholic hands in 1661 would not have been possible.

Nonetheless, the overall impression which emerges is of a confessional community which successfully retained the attachment of the majority of its members throughout the period running from the Edict of Nantes to its Revocation—although significant regional differences distinguished much of western and southwestern France, where the erosion of Protestant strength was not inconsiderable, from other regions of Huguenot strength, where the ranks of the faithful held up much better. The dizzying expansion which Protestantism knew for a brief moment on the eve of the Wars of Religion was halted and reversed by the civil wars and the violence which accompanied them. Once a measure of peace was finally established nearly four decades later, confessional identity had been more or less firmly fixed throughout the kingdom of France properly speaking. The Reformed churches might still win over a few converts. They might lose a few more, particularly in regions such as Aquitaine and Saintonge. Most people, however, continued to identify with what had by now become the faith of their ancestors, despite continuing Catholic missionary efforts and mounting legal pressure to return to the Roman fold. Furthermore, most of the causes of the gradual numerical erosion which did occur within the Protestant ranks are not ones which suggest fundamental weaknesses in the community's institutional fiber, although they do perhaps reflect poorly on the wisdom of political decisions made in the 1620s. It certainly seems exaggerated to suggest that the Protestant community would have died out over the long run had it not been for the reinvigorating shock of the Revocation.

The impression of a well-structured community also emerges from evidence assembled about Huguenot religious comportment. The rapid rejection of prohibitions against Lent and Advent marriages, the steady advance of a Protestant understanding of baptism, and the low rates of extramarital sexual activity all suggest a religious community in which the moral and theological principles articulated by the church leaders were widely shared among the faithful. Such a conclusion, it is worth stressing, could only be reached through the use of statistical methods such as those employed here. The archives of repression, notably consistory records, can indicate the forms of behavior which the church sought to eliminate, but they can never indicate with certainty how widespread such practices might have been and whether they increased or diminished with time, for the simple reason that one can never be certain whether changes in the number of recorded cases concerning a specific offense indicate alterations in the frequency of the offense or in the amount of attention devoted to it by those doing the repressing. Such records can provide evidence about the persistence of Catholic practices, but they cannot demonstrate their gradual abandonment. A satisfactory history of Protestant religious practice must exploit more than these documents alone.

While commitment to Protestant tenets was widespread, Calvinism was by no means a total ideology. The emergence of the *creux de Mai* in Protestant marital patterns throughout the Midi shows that the members of the faith were at least as receptive as their Catholic neighbors to extra-ecclesiastical cultural beliefs about lucky and unlucky seasons. The reappearance of a tendency to avoid marriages during Lent in many regions shows that, where the Protestants were a relatively small and cowed minority, they accepted certain Catholic rhythms of life rather than risking offense against ingrained religious sensibilities. At the same time, the fact that the Catholic inhabitants of certain heavily Protestant regions also began to postpone the baptism of their children for a week or more shows that other Catholic religious sensibilities were not as deeply ingrained as might previously have been thought. A degree of interpenetration of religious practices clearly occurred between the two confessional groups living side by side in seventeenth-century France. They were not hermetically sealed communities of belief and practice.

Perhaps as important as any of the broader conclusions which can be drawn from this study are the unresolved, and previously unseen, questions to which it calls attention. Was the inability displayed by the rural and small-town congregations of much of western France to resist significant numerical erosion as successfully as their counterparts in Languedoc or Dauphiné the product of different patterns of Protestant-Catholic interaction? Of the force of seigneurial influence in the initial establishment of Reformed churches in the West? Of other salient differences between churches in different regions? Does the rapid falling away from Protestantism once Catholic worship was re-established in Béarn testify to the superficial protestantization inherent in all attempts to impose a Reformation from above on a predominantly rural population, or to particular failings in the way in which the Reformation was implemented in this particular statelet? Why did the population of the Cévennes stagnate in the seventeenth century? Can any persuasive correlations, either positive or negative, be established between the belief in the unluckiness of May marriages and either Calvinism or the Counter-Reformation? As Joseph Schumpeter once wrote, "We need statistics not only for explaining things, but also in order to know precisely what there is to explain." In the process of establishing the changing numerical contours of the Protestant community in seventeenth-century France, this study has also tried to suggest some new things to explain. If the social history of French Protestantism in this era is to be invigorated, such new problems may be precisely what is needed.

APPENDIX

DATA AND SOURCES

This appendix presents the basic evidence about the changing size of the 120 Protestant congregations or localities examined in this study, along with full archival references. In the tables which follow, numbers in parentheses denote the number of complete months for which figures are available in cases of years for which a church's registers cover only part of the year. Bracketed figures indicate years which were excluded from the calculations of the long-term movement of baptismal levels in the church in question. The reasons why these years were excluded—most commonly, registration of questionable accuracy or changes in the geographic area from which the church attracted worshippers—are indicated in the notes. Unless otherwise indicated, the annual figures refer to baptisms per year.

The localities are arranged by synod. Figures for the church of Metz, which enjoyed special legal status and did not participate in the synodal assemblies of the national Reformed church, have been placed at the end of the synod of Ile-de-France–Champagne–Picardy.

SYNOD: ILE-DE-FRANCE-CHAMPAGNE-PICARDY

AMIENS (colloque de Picardie)

Avg. baps. p.a.		*Annual figures*			
1605–10	56.2	1605 53	1630 75	1646 50	1671 29
1624–29	57	–	1631 55	1647 41	–
1630–39	62.3	1607 55	1632 39	1648 48	1675 28
1640–49	56.2	1608 52	–	1649 44	1676 22
1650–59	43.5	1609 71	1634 67		1677 29
1670–79	25.5	1610 50	1635 67	1650 40	1678 18
1680–81	15.5	–	–	1651 50	1679 27
		1624 51	1638 70	1652 37	
		1625 53	1639 63	1653 31	1680 15
		1626 48		1654 42	1681 16
		1627 61	1640 75	1655 48	
		1628 56	1641 51	1656 47	
		1629 73	1642 70	1657 60	
			1643 65	1658 41	
			1644 62	1659 39	
			1645 56	–	

SOURCES: A.D. Somme, I 3–9.

NOTE: The complete registers cover the years 1601–60 and 1670–85, but they are clearly incomplete for many years. I have retained for use only those years for which the format of the register and the number of baptisms recorded suggest that registration was most complete.

AUTHON-DU-PERCHE (colloque de la Beauce)

Avg. baps. p.a.		*Annual figures*			
1600–09	12.9	1600 15	1620 11	1640 6	1660 11
1610–19	10.4	1601 12	1621 18	1641 15	1661 6
1620–29	13.5	1602 13	1622 15	1642 10	1662 3
1630–39	13.7	1603 12	1623 12	1643 16	1663 7
1640–49	9.7	1604 14	1624 16	1644 10	1664 4
1650–59	7.8	1605 15	1625 10	1645 7	1665 10
1660–69	7.5	1606 13	1626 17	1646 8	1666 9
1670–79	10.1	1607 12	1627 12	1647 8	1667 7
1680–84	5.6	1608 15	1628 10	1648 6	1668 9
		1609 8	1629 14	1649 11	1669 9
		1610 13	1630 13	1650 7	1670 10
		1611 6	1631 17	1651 11	1671 10
		1612 12	1632 9	1652 5	1672 16
		1613 6	1633 18	1653 5	1673 13
		1614 13	1634 13	1654 7	1674 10
		1615 11	1635 12	1655 6	1675 6
		1616 7	1636 20	1656 10	1676 12
		1617 13	1637 9	1657 8	–
		1618 9	1638 13	1658 12	1678 5
		1619 14	1639 13	1659 7	1679 9
			1680 9		
			1681 7		
			1682 4		
			1683 6		
			1684 2 (4)		

SOURCE: A.D. Eure-et-Loir, 3 E 473/1.

CHALANDOS (colloque d'Ile-de-France)

Avg. baps. p.a.

1631–39	12.7
1640–49	12.3
1650–59	8.1
1660–69	11
1670–79	15.9
1680–84	9.2

Annual figures

		1650	13	1670	18
1631	8	1651	5	1671	18
1632	11	1652	1	1672	19
1633	12	1653	22	1673	19
1634	13	1654	1	1674	18
1635	18	1655	4	1675	14
1636	17	1656	10	1676	18
1637	14	1657	8	1677	14
1638	8	1658	12	1678	7
1639	13	1659	5	1679	14
1640	10	1660	13	1680	10
1641	9	1661	2	1681	6
1642	26	1662	5	1682	13
1643	15	1663	9	1683	11
1644	19	1664	12	1684	6
1645	16	1665	9		
1646	10	1666	16		
1647	12	1667	11		
1648	4	1668	17		
1649	2	1669	16		

SOURCE: Eva Telkès, "Les Protestants en Brie au 17ème siècle: Approche démographique et socio-économique" (unpublished *mémoire de maîtrise,* Université de Paris, 1971), unpaginated.

CHALONS-SUR-MARNE (colloque de Champagne)

Avg. baps. p.a.

1600–09	33.1
1610–19	32.7
1620–29	30.9
1630–39	45.5
1640–43	38.3
1668–71	33.7
1680–83	27.8

Annual figures

1600	34	1620	27	1640	36
1601	32	1621	32	1641	36
1602	32	1622	27	1642	41
1603	31	1623	27	1643	40
1604	38	1624	31	–	
1605	28	1625	35	1668	34
1606	38	1626	29	1669	30
1607	31	1627	32	1670	39
1608	35	1628	34	1671	1 (1)
1609	32	1629	35	–	
				1680	3 (2)
1610	44	1630	36	1681	24
1611	28	1631	40	1682	35
1612	35	1632	39	1683	26
1613	33	1633	43		
1614	32	1634	46		
1615	34	1635	53		
1616	25	1636	47		
1617	37	1637	50		
1618	34	1638	50		
1619	25	1639	51		

SOURCES: A.D. Marne, 2 E 119/42, 2 E 180/7.

CHALTRAIT (colloque de Champagne)

Avg. baps. p.a.	*Annual figures*			
1603–12 24.1	1603 5 (1)	1613 25	1661 21	1677 26
1613–22 19.8	1604 28	1614 15	1662 14	–
1661–65 19.4	1605 26	1615 24	1663 19 (10)	1679 16
1674–79 18.6	1606 28	1616 18	1664 21	
1680–84 13.8	1607 23	1617 20	1665 14 (9)	1680 12
	1608 21	1618 30	–	1681 16
	1609 19	1619 22	1674 13	1682 16
			1675 22	1683 11
	1610 21	1620 15	1676 16	1684 [31]
	1611 23	1621 16		
	1612 25	1622 10 (3)		

SOURCES: B.P.F., Ms E 34; A.D. Marne 2 E 122/3.

COMPIEGNE (colloque de Picardie)

Avg. baps. p.a.	*Annual figures*		
1632–39 9.1	1632 9	1640 10	1669 8
1640–44 11.4	1633 4	1641 15	–
1669–73 8.5	1634 11	1642 13	1671 8
1679–84 9.2	1635 7	1643 12	1672 9
	1636 5	1644 7	1673 9
	1637 15	–	–
	1638 14		1679 10
	1639 8		–
			1681 11
			1682 9
			1683 6
			1684 10

SOURCE: A.D. Oise, 3 E Compiègne.
NOTE: A register also exists for the years 1651–58, but it appears to be incomplete.

FONTAINE-SOUS-PREMONT (colloque de la Beauce)

Avg. baps. p.a.	*Annual figures*	
1618–22 25.8	1654 8 (10)	1670 25
1654–59 17.3	1655 11	1671 17
1660–69 16.7	1656 23	1672 27
1670–82 21.2	1657 22	1673 17
	1658 15	1674 23
	1659 22	1675 21
		1676 18
	1660 18	1677 16
	1661 16	1678 20
	1662 13	1679 19
	1663 10	
	1664 1 (2)	1680 17
	1665 15	1681 31
	1666 17	1682 24
	1667 17	
	1668 15	
	1669 31	

SOURCES: A.D. Eure-et-Loir, 3 E 473/7; Henry Lehr, ed., "Les registres paroissiaux de Fontaine-sous-Prémont," *B.S.H.P.F.*, LXIV (1915), 561–9. The baptismal register of the early seventeenth century for which Lehr provides the total number of acts appears to have been lost.

LANDREVILLE (colloque de Champagne)

Avg. baps. p.a.		*Annual figures*					
1620–22	36.7	1620–22	77	1668	24	1674	27
1647–48	37	1647–48	37	1669	28	1675	32
1668–78	29.3			1670	24	1676	23 (9)
				1671	39	1677	22 (8)
				1672	24	1678	25
				1673	37	1679	10 (8)

Source: Auguste Pétel, "Le temple protestant de Landreville: contribution à l'histoire du Protestantisme dans l'arrondissement de Bar-sur-Seine," *Mémoires de la Société Académique d'Agriculture, des Sciences, Arts et Belles-Lettres du Département de l'Aube*, LXXI (1907), 99–130.
Note: Pétel does not provide the annual figures for the earliest registers, which cover the periods April 26, 1620, through May 31, 1622, and May 1647 through May 10, 1648.

LEHAUCOURT (colloque de Picardie)

Avg. baps. p.a.		*Annual figures*					
1610–15	59.7	1610	52	1668	41	1677	40
1668–75	40.1	1611	69	1669	52	1678	24
1676–83	26.2	1612	63	1670	30	1679	30
		1613	45	1671	43	1680	39
		1614	63	1672	38	1681	18
		1615	44 (8)	1673	48	1682	23
		1616	22 (4)	1674	37	1683	30
		1617	32 (6)	1675	32	1684	[6]
				1676	32	1685	[20]

Source: Alfred Daullé, *La Réforme à Saint-Quentin et aux environs du XVIe siècle à la fin du XVIIIe siècle* (Le Cateau, 1905), 93, 197. Jacques Pannier, "La Réforme en Vermandois: L'Eglise de Saint-Quentin," *B.S.H.P.F.*, XLV (1896), 228–9, provides slightly different figures.
Note: The temple at Lehaucourt drew worshippers both from Saint-Quentin and from much of the surrounding region of the Vermandois. The increase in Saint-Quentin's Protestant population (see below) means that the decline in the rural component of this church must have been particularly marked. Registers also exist from the first decade of the century, but the sharp fluctuations in the number of acts they record suggest that they may not be trustworthy. One might also wonder about the completeness of registration in 1684. Neither source indicates the number of months covered by the registers in 1685.

MEAUX-NANTEUIL (Colloque d'Ile-de-France)

Avg. baps. p.a.		*Annual figures*					
1600–09	87.3	1600	91	1620	62	1670	77
1610–19	77.6	1601	71	1621	67	1671	110
1620–32	63	1602	83	1622	46	1672	79
1669–75	88.7	1603	79	1623	57	1673	100
1676–84	67.8	1604	99	1624	70	1674	86
		1605	88	1625	69	1675	69
		1606	93	1626	62	1676	83
		1607	107	1627	54	1677	69
		1608	82	1628	74	1678	87
		1609	80	1629	53	1679	58
		1610	94	1630	67	1680	55
		1611	79	1631	66	1681	61
		1612	90	1632	72	1682	60
		1613	87	–		1683	74
		1614	76	1669	100	1684	63
		1615	74			1685	[53]
		1616	56				
		1617	78				
		1618	72				
		1619	70				

Source: Telkès, "Les Protestants en Brie," unpaginated.
Note: The source does not indicate how many months the registers cover in 1685.

SAINT-QUENTIN (colloque de Picardie)

Protestant population acc. censuses

1599	233 people
1624	553 people
1632	424 people
1664	"over 800" people, 130 families
1684	"nearly 120" families

SOURCE: Daullé, *La Réforme à Saint-Quentin*, 63-5, 103-12, 144.

WASSY (colloque de Champagne)

Avg. baps. p.a.

1626–32	43.3
1633–39	37
1644–51	40.8
1656–65	33.3
1666–75	31.4
1676–85	31.2

Annual figures

1626	26 (7)	–		1660	31	1675	27
1627	45	1644	40	1661	29	1676	26
1628	50	–		1662	33	1677	31
1629	43	1647	38 (9)	1663	34	1678	33
		1648	39	1664	38	1679	43
1630	49	1649	50	1665	22		
1631	36			1666	40	1680	28
1632	36	1650	33	1667	31	1681	31
1633	34	1651	21 (8)	1668	40	1682	17
1634	43	–		1669	33	1683	33
1635	45	1656	32			1684	37
1636	38	1657	38	1670	33	1685	15 (5)
1637	44	1658	37	1671	31		
1638	29	1659	39	1672	25		
1639	23 (11)			1673	30		
				1674	24		

SOURCE: A.D. Haute-Marne, Wassy, Protestants 1626–85.

METZ

1.) Citydwellers

Avg. baps. p.a.

1600–09	299.3
1610–19	290.5
1620–29	320.1
1630–39	296.4
1640–49	229.5
1650–59	186.9
1660–69	183
1670–79	220.2
1680–85	205.4

Annual figures

1600	288	1620	310	1640	222	1660	172
1601	275	1621	319	1641	205	1661	170
1602	295	1622	310	1642	247	1662	178
1603	283	1623	330	1643	223	1663	171
1604	309	1624	337	1644	232	1664	198
1605	295	1625	316	1645	220	1665	182
1606	328	1626	326	1646	262	1666	203
1607	301	1627	326	1647	222	1667	190
1608	315	1628	325	1648	231	1668	185
1609	304	1629	302	1649	231	1669	181
1610	331	1630	325	1650	199	1670	229
1611	282	1631	300	1651	189	1671	193
1612	313	1632	284	1652	177	1672	212
1613	296	1633	288	1653	187	1673	200
1614	262	1634	361	1654	178	1674	209
1615	276	1635	333	1655	203	1675	235
1616	279	1636	278	1656	184	1676	221
1617	284	1637	338	1657	202	1677	236
1618	295	1638	238	1658	176	1678	222
1619	287	1639	219	1659	174	1679	245

1680	180
1681	212
1682	213
1683	224
1684	213
1685	156 (10)

Protestant population acc. censuses

1635	6329
1684	4380

2.) "Villageois"

Avg. baps. p.a.	
1600–09	122.4
1610–19	106.2
1620–29	108
1630–39	101.5
1640–49	74.3
1656–59	69
1660–69	69.2
1670–79	76.6
1680–85	81.1

Annual figures

1600	125	1620	95	1640	78	1660	64
1601	115	1621	103	1641	73	1661	64
1602	146	1622	103	1642	78	1662	67
1603	111	1623	92	1643	70	1663	64
1604	115	1624	118	1644	73	1664	74
1605	119	1625	117	1645	55	1665	68
1606	117	1626	104	1646	89	1666	76
1607	135	1627	126	1647	68	1667	71
1608	122	1628	126	1648	87	1668	92
1609	119	1629	96	1649	72	1669	52
1610	103	1630	140	–		1670	75
1611	110	1631	90	1656	69	1671	67
1612	119	1632	116	1657	76	1672	69
1613	103	1633	107	1658	66	1673	60
1614	119	1634	113	1659	65	1674	87
1615	87	1635	142			1675	79
1616	103	1636	65			1676	80
1617	103	1637	115			1677	103
1618	91	1638	73			1678	72
1619	124	1639	54			1679	74

1680	70
1681	90
1682	74
1683	86
1684	94
1685	59 (10)

SOURCES: A. C. Metz, GG 236–58; Jean-Louis Calbat, "La communauté réformée de Metz. Approche démographique," in François-Yves Le Moigne and Gérard Michaux, eds., *Protestants messins et mosellans, XVIe–XXe siècles* (Metz, 1988), 89–90; Jean Rigault, "La population de Metz au XVIIe siècle: quelques problèmes de démographie," *Annales de l'Est*, 5th ser., 11 (1951), 307–16.

NOTES: For most of the seventeenth century, two separate baptismal registers were maintained for the church of Metz, a "livre des enfants des villageois" and one for the inhabitants of the city. After 1655, baptisms of both citydwellers and inhabitants of the surrounding *pays messin* were recorded together; from late 1667 onward, the common registers indicate the place of residence of parents bringing their children to baptism. For the years 1655–67, the number of baptisms recorded in the common register has been divided among city- and countrydwellers on the assumption that the distribution of acts between city and countryside was similar to that found in the years immediately preceding and following this period. For the years 1637–49, the number of recorded rural baptisms has been reduced by 28 percent to compensate for the closure of the nearby temple of Courcelles, destroyed in 1636 amid the fighting of the Thirty Years' War and not reopened until some point in the 1650s. This correction has been determined by comparing the number of baptisms celebrated in Courcelles between 1669 and 1672 recorded in A.D. Moselle, 5 E 5831, with the number of baptisms of countrydwellers recorded in Metz's registers during the same years. I owe the breakdown of acts between city- and countrydwellers for the years 1668–85 to the kindness of Jean-Louis Calbat, whose published figures for the entire period are also modified here slightly on the basis of corrections which he has provided me and my own baptismal counts. The Protestant baptismal figures offered by Rigault are unreliable, for they fail to distinguish between those years for which separate registers were kept for towndwellers and *villageois* and those for which the acts for these two groups were confounded. The figures he offers for the number of Catholic baptisms in the city, it should also be noted, are extrapolated from very incomplete registers according to methods which are not explained.

ALENCON (colloque d'Alençon)

Avg. baps. p.a.		*Annual figures*			
1616–29	64.6	1616 36 (10)	–	1650 43	1670 49
1631–39	59.4	1617 67	1631 56	1651 54	1671 45
1640–49	54	1618 63	1632 54	1652 49	1672 41
1650–59	55	1619 67	1633 68	1653 49	1673 27
1660–69	52.6		1634 49	1654 60	1674 38
1670–79	36.8	1620 64	1635 57	1655 58	1675 40
1680–85	30.9	1621 84	1636 65	1656 62	1676 34
		1622 63	1637 65	1657 59	1677 30
		1623 58	1638 59	1658 66	1678 33
		1624 66	1639 62	1659 50	1679 31
		1625 64			
		1626 60	1640 58	1660 50	1680 29
		1627 63	1641 53	1661 48	1681 29
		1628 71	1642 58	1662 47	1682 43
		1629 68	1643 53	1663 58	1683 31
			1644 66	1664 55	1684 32
			1645 54	1665 62	1685 26 (10)
			1646 50	1666 49	
			1647 45	1667 51	
			1648 52	1668 50	
			1649 51	1669 56	

SOURCES: A.D. Orne, I 1–3, 6–21; B.P.F., Fonds Robert.

CAEN (colloque de Caen)

Avg. baps. p.a.	
1600–11	229
1639–48	133
1649–58	128
1659–68	119

SOURCE: A. Galland, *Essai sur l'histoire du Protestantisme à Caen et en Basse-Normandie de l'Edit de Nantes à la Révolution (1598–1791)* (Paris, 1898), 157. The original registers were destroyed during the Second World War.

FECAMP (colloque de Caux)

Avg. baps. p.a.		*Annual figures*		
1613–19	23.9	1613 26	1630 30	1650 25
1620–29	24.3	1614 12	1631 23	1651 22
1630–39	26.6	1615 20	1632 21	1652 21
1640–49	25.8	1616 27	1633 36	1653 25
1650–59	21.8	1617 32	1634 27	1654 22
1660–67	15	1618 25	1635 36	1655 22
		1619 25	1636 26	1656 26
			1637 22	1657 18
		1620 29	1638 21	1658 15
		1621 24	1639 24	1659 22
		1622 21		
		1623 24	1640 25	1660 9
		1624 21	1641 21	1661 13
		1625 24	1642 26	1662 9
		1626 23	1643 17	1663 18
		1627 27	1644 30	1664 17
		1628 24	1645 25	1665 29
		1629 26	1646 30	1666 13
			1647 34	1667 12
			1648 24	
			1649 26	

SOURCE: A.C. Fécamp, état civil réformé. Figures kindly supplied by Denis Vatinel.

LAIGLE (colloque d'Alençon)

Avg. baps. p.a.		*Annual figures*			
1602–09	4.6	1602 2	1620 5	1640 4	1660 1
1610–19	3.4	1603 3	1621 5	1641 4	1661 1
1620–29	2.6	1604 1	1622 4	1642 5	1662 0
1630–39	2.4	1605 5	1623 1	1643 3	1663 1
1640–49	3.6	1606 6	1624 0	1644 2	–
1650–59	1.6	1607 3	1625 1	1645 3	1668 1
1660–69	1	1608 9	1626 0	1646 5	1669 2
1670–71	0.5	1609 8	1627 3	1647 5	
			1628 5	1648 3	1670 1
		1610 5	1629 2	1649 2	1671 0
		1611 6			–
		1612 7	1630 1	1650 2	1683 [9]
		1613 5	1631 5	1651 2	1684 [12]
		1614 4	1632 0	1652 1	1685 [3 (4)]
		1615 0	1633 5	1653 1	
		1616 0	1634 0	1654 3	
		1617 1	1635 1	1655 3	
		1618 2	1636 4	1656 2	
		1619 4	1637 3	1657 0	
			1638 3	1658 1	
			1639 2	1659 1	

SOURCES: B. P. F., Ms E 22; A.D. Orne, I 35–6.
NOTE: Many acts between 1683 and 1685 involve inhabitants of other nearby localities.

LE HAVRE (colloque de Caux)

Avg. baps. p.a.		*Annual figures*			
1600–09	52.6	1600 43	1620 60	1640 53	1660 50
1610–19	54.4	1601 55	1621 56	1641 46	1661 42
1620–29	50	1602 47	1622 50	1642 55	1662 30
1630–39	46.6	1603 45	1623 41	1643 43	1663 32
1640–49	46.1	1604 54	1624 56	1644 49	1664 19
1650–59	53.1	1605 36	1625 45	1645 38	1665 34
1660–69	35.2	1606 55	1626 46	1646 49	1666 34
1670–79	35.5	1607 53	1627 48	1647 35	1667 42
1680–81	33	1608 63	1628 49	1648 45	1668 36
		1609 75	1629 49	1649 48	1669 33
		1610 72	1630 43	1650 72	1670 31
		1611 65	1631 59	1651 53	1671 42
		1612 52	1632 37	1652 67	1672 22
		1613 57	1633 52	1653 44	1673 44
		1614 59	1634 45	1654 39	1674 35
		1615 55	1635 60	1655 62	1675 28
		1616 46	1636 50	1656 50	1676 37
		1617 52	1637 48	1657 51	1677 38
		1618 42	1638 33	1658 45	1678 45
		1619 44	1639 39	1659 48	1679 33

1680	35
1681	31
1682	[84]
1683	[72]
1684	[52]
1685	[68]

SOURCE: Robert Richard and Denis Vatinel, "Le consistoire de l'Eglise réformée du Havre au XVIIe siècle: les pasteurs," *B.S.H.P.F.*, CXXVII (1981), 76–7.
NOTE: The increase in the number of baptisms from 1682 onward resulted from the closure of the nearby temple of Sénitot. The authors do not indicate for how many month baptisms were recorded in 1685.

LINTOT (colloque de Caux)

Avg. baps. p.a.		*Annual figures*			
1609–19	237.2	1609 76 (3)			
1620–29	204.3	1610 262	1630 223	1650 164	1670 184
1630–39	202.1	1611 280	1631 202	1651 131	1671 184
1640–49	193.5	1612 264	1632 192	1652 164	1672 202
1650–59	177.6	1613 237	1633 227	1653 152	1673 182
1660–69	176.5	1614 259	1634 221	1654 187	1674 187
1670–79	173.1	1615 228	1635 240	1655 204	1675 172
1680–81	149.7	1616 222	1636 186	1656 234	1676 155
		1617 199	1637 195	1657 164	1677 158
		1618 189	1638 166	1658 202	1678 174
		1619 215	1639 169	1659 174	1679 133
		1620 229	1640 199	1660 160	1680 145
		1621 220	1641 190	1661 177	1681 105 (8)
		1622 204	1642 209	1662 135	
		1623 192	1643 198	1663 162	
		1624 159	1644 198	1664 164	
		1625 185	1645 212	1665 206	
		1626 211	1646 196	1666 188	
		1627 192	1647 201	1667 192	
		1628 213	1648 154	1668 189	
		1629 238	1649 178	1669 192	

SOURCES: A.D. Seine-Maritime, 4 E 3381–86. Figures kindly supplied by Denis Vatinel.

LUNERAY (colloque de Caux)

Avg. baps. p.a.		*Annual figures*			
1624–29	61.8	1623 [16]	1640 81	1660 63	–
1630–39	46.8	1624 52	1641 72	1661 51	1681 25 (6)
1640–49	67.1	1625 [10]	1642 72	1662 61	
1650–59	57.1	1626 73	1643 65	1663 46	
1660–69	63.8	1627 55	1644 52	1664 65	
1671–79	66.4	1628 75	1645 68	1665 62	
1681	50	1629 54	1646 67	1666 82	
			1647 68	1667 52	
		1630 52	1648 58	1668 70	
		1631 46	1649 68	1669 86	
		1632 40		–	
		1633 65	1650 55	1671 76	
		1634 48	1651 51	1672 67	
		1635 36	1652 47	1673 76	
		1636 49	1653 41	1674 66	
		1637 39	1654 63	1675 67	
		1638 49	1655 64	1676 58	
		1639 44	1656 75	1677 74	
			1657 58	1678 67	
			1658 67	1679 47	
			1659 50		

SOURCE: Isabelle Michalkiewicz, "La communauté protestante de Luneray au XVIIème siècle (1623–1710)," (unpublished *mémoire de maîtrise*, Université de Haute-Normandie, 1985), appendix 1.

PONTORSON-CORMERAY (colloque du Cotentin)

Avg. baps. p.a.		*Annual figures*							
1600–09	10.4	1600	8	1620	15	1640	4	1660	6
1610–19	11.1	1601	11	1621	7	1641	7	1661	5
1620–29	5	1602	6	1622	1	1642	6	1662	2
1630–39	4.3	1603	10	1623	2	1643	7	1663	5
1640–49	3.8	1604	2	–		1644	4	1664	4
1650–59	5	1605	12	1627	4 (5)	1645	3	1665	5
1660–69	4.3	1606	12	1628	2	1646	3	1666	5
		1607	15	1629	2	1647	2	1667	2
		1608	14			1648	1	1668	5
		1609	14	1630	4	1649	1	1669	4
				1631	3				
		1610	15	1632	2	1650	5		
		1611	7	1633	4	1651	5		
		1612	13	1634	5	1652	3		
		1613	11	1635	4	1653	5		
		1614	15	1636	4	1654	5		
		1615	11	–		1655	6		
		1616	11	1638	9 (10)	1656	6		
		1617	9	1639	3	1657	7		
		1618	14			1658	4		
		1619	5			1659	4		

SOURCE: B.P.F., Ms 979/1. See also A. Galland, "L'ancienne Eglise réformée de Pontorson-Cormeray d'après un registre d'état civil inédit," *B.S.H.P.F.*, LVIII (1909), 448–63.

ROUEN (colloque de Rouen)

Avg. baps. p.a.		*Annual figures*							
1600–03	175	1600	157	1620	232	1640	259	1660	210
1610–19	190	1601	156	1621	230	1641	244	1661	223
1620–29	213	1602	192	1622	196	1642	238	1662	182
1630–39	247	1603	195	1623	294	1643	260	1663	184
1640–49	238	–		–		1644	239	1664	207
1650–59	219	1610	187	1631	234	1645	226	1665	203
1660–69	198	1611	159	1632	257	1646	241	1666	189
1670–79	174	1612	181	1633	234	1647	233	1667	207
1680–84	153	1613	156	1634	275	1648	221	1668	191
		1614	220	1635	242	1649	222	1669	188
		1615	207	1636	250				
		1616	206	1637	203	1650	200	1670	195
		1617	203	1638	240	1651	199	1671	197
		1618	183	1639	233	1652	227	1672	182
		1619	202			1653	213	1673	176
						1654	226	1674	179
						1655	226	1675	159
						1656	247	1676	165
						1657	204	1677	166
						1658	224	1678	168
						1659	228	1679	152
						1680	158		
						1681	160		
						1682	140		
						1683	157		
						1684	151		

SOURCE: Jean-Pierre Bardet, *Rouen aux XVIIe et XVIIIe siècles: Les mutations d'un espace social*, 2 vols. (Paris, 1983), II, 27.

SAINT-LO (colloque du Cotentin)

Avg. baps. p.a.		*Annual figures*			
1600–09	64.2	1600 62	1620 64	1640 55	1660 32
1610–19	58.7	1601 69	1621 57	1641 54	1661 43
1620–29	51.2	1602 74	1622 67	1642 59	1662 36
1630–39	52.7	1603 43	1623 41	1643 54	1663 47
1640–49	52.2	1604 59	1624 48	1644 57	1664 48
1650–59	44.8	1605 72	1625 50	1645 50	1665 44
1660–69	42.2	1606 74	1626 37	1646 45	1666 53
1670–79	35.6	1607 73	1627 53	1647 58	1667 50
1680–84	33	1608 52	1628 38	1648 44	1668 37
		1609 64	1629 57	1649 46	1669 32
		1610 55	1630 49	1650 52	1670 40
		1611 56	1631 44	1651 38	1671 41
		1612 60	1632 58	1652 43	1672 42
		1613 57	1633 54	1653 53	1673 46
		1614 59	1634 55	1654 35	1674 47
		1615 65	1635 51	1655 53	1675 32
		1616 57	1636 52	1656 43	1676 34
		1617 61	1637 60	1657 43	1677 28
		1618 61	1638 45	1658 49	1678 23
		1619 56	1639 59	1659 39	1679 23
			1680 31		
			1681 34		
			1682 31		
			1683 35		
			1684 34		
			1685 [62]		

SOURCE: R. Leclerc, "Le Protestantisme à Saint-Lô," *Notices, mémoires et documents publiés par la Société d'archéologie de la Manche*, XXXVIII (1926), 35–38.
NOTE: The author does not indicate the number of months covered by the registers in 1685.

SAINT-PIERRE-SUR-DIVES (colloque de Falaise)

Avg. baps. p.a.		*Annual figures*			
1624–32	5.5	1624 4 (9)	1646 4	1661 5	1673 5
1646–56	3.8	1625 6	–	1662 3	1674 5
1661–68	4.5	1626 3	1654 2	1663 4	–
1673–81	4.2	1627 6	1655 3	1664 3	1677 5
		1628 4	1656 4 (5)	1665 5	1678 6
		1629 5		1666 4	1679 1
		1630 10		1667 7	–
		1631 5		1668 2 (4)	1681 3
		1632 5			

SOURCES: A.D. Calvados, I 58, 60–65.

VITRE

Avg. baps. p.a.

1600–09	22.5
1610–19	24.2
1620–29	25.4
1630–39	33.5
1640–49	23.3
1650–59	21.3
1660–69	18.6
1670–79	13.8
1680–85	12.7

Annual figures

1600	27	1620	26	1640	26	1660	28
1601	21	1621	32	1641	22	1661	20
1602	25	1622	[17]	1642	26	1662	10
1603	25	1623	16	1643	25	1663	21
1604	20	1624	27	1644	22	1664	19
1605	23	1625	23	1645	25	1665	17
1606	21	1626	24	1646	28	1666	18
1607	25	1627	20	1647	21	1667	22
1608	21	1628	36	1648	21	1668	16
1609	17	1629	25	1649	17	1669	15
1610	21	1630	31	1650	15	1670	18
1611	22	1631	31	1651	28	1671	13
1612	22	1632	32	1652	21	1672	17
1613	22	1633	31	1653	18	1673	9
1614	26	1634	34	1654	23	1674	20
1615	29	1635	35	1655	25	1675	10
1616	24	1636	41	1656	21	1676	13
1617	24	1637	41	1657	25	1677	12
1618	25	1638	40	1658	18	1678	14
1619	27	1639	19	1659	19	1679	12

1680	12
1681	16
1682	16
1683	10
1684	10
1685	10 (10)

SOURCES: A.D. Ille-et-Vilaine, 3 E Vitré; Alain Croix, "La mort quotidienne en Bretagne (1450–1670)," *thèse de doctorat d'état,* typescript copy at A.D. Ille-et-Vilaine, vol. 5.
NOTE: Possible gap in register 1622.

ANGERS (colloque d'Anjou)

Avg. baps. p.a.	
1600–09	15.6
1610–19	16
1620–29	13
1630–39	11.5
1640–49	9.6
1650–59	11.1
1660–69	17.7
1670–79	15
1680–84	13.6

Annual figures

1600 11	1620 16	1640 13	1660 20
1601 8	1621 16	1641 9	1661 15
1602 11	1622 15	1642 9	1662 12
1603 12	1623 9	1643 7	1663 21
1604 18	1624 15	1644 11	1664 16
1605 20	1625 15	1645 14	1665 18
1606 21	1626 10	1646 14	1666 16
1607 15	1627 12	1647 10	1667 21
1608 20	1628 7	1648 4	1668 18
1609 20	1629 15	1649 5	1669 20
1610 16	1630 12	1650 5	1670 10
1611 22	1631 6	1651 11	1671 15
1612 12	1632 5	1652 8	1672 14
1613 20	1633 13	1653 8	–
1614 23	1634 11	1654 18	1674 15
1615 12	1635 13	1655 13	1675 18
1616 10	1636 12	1656 11	1676 15
1617 15	1637 14	1657 15	1677 14
1618 14	1638 16	1658 10	1678 18
1619 16	1639 13	1659 12	1679 16
		1680 14	
		1681 11	
		1682 17	
		1683 16	
		1684 10	

SOURCE: A.D. Maine-et-Loire, I 1. Figures kindly supplied by Jean-Noël Biraben on the basis of Y. Chauvin, "La communauté protestante d'Angers de 1600 à 1685" (unpublished *diplôme d'études supérieures*, Université de Rennes, 1961). See also François Lebrun, *Les hommes et la mort en Anjou aux 17e et 18e siècles: Essai de démographie et de psychologie historiques* (Paris–The Hague, 1971), 162.

BELLEME (colloque du Maine)

Avg. baps. p.a.	
1634–39	16.4
1640–49	12
1650–59	7
1660–69	7.1
1670–79	6.1
1680–83	4

Annual figures

1634 12 (8)	1650 7	1670 6
1635 13	1651 7	1671 9
1636 15	1652 3	1672 8
1637 18	1653 4	1673 5
1638 19	1654 5	1674 7
1639 16	1655 10	1675 8
	1656 7	1676 7
1640 15	1657 7	1677 1
1641 19	1658 10	1678 6
1642 11	1659 10	1679 4
1643 11		
1644 11	1660 4	1680 3
1645 10	1661 6	1681 6
1646 12	1662 4	1682 3
1647 11	1663 5	1683 4
1648 10	1664 10	
1649 10	1665 5	
	1666 10	
	1667 8	
	1668 7	
	1669 12	

SOURCES: A.D. Orne, I 43–59.

CHATEAU-DU-LOIR (colloque du Maine)

Avg. baps. p.a.	
1610–19	2.1
1620–29	2.8
1630–39	1.9
1640–49	1.9
1650–59	1.6
1660–71	1.4

Annual figures

1610	5	1630	1	1650	2	1670	1
1611	2	1631	0	1651	2	1671	1
1612	2	1632	1	1652	2		
1613	2	1633	0	1653	0		
1614	0	1634	5	1654	3		
1615	1	1635	6	1655	1		
1616	0	1636	0	1656	2		
1617	5	1637	1	1657	2		
1618	1	1638	1	1658	1		
1619	3	1639	4	1659	1		
1620	2	1640	1	1660	0		
1621	4	1641	1	1661	3		
1622	4	1642	0	1662	0		
1623	4	1643	2	1663	2		
1624	6	1644	4	1664	3		
1625	1	1645	1	1665	2		
1626	2	1646	3	1666	2		
1627	0	1647	1	1667	3		
1628	2	1648	1	1668	0		
1629	3	1649	5	1669	0		

SOURCE: B.P.F., Ms E 47.

LAVAL (colloque du Maine)

Avg. baps. p.a.	
1601–09	3.8
1610–19	1.5
1620–29	0.8
1630–39	1.9
1640–49	0.7
1650–59	0
1660–69	2.3
1670–79	0.9
1680–83	1

Annual figures

		1620	1	1640	1	1660	1
1601	5	1621	0	1641	2	1661	3
1602	1	1622	0	1642	2	1662	3
1603	8	1623	1	1643	2	1663	3
1604	2	1624	0	1644	0	1664	2
1605	5	1625	1	1645	0	1665	2
1606	3	1626	0	1646	0	1666	4
1607	0	1627	2	1647	0	1667	1
1608	8	1628	0	1648	0	1668	2
1609	2	1629	3	1649	0	1669	2
1610	3	1630	0	1650	0	1670	0
1611	2	1631	1	1651	0	1671	1
1612	3	1632	3	1652	0	1672	2
1613	1	1633	4	1653	0	1673	2
1614	2	1634	1	1654	0	1674	1
1615	0	1635	2	1655	0	1675	1
1616	0	1636	2	1656	0	1676	0
1617	1	1637	2	1657	0	1677	1
1618	0	1638	1	1658	0	1678	0
1619	3	1639	3	1659	0	1679	1

1680	0
1681	2
1682	1
1683	1

SOURCE: André Joubert, *Histoire de l'Eglise réformée de Laval* (Laval-Paris, 1889), *passim*. This volume, which claims to reproduce every act in the church's register, offers no reason to suspect that services ceased between 1643 and 1660. One marriage was celebrated between those dates.

LOUDUN (colloque d'Anjou)

Avg. baps. p.a.	
1600–08	110.4
1621–29	97.2
1630–39	95.6
1640–49	86.7
1650–59	76
1660–69	62.8
1670–79	51.5
1680–85	33

Annual figures

1600	128	1630	97	1650	87	1670	65
1601	114	1631	90	1651	86	1671	63
1602	111	1632	81	1652	75	1672	56
1603	115	1633	82	1653	69	1673	61
1604	96	1634	101	1654	81	1674	53
1605	104	1635	107	1655	77	1675	49
1606	104	1636	94	1656	72	1676	53
1607	111	1637	99	1657	72	1677	39
1608	37 (4)	1638	104	1658	71	1678	39
–		1639	101	1659	70	1679	37
1621	23 (3)	1640	100	1660	65	1680	35
1622	100	1641	86	1661	68	1681	44
1623	104	1642	84	1662	55	1682	28
1624	105	1643	96	1663	55	1683	28
1625	106	1644	77	1664	66	1684	30
1626	102	1645	87	1665	67	1685	19 (7)
1627	74	1646	91	1666	68		
1628	97	1647	84	1667	56		
1629	91	1648	81	1668	73		
		1649	81	1669	55		

SOURCES: A.C. Loudun, GG 195–7 (manuscript tables in the back of the city's Catholic parish registers). The original registers to which these tables refer have been lost.
NOTE: Fragments of the original registers survive for the sixteenth century and were published by C.E. Lart, *The Registers of the Protestant Church, 1566–1582* (Lymington, 1905). When checked against this work, the tables appear to be a complete listing of the original acts.

PREUILLY-SUR-CLAISE (colloque de Touraine)

Avg. baps. p.a.	
1600–09	12.8
1610–19	14.2
1620–29	11.9
1630–39	11.1
1640–49	11.3
1650–59	10.2
1660–69	8.5
1670–79	8.5
1680–83	10.8

Annual figures

1600	15	1620	13	1640	6	1660	11
1601	11	1621	10	1641	9	1661	7
1602	21	1622	11	1642	13	1662	8
1603	17	1623	9	1643	9	1663	6
1604	10	1624	11	1644	13	1664	8
1605	18	1625	12	1645	8	1665	6
1606	6	1626	9	1646	10	1666	8
1607	10	1627	13	1647	17	1667	11
1608	14	1628	15	1648	13	1668	10
1609	6	1629	16	1649	15	1669	10
1610	20	1630	19	1650	12	1670	7 (9)
1611	11	1631	9	1651	18	1671	2 (1)
1612	11	1632	9	1652	10	1672	9
1613	18	1633	10	1653	12	1673	9
1614	15	1634	6	1654	10	–	
1615	14	1635	13	1655	10	1676	5
1616	8	1636	11	1656	9	1677	8
1617	15	1637	14	1657	8	1678	7
1618	9	1638	12	1658	8	1679	11
1619	21	1639	8	1659	5		

1680	6
1681	10
1682	12
1683	15

SOURCES: A.C. Preuilly-sur-Claise, registres paroissiaux; A.C. Tours, E, Protestants (includes Preuilly's register for 1673); A.D. Indre-et-Loire, 5 Mi 1821–22; F. Béraudy, "Les Protestants en Touraine, 1650–1700" (unpublished *diplôme d'études supérieures*, Université de Tours, n.d.), 81–2.

SAUMUR (colloque d'Anjou)

Avg. baps. p.a.		*Annual figures*							
1600–09	38.9	1600	37	1620	48	1640	43	1660	38
1610–19	54.3	1601	23	1621	64	1641	44	1661	38
1620–29	32.4	1602	42	1622	40	1642	42	1662	32
1630–39	40	1603	41	1623	28	1643	34	1663	33
1640–49	36.4	1604	46	1624	33	1644	25	1664	32
1650–59	36.3	1605	43	1625	20	1645	28	1665	32
1660–69	33.7	1606	30	1626	22	1646	38	1666	32
1670–79	28.3	1607	41	1627	18	1647	31	1667	38
1680–84	22.2	1608	41	1628	21	1648	46	1668	29
		1609	45	1629	30	1649	33	1669	39
		1610	54	1630	40	1650	36	1670	30
		1611	68	1631	39	1651	21	1671	39
		1612	49	1632	38	1652	26	1672	38
		1613	52	1633	17	1653	34	1673	28
		1614	51	1634	41	1654	37	1674	26
		1615	56	1635	56	1655	37	1675	22
		1616	52	1636	41	1656	36	1676	25
		1617	50	1637	39	1657	41	1677	25
		1618	51	1638	37	1658	50	1678	22
		1619	60	1639	52	1659	45	1679	28
				1680	15				
				1681	27				
				1682	22				
				1683	28				
				1684	19				

SOURCES: A.D. Maine-et-Loire, I 4–8. Figures kindly supplied by Jean-Noël Biraben.

TOURS (colloque de Touraine)

Avg. baps. p.a.		*Annual figures*					
1632–39	54.6			1650	39	1670	40
1640–49	50.9			1651	38	1671	51
1650–59	36.9	1632	41	1652	23	1672	43
1660–69	39.7	1633	51	1653	29	1673	36
1670–79	42.5	1634	57	1654	32	1674	43
1680–84	32.6	1635	62	1655	41	1675	45
		1636	54	1656	37	1676	44
		1637	62	1657	48	1677	40
		1638	52	1658	41	1678	47
		1639	58	1659	41	1679	33
		1640	59	1660	35	1680	37
		1641	56	1661	38	1681	35
		1642	67	1662	24	1682	27
		1643	46	1663	36	1683	34
		1644	52	1664	50	1684	30
		1645	46	1665	32 (9)		
		1646	51	–			
		1647	46	1668	46		
		1648	45	1669	47		
		1649	41				

SOURCE: A.C. Tours, E, Protestants. Figures kindly supplied by Brigitte Maillard. See also Maillard, "Religion et démographie: Les Protestants de Tours au XVIIe siècle," *Annales de Bretagne et des Pays de l'Ouest*, LXXXX (1983), 543–4; Alexandre Giraudet, *Recherches historiques et statistiques sur l'hygiène de la ville de Tours et sur le mouvement de sa population, depuis 1632 jusqu'à l'époque actuelle* (Tours, 1853), 84–5; Béraudy, "Les Protestants en Touraine," 85; "L'Eglise réformée de Tours," *B.S.H.P.F.*, XXV (1876), 141

AUBUSSON (colloque du Berry)

Avg. baps. p.a.		*Annual figures*		
1620–29	29	1620 41	1640 30	1660 35
1630–39	30.2	1621 39	1641 33	1661 25
1640–49	35	1622 31	1642 43	1662 35
1650–59	25.2	1623 40	1643 31	1663 22
1660–67	28.4	1624 31	1644 38	1664 28
1679–82	28.5	1625 15	–	1665 23
		1626 20	1648 33	1666 36
		1627 13	1649 37	1667 23
		1628 29		–
		1629 31	1650 28	1674 28
			1651 32	–
		1630 28	1652 26	1679 24
		1631 27	1653 14	1680 33
		1632 30	1654 30	1681 29
		1633 30	1655 22	1682 29
		1634 36	1656 24	
		1635 32	1657 25	
		1636 24	1658 28	
		1637 25	1659 23	
		1638 34		
		1639 31		

SOURCE: A.C. Aubusson, état civil réformé. Figures kindly supplied by Yves Gueneau.

BLOIS (colloque de l'Orléanais)

Avg. baps. p.a.		*Annual figures*			
1600–09	37	1600 29	1620 44	1640 35	1660 30
1610–19	35.4	1601 42	1621 44	1641 39	1661 24
1620–29	38.7	1602 39	1622 35	1642 39	1662 29
1630–39	42.8	1603 31	1623 39	1643 40	1663 32
1640–49	34.8	1604 32	1624 28	1644 35	1664 28
1650–59	25.9	1605 46	1625 44	1645 31	–
1660–69	28	–	1626 38	1646 32	1668 30
1670–79	20.1	1607 37	1627 32	1647 40	1669 24
1680–82	15.7	1608 34	1628 38	1648 29	
		1609 39	1629 45	1649 28	1670 24
					1671 27
		1610 36	1630 36	1650 24	1672 24
		1611 37	1631 37	1651 18	1673 19
		1612 37	1632 29	1652 31	1674 22
		1613 36	1633 33	1653 21	1675 18
		1614 31	1634 55	1654 23	1676 16
		1615 39	1635 52	1655 21	1677 13
		1616 27	1636 40	1656 32	1678 23
		1617 36	1637 51	1657 32	1679 15
		1618 40	1638 44	1658 30	
		1619 35	1639 51	1659 27	1680 21
					1681 13
					1682 13

SOURCES: A.D. Loir-et-Cher, I 6–12; Liliane Bariteaud, "Les Protestants en pays blésois au XVIIème siècle" (unpublished *diplôme d'études supérieures*, Université de Tours, 1973), figure following p. 75.

CHATEAUDUN (colloque de l'Orléanais)

Avg. baps. p.a.	
1600–09	23.5
1610–19	16.7
1620–29	20.7
1630–39	17.2
1640–49	16.3
1650–59	16
1660–69	12.2
1670–79	10.2
1680–82	8

Annual figures

1600 25	1620 17	1640 22	1660 13
1601 25	1621 23	1641 16	1661 9
1602 19	1622 26	1642 13	1662 7
1603 41	1623 19	1643 22	1663 7
1604 35	1624 16	1644 14	1664 9
1605 24	1625 23	1645 16	1665 9
1606 12	1626 17	1646 13	1666 15
1607 17	1627 21	1647 16	1667 16
1608 15	1628 22	1648 13	1668 18
1609 22	1629 23	1649 18	1669 19
1610 13	1630 19	1650 15	1670 13
1611 20	1631 16	1651 14	1671 13
1612 16	1632 16	1652 11	1672 20
1613 15	1633 11	1653 14	1673 13
1614 15	1634 17	1654 13	1674 14
1615 11	1635 24	1655 19	1675 5
1616 19	1636 14	1656 15	1676 10
1617 16	1637 21	1657 22	1677 7
1618 13	1638 16	1658 19	1678 9
1619 29	1639 18	1659 18	1679 2

1680	13
1681	6
1682	5

SOURCE: A.D. Eure-et-Loir, 3 E 473/5. Figures kindly supplied by Yves Gueneau. See also Henry Lehr, *La Réforme et les Eglises réformées dans le département actuel d'Eure-et-Loir (1523–1911)* (Chartres–Paris, 1912), 370.

CHATILLON-SUR-LOING (colloque du Berry)

Avg. baps. p.a.	
1608–19	15.7
1620–29	16.6
1630–39	17.2
1640–49	16.8
1650–57	21.6
1673–79	15
1681–84	8.8

Annual figures

1608 9	1620 15	1640 18	1673 19
1609 15	1621 15	1641 13	1674 20
	1622 25	1642 13	1675 18
1610 22	1623 17	1643 18	1676 14
1611 13	1624 19	1644 15	1677 13
1612 15	1625 17	–	1678 9
1613 19	1626 14	1647 12	1679 12
1614 18	1627 15	1648 22	–
1615 17	1628 17	1649 23	1681 9
1616 9	1629 12		1682 10
1617 19		1650 18	1683 8
1618 17	1630 15	1651 29	1684 8
1619 15	1631 18	1652 21	
	1632 13	1653 18	
	1633 20	1654 15	
	1634 22	1655 24	
	1635 16	1656 25	
	1636 19	1657 23	
	1637 11	–	
	1638 21		
	1639 17		

SOURCES: A.C. Chatillon-Coligny, GG 25–6. Figures kindly supplied by Yves Gueneau.

CHATILLON-SUR-LOIRE (colloque du Berry)

Avg. baps. p.a.

1600–10	69.8
1669–79	61.3
1680–83	47

Annual figures

1600	89	1669	70	1680	55
1601	54	1670	57	1681	42
1602	63	1671	77	1682	48
1603	69	1672	70	1683	43
1604	85	1673	55		
1605	48	1674	71		
1606	86	1675	63		
1607	77	1676	50		
1608	63	1677	68		
1609	65	1678	55		
1610	69	1679	38		

SOURCES: A.N., TT 232 (16); B.P.F., Ms 1082. Figures kindly supplied by Yves Gueneau.

DANGEAU (colloque de l'Orléanais)

Avg. baps. p.a.

1622–29	7.6
1630–39	10.3
1640–49	11.5
1650–59	10.3
1660–69	10.7
1670–79	8.6
1680–83	4

Annual figures

1622	2	1640	8	1660	13	1680	3
1623	15	1641	8	1661	10	1681	6
1624	6	1642	11	1662	7	1682	6
1625	2	1643	8	1663	10	1683	1
1626	13	1644	12	1664	12		
1627	5	1645	12	1665	17		
1628	11	1646	9	1666	7		
1629	7	1647	18	1667	12		
		1648	15	1668	6		
1630	12	1649	14	1669	13		
1631	19						
1632	9	1650	9	1670	11		
1633	5	1651	13	1671	4		
1634	10	1652	10	1672	14		
1635	11	1653	13	1673	16		
1636	8	1654	13	1674	5		
1637	8	1655	11	1675	9		
1638	9	1656	5	1676	6		
1639	12	1657	6	1677	9		
		1658	10	1678	7		
		1659	13	1679	5		

SOURCE: A.D. Eure-et-Loir, 3 E 473/6. Figures kindly supplied by Yves Gueneau.

GIEN (colloque du Berry)

Avg. baps. p.a.	
1600–09	50.1
1610–19	44.6
1620–29	40.1
1630–39	39.3
1640–49	35.6
1650–59	38.3
1660–67	45.8
1670–75	36.8

Annual figures

1600 55	1620 49	1640 35	1660 53
1601 53	1621 57	1641 36	1661 40
1602 56	1622 51	1642 28	1662 27
1603 58	1623 48	1643 38	1663 51
1604 50	1624 26	1644 29	1664 49
1605 49	1625 47	1645 32	1665 51
–	1626 21	1646 37	1666 52
1608 34	1627 29	1647 36	1667 43
1609 46	1628 42	1648 48	–
	1629 31	1649 37	1670 36
1610 52			1671 37
1611 33	1630 44	1650 37	1672 39
1612 55	1631 38	1651 45	1673 33
1613 45	1632 35	1652 18	–
1614 44	1633 38	1653 38	1675 39
1615 47	1634 45	1654 38	
1616 42	1635 39	1655 40	
1617 42	1636 41	1656 43	
1618 37	1637 39	1657 47	
1619 49	1638 36	1658 36	
	1639 38	1659 41	

SOURCES: A.N., TT 244; B.P.F., Ms 1082. Figures kindly supplied by Yves Gueneau.

ISSOUDUN (colloque du Berry)

Avg. baps. p.a.	
1609–14	17
1620–28	21.3
1631–39	27.8
1640–49	29.8
1650–59	24.9
1660–69	18.2
1670–79	19.3
1680–84	11.4

Annual figures

1609 26	1631 23	1650 31	1670 22
1610 22	–	1651 23	1671 21
1611 10	1634 31	1652 11	1672 28
1612 19	1635 22	1653 22	1673 22
1613 15	1636 33	1654 21	1674 24
1614 10	–	1655 35	1675 13
–	1638 29	1656 29	1676 16
1620 26	1639 29	1657 29	1677 14
1621 18		1658 24	1678 19
1622 12	1640 31	1659 24	1679 14
1623 20	1641 29		
1624 31	1642 30	1660 27	1680 8
1625 18	1643 38	1661 24	1681 8
1626 27	1644 29	1662 9	1682 10
1627 19	1645 25	1663 12	1683 16
1628 21	1646 34	1664 29	1684 15
–	1647 32	1665 17	
	1648 30	1666 17	
	1649 20	1667 20	
		1668 11	
		1669 21	

SOURCE: A.D. Indre, I 4. Figures kindly supplied by Yves Gueneau.

LA CELLE-SAINT-CYR-DOLLOT (colloque du Berry)

Avg. baps. p.a.		*Annual figures*					
1614–21	7.5	1614	1	1630	8	1650	1
1623–30	8.3	1615	10	–		1651	8
1632–40	7.6	1616	8	1632	9	1652	2
1641–49	4.2	1617	7	1633	13	1653	2
1650–59	4.4	1618	5	1634	6	1654	5
1660–69	5.4	1619	11	1635	10	1655	2
				1636	3	1656	7
		1620	12	1637	7	1657	5
		1621	6	1638	7	1658	6
		–		1639	5	1659	6
		1623	5				
		1624	11	1640	8	1660	6
		1625	12	1641	2	1661	9
		1626	9	1642	8	1662	5
		1627	7	1643	9	1663	4
		1628	7	1644	5	1664	6
		1629	7	1645	5	1665	8
				1646	6	1666	4
				1647	3	1667	4
				1648	3	1668	6
				1649	1	1669	2

SOURCE: A.C. Chatillon-Coligny, état civil réformé. Figures kindly supplied by Yves Gueneau.

LA CHARITE (colloque du Berry)

Avg. baps. p.a.		*Annual figures*					
1637–42	2.2	1637	2	1650	3	1669	5
1643–49	4	1638	1	1651	3	1670	6
1650–59	4.4	1639	2	1652	2	1672	8
1669–77	4.6			1653	7	1673	1
1681–84	4	1640	1	1654	4	1674	2
		1641	1	1655	3	1675	4
		1642	6	1656	5	1676	9
		1643	3	1657	4	1677	2
		1644	3	1658	6	1681	4
		1645	1	1659	7	1684	4
		1646	4				
		1647	5	1660	1		
		1648	7	1661	2		
		1649	5				

SOURCE: Figures kindly supplied by Yves Gueneau.

MER (colloque de l'Orléanais)

Avg. baps. p.a.		*Annual figures*							
1615–24	65.3	1615	57	1625	73	1669	61	1680	48
1625–33	70	1616	46	1626	75			1681	46
1669–75	62.6	1617	67	1627	78	1670	61	1682	43
1676–82	51.7	1618	65	1628	69	1671	66		
		1619	64	1629	73	1672	62		
						1673	68		
		1620	83	1630	97	1674	65		
		1621	76	1631	51	1675	55		
		1622	64	1632	41	1676	65		
		1623	56	1633	73	1677	59		
		1624	75	–		1678	60		
						1679	41		

SOURCES: A.D. Loir-et-Cher, I 34,36; Bariteaud, "Protestants en pays blésois," figure following p. 75.

NOTE: The church of Beaugency closed in 1636, and the Protestants of that town subsequently worshipped at Mer. Figures for the period 1669–82 have been corrected to eliminate the small number of baptisms concerning inhabitants of Beaugency.

SANCERRE (colloque du Berry)

Avg. baps. p.a.	
1618–22	84.8
1636–39	78.8
1641–51	11.7
1652–59	48.3
1668–79	47.1
1680–84	47.4

Annual figures

1618 89	–	1650 18	1668 59
1619 85	1641 3	1651 13	–
1620 78	1642 8	1652 27	1670 52
1621 73	1643 11	1653 31	–
1622 99	1644 22	1654 45	1674 32
–	1645 13	1655 48	1675 53
1636 84	1646 8	1656 56	1676 55
1637 74	1647 9	1657 66	1677 48
1638 77	1648 15	1658 50	1678 35
1639 80	1649 9	1659 63	1679 43

1680	42
1681	35
1682	56
1683	57
1684	47

SOURCE: Archives de l'Eglise réformée de Sancerre, état civil. Figures kindly supplied by Yves Gueneau.
NOTE: Between 1640 and 1651, Sancerre's temple was closed. The baptisms noted here were performed at the temple of La Charité.

SYNOD: BURGUNDY

BAILLIAGE DE BRESSE (colloque de Lyon)

Protestant population acc. censuses

1621	265 families
1682	129 families (609 individuals)

SOURCE: Sylvie Cadier-Sabatier, *Les Protestants de Pont-de-Veyle et lieux circonvoisins au XVIIe siècle* (Trévoux, 1975), 70, 72.
NOTE: Three temples existed in the Bresse at one point or another during the century: Pont-de-Veyle, closed in 1661, Bourg, closed in 1618, and Reyssouze, whose existence was precarious for much of the period. Inhabitants of the region are also known to have worshipped at the nearby temple of Mâcon. Although registers exist for Pont-de-Veyle and Reyssouze, the impermanence of these churches and the fluidity of their boundaries make the census data a surer guide to Protestantism's numerical evolution in the region.

IS-SUR-TILLE (colloque de Dijon)

Avg. baps. p.a.	
1607–16	47.3
1632–39	31.6
1640–49	43.6
1650–59	40.3
1660–69	38.7
1670–79	35.4
1680–84	38.3

Annual figures

1632 21	1650 43	1670 43
1633 17	1651 41	1671 28
1634 13	1652 42	1672 40
1635 57	1653 41	1673 33
1636 32	1654 39	1674 37
1637 20	1655 39	1675 36
1639 32	1656 45	1676 30
	1657 32	1677 39
1640 36	1658 37	1678 36
1641 40	1659 44	1679 32
1642 36		
1643 33	1660 38	1680 42
1644 42	1661 41	1681 39
1645 46	1662 33	1682 28
1646 58	1663 31	1683 47
1647 47	1664 38	1684 35
1648 51	1665 43	
1649 47	1666 43	
	1667 40	
	1668 39	
	1669 25 (7)	

SOURCES: B. P. F., Ms 437 (copy of register covering the years 1631–85; the original is at the *mairie*); Jacques Fromental, *La Réforme en Bourgogne aux XVIe et XVIIe siècles* (Paris, 1968), 11, 171.

LYON (colloque de Lyon)

Avg. baps. p.a.		*Annual figures*			
1601–11	41	1601 29	–	1650 51	1670 59
1619–28	35.5	1602 27	1632 13	1651 48	1671 61
1632–39	45.3	1603 52	–	1652 55	1672 63
1640–49	45.1	1604 33	1634 51	1653 47	1673 48
1650–59	49.5	1605 43	1635 46	1654 54	1674 45
1660–69	48.2	1606 51	1636 56	1655 49	1675 46
1670–79	53	1607 38	1637 44	1656 48	1676 54
1680–84	50	1608 44	1638 55	1657 48	1677 50
		1609 35	1639 52	1658 55	1678 68
				1659 40	1679 36
		1610 49	1640 47		
		1611 50	1641 46	1660 37	1680 60
		–	–	1661 44	1681 54
		1619 37	1643 46	1662 47	1682 46
		–	1644 41	1663 47	1683 44
		1623 28	1645 43	1664 52	1684 46
		1624 48	1646 36	1665 48	
		1625 46	1647 51	1666 49	
		1626 33	1648 49	1667 53	
		–	1649 47	1668 54	
		1628 21		1669 51	

SOURCES: A.C. Lyon, 714, 718–20. Figures kindly supplied by Jean-Noël Biraben.

PARAY-LE-MONIAL (colloque de Chalon-sur-Sâone)

Avg. baps. p.a.		*Annual figures*			
1602–09	8.8		1620 8 (9)	1640 11	1673 10 (10)
1610–19	11.3	1601 21	–	1641 6	1674 6
1620–29	9.6	1602 10	1622 4 (3)	1642 14	–
1630–39	9	1603 6	1623 13	1643 9	1676 11
1640–49	12.3	1604 6	1624 4	1644 16	1677 10
1650–53	10.9	1605 5	1625 10	1645 11	1678 12
1673–80	10.5	1606 7	1626 11	1646 16	1679 14
		1607 14	1627 10	1647 15	1680 6 (7)
		1608 7	1628 7	1648 10	
		1609 15	1629 10	1649 15	
		1610 10	1630 9	1650 10	
		1611 13	1631 9	1651 12	
		1612 10	1632 7	1652 13	
		1613 12	1633 4	1653 8 (9)	
		1614 11	1634 13		
		1615 10	1635 8		
		1616 9	1636 10		
		1617 15	1637 12		
		1618 16	1638 11		
		1619 7	1639 8		

SOURCES: B. P. F., Mss 438, E 30. The former is an original register covering the years 1601–53, the latter a photocopy of registers in the *mairie*.

CHEF-BOUTONNE (colloque du Moyen-Poitou)

Avg. baps. p.a.		*Annual figures*			
1602–09	42.5	1602 37	1623 39	1640 39	1660 26
1610–18	47	1603 41	1624 50	1641 25	1661 21 (11)
1623–30	36.5	1604 59	1625 33	1642 42	–
1631–40	37.6	1605 48	1626 35	1643 37	1669 26 (9)
1641–50	32.1	1606 37	1627 47	1644 28	
1651–61	29.7	1607 32	1628 34	1645 43	1670 31
1669–76	29.9	1608 41	1629 34	1646 28	1671 29
1677–84	25.2	1609 45		1647 33	1672 28
			1630 20	1648 37	1673 33
		1610 61	1631 32	1649 23	1674 29
		1611 52	1632 31		1675 27
		1612 54	1633 25	1650 25	1676 32
		1613 36	1634 51	1651 24	1677 29
		1614 36	1635 51	1652 40	1678 29
		1615 49	1636 34	1653 41	1679 18
		1616 41	1637 41	1654 28	
		1617 51	1638 32	1655 36	1680 17
		1618 43	1639 40	1656 23	1681 35
		–		1657 30	1682 21
				1658 28	1683 8
				1659 29	1684 48

SOURCES: A. D. Deux-Sèvres, 4E² 64/2–8; Raymond Proust, "Chef-Boutonne: Les protestants au XVIIe siècle," *Bulletin de la Société des Antiquaires de l'Ouest*, 4th ser., III (1956), 545–62, esp. 562.
NOTE: I have corrected Proust's figures to take into account the slight shifts in the boundary of the church after 1669.

LA-MOTHE-SAINT-HERAY-EXOUDUN (colloque du Moyen-Poitou)

Avg. baps. p.a.		*Annual figures* register 1 (*La-Mothe-Saint-Héray?*)	register 2 (*Exoudun?*)	register 4 (*two churches combined*)
1618–30	367	1618 150 (7)	1630 121	1675 345 (11)
1675–77	355.4	1619 229	1631 63 (8)	1676 309
		1620 240		1677 382
		1621 246		
		1622 241		1681 277
		1623 248		
		1624 322		
		1625 269		
		1626 319		
		1627 249		
		1628 253		
		1629 225		
		1630 281		
		1631 145 (7)		

SOURCE: A.D. Deux-Sèvres, 4E² 133.
NOTE: Neither of the early registers indicates either the church to which it belonged or the place of residence of those bringing children to be baptized, although these registers are contained in a liasse marked "La-Mothe-Saint-Héray-Exoudun." Where the two registers overlap, the acts concern different individuals. I have assumed that the two early registers concern the once separate churches of La-Mothe-Saint-Héray and Exoudun and that the relative size of the two churches as indicated by the number of baptisms in 1630–31 was constant throughout the period 1618–31. The acts in the final register clearly concern the church of La-Mothe-Saint-Héray-Exoudun, Exoudun's temple having been closed in 1666. A register also exists for one of the churches, probably Exoudun, for the years 1647–54.

MOUGON (colloque du Moyen-Poitou)

Avg. baps. p.a.		*Annual figures*	
1600–05	240.5	1600 219	1677 100 (9)
1677–78	170.8	1601 217	1678 85 (4)
		1602 203	
		1603 198	
		1604 266	
		1605 158 (8)	

Source: A.D. Deux-Sèvres, 4E[2] 196.

ROCHECHOUART (colloque du Haut-Poitou)

Avg. baps. p.a.		*Annual figures*		
1600–08	34.3	1600 31 (10)	1620 37	1650 23
1611–20	37.1	–	1621 43	1651 13
1621–30	28.2	1602 16 (6)	1622 35	1652 [5]
1649–59	20.2	1603 22	1623 37	1653 [2]
1660–69	14.9	1604 [22 (6)]	1624 26	1654 [2]
		1605 [18]	1625 36	1655 [10]
		1606 39	1626 20	1656 [23]
		1607 40	1627 20	1657 11 (6)
		1608 18 (6)	1628 22	1658 23
		–	1629 19	1659 18
		1611 17 (4)	1630 17 (9)	1660 19
		1612 38	–	1661 21
		1613 44	1649 8 (3)	1662 17
		1614 32		1663 17
		1615 45		1664 10
		1616 31		1665 6
		1617 35		1666 17
		1618 27		1667 10
		1619 40		1668 16
				1669 4 (2)

Source: A.D. Haute-Vienne, Etat civil protestant, Rochechouart.
Note: This church was troubled by conflicts between its pastors and members and an inability to retain ministers. The years in brackets are ones when the church had no resident minister; baptisms were performed at irregular intervals by ministers from other localities in the region.

SYNOD: AUNIS-SAINTONGE-ANGOUMOIS

BARBEZIEUX (colloque de Saintes)

Avg. baps. p.a.		*Annual figures*			
1600–04	164.9	1600 172	1620 90	1630 135	1670 84 (11)
1613–22	110.2	1601 151	1621 97	1631 111	1671 80
1623–33	112.4	1602 165	1622 98	1632 108	1672 94
1670–80	73.6	1603 179	1623 132	1633 68 (10)	1673 74
		1604 61 (5)	1624 120	–	1674 85
		–	1625 101		1675 86
		1613 127	1626 122		1676 60
		1614 121	1627 111		1677 70
		1615 125	1628 109		1678 36
		1616 111	1629 101		1679 58
		1617 102			
		1618 116			1680 58 (9)
		1619 115			–
					1683 89

Sources: A. C. Barbézieux, regs. II–VI, IX, XII.

DOMPIERRE-BOURGNEUF (colloque d'Aunis)

Avg. baps. p.a.		*Annual figures*			
1636–39	11	1636 3 (4)	1650 15	1660 15	1670 18
1640–49	11.9	1637 15	1651 14	1661 18	1671 9
1650–59	12.6	1638 15	1652 10	1662 25	1672 20
1660–69	19.1	1639 11	1653 9	1663 15	1673 15
1670–79	11.2		1654 17	1664 24	1674 10
1680–83	12.3	1640 8	1655 12	1665 20	1675 9
		1641 9	1656 12	1666 22	1676 13
		1642 18	1657 14	1667 19	1677 1
		1643 16	1658 12	1668 20	1678 7
		1644 4	1659 11	1669 13	1679 10
		1645 10			
		1646 16			1680 19
		1647 15			1681 9
		1648 9			1682 13
		1649 14			1683 8
					1684 1 (3)

SOURCES: A. D. Charente-Maritime, I 102–12.

LA ROCHEFOUCAULD (colloque de l'Angoumois)

Avg. baps. p.a.		*Annual figures*			
1608–19	36.1	1608 10 (3)	1620 40	1640 24	1660 12
1620–29	30.9	1609 40	1621 35	1641 24	1661 16
1630–39	26.6		1622 35	1642 23	1662 14
1640–49	22.4	1610 25	1623 28	1643 21	1663 14 (10)
1650–59	18.4	1611 18 (8)	1624 30	1644 26	
1660–63	14.6	1612 43	1625 27	1645 21	
		1613 42	1626 32	1646 22	
		1614 29	1627 32	1647 25	
		1615 41	1628 20	1648 20	
		1616 30	1629 30	1649 18	
		1617 38			
		1618 35	1630 29	1650 20	
		1619 43	1631 18	1651 14	
			1632 23	1652 27	
			1633 30	1653 17	
			1634 26	1654 24	
			1635 32	1655 19	
			1636 32	1656 17	
			1637 28	1657 28	
			1638 28	1658 13	
			1639 20	1659 15	

SOURCE: A.D. Charente, I 305.

LA ROCHELLE (colloque d'Aunis)

Avg. baps. p.a.		*Annual figures*							
1610–19	671.2	1610	776	1630	292	1650	262	1670	220
1620–29	541.9	1611	649	1631	287	1651	262	1671	242
1630–39	317.4	1612	635	1632	349	1652	256	1672	220
1640–49	313.7	1613	702	1633	324	1653	194	1673	243
1650–59	256.2	1614	673	1634	326	1654	245	1674	239
1660–69	235.1	1615	700	1635	310	1655	263	1675	225
1670–79	222	1616	634	1636	325	1656	263	1676	240
1680–84	170.3	1617	663	1637	313	1657	276	1677	198
		1618	674	1638	350	1658	264	1678	211
		1619	606	1639	298	1659	277	1679	182
		1620	679	1640	351	1660	272	1680	184
		1621	728	1641	324	1661	296	1681	189
		1622	651	1642	350	1662	188	1682	152
		1623	621	1643	325	1663	200	1683	156
		1624	655	1644	309	1664	237		
		1625	624	1645	326	1665	237		
		1626	422	1646	324	1666	237		
		1627	480	1647	298	1667	222		
		1628	402	1648	259	1668	238		
		1629	157	1649	271	1669	224		

Sources: A.D. Charente-Maritime, I 23, 25–8, 30–3, 35–7, 39–42, 44–59. Figures kindly supplied by Jean-Noël Biraben. See also Louis Perouas, "Sur la démographie rochelaise," *Annales: E.S.C.* (1961), 1131–40.

MARENNES (colloque des Iles)

Avg. baps. p.a.		*Annual figures*					
1636–39	346			1650	255	1670	281
1640–49	301.1	1631	[285 (10)]	1651	241	1671	312
1650–59	246.1	1632	[419]	1652	202	1672	281
1660–69	256	1633	[462]	1653	158	1673	271
1670–79	260.5	1634	[513]	1654	18 (1)	1674	123 (6)
		1635	[478]	1655	248	1675	273
		1636	361	1656	290	1676	261
		1637	350	1657	279	1677	243
		1638	351	1658	273	1678	218
		1639	323	1659	269	1679	212
		1640	289	1660	233	1680	103 (8)
		1641	358	1661	247		
		1642	325	1662	195		
		1643	330	1663	246		
		1644	308	1664	270		
		1645	299	1665	276		
		1646	305	1666	266		
		1647	277	1667	258		
		1648	275	1668	273		
		1649	245	1669	296		

Source: A.D. Charente-Maritime, I 125.
Note: Between 1631 and 1635, several churches in the region were closed in the wake of the civil wars, swelling the number of baptisms celebrated at the temple of Marennes.

MORTAGNE-SUR-GIRONDE (colloque de Saintes)

Avg. baps. p.a.		*Annual figures*			
1613–20	35.9	1613 10 (4)	1620 38	1630 18	1660 20
1621–33	19.1	1614 52	1621 9	1631 16	1661 30
1655–59	24.4	1615 54	1622 11 (2)	1632 14	1662 26
1660–68	25.4	1616 25	–	1633 24	1663 24
		1617 31	1625 13 (6)	–	1664 26
		1618 15	1626 20	1655 14 (7)	1665 23
		1619 38	1627 16	1656 20	–
			1628 20	1657 24	1667 7 (2)
			1629 21	1658 22	1668 13 (6)
				1659 32	

SOURCE: Charleston Library Society (Charleston, South Carolina), Crottet Collection, Vol. 1.

PONS (colloque de Saintes)

Avg. baps. p.a.		*Annual figures*			
1596–1600	69.8	1596 60	1653 38	1660 51	1672 75
1653–59	47.6	1597 85	1654 43	1661 29	1673 60
1660–67	52.3	1598 84	1655 55	1662 35	1674 60
1672–80	53.3	1599 54	1656 44	1663 45	1675 47
		1600 34 (7)	1657 54	1664 61	1676 49
		–	1658 52	1665 57	1677 63
			1659 47	1666 72	1679 50
				1667 68	1680 42

SOURCES: A. N. TT 262 (2); A. D. Charente-Maritime, I 14.

SAINT-JEAN-D'ANGLE (colloque des Iles)

Avg. baps. p.a.		*Annual figures*		
1636–39	51.3	1635 [96]	1650 26	1670 22
1640–49	36.9	1636 59	1651 31	1671 34
1650–59	25	1637 58	1652 10 (9)	1672 28
1660–69	30.9	1638 36	1653 5	1673 32
1670–81	24.7	1639 52	1654 23	1674 24
			1655 27	1675 17
		1640 41	1656 31	1676 28
		1641 49	1657 36	1677 29
		1642 47	1658 28	1678 13
		1643 32	1659 27	1679 28
		1644 38		
		1645 29	1660 24	1680 [190]
		1646 34	1661 30	1681 14
		1647 38	1662 34	
		1648 30	1663 29	
		1649 31	1664 34	
			1665 30	
			1666 32	
			1667 27	
			1668 32	
			1669 37	

SOURCE: A. D. Charente-Maritime, I 134.
NOTES: The figure for 1635 includes many acts involving inhabitants of Saint-Just, that for 1680 includes many acts concerning residents of Marennes, Saint-Just, and La Tremblade.

SAINT-JUST (colloque des Iles)

Avg. baps. p.a.		*Annual figures*							
1601–09	173.8	1601	110 (9)	1620	150	1640	140	1660	90
1610–19	139.3	1602	195	1621	189	1641	156	1661	106
1620–26	158.4	1603	186	1622	[301]	1642	129	–	
1635–44	145.1	1604	168	1623	90	1643	159	1666	133
1645–54	103.9	1605	87 (7)	1624	115	1644	122	1667	120
1655–63	103.9	1606	137	1625	128	1645	125	1668	123
1666–74	107	1607	176	1626	109 (10)	1646	116 (10)	1669	86
1675–81	77.7	1608	210	–		1648	100		
		1609	121 (8)	1635	69 (4)	1649	138	1670	105
				1636	145			1671	108
		1610	188	1637	159	1650	94	1672	92
		1611	122	1638	133	1651	128	1673	112
		1612	154	1639	142	1652	81	1674	84
		1613	166			1653	56	1675	95
		1614	131			1654	48	1676	97
		1615	105 (11)			1655	109	1677	80
		–				1656	119	1678	81
		1617	101			1657	117	1679	56
		1618	123			1658	121		
		1619	130			1659	103	1680	68
								1681	67
								1682	[177]
								1683	[249]

SOURCE: Source: A. D. Charente-Maritime, I 135.
NOTE: Although the registers do not indicate the place of residence of those bringing their children for baptism, the numbers seem clearly swollen in certain years by residents of nearby communities.

SALLES (colloque d'Aunis)

Avg. baps. p.a.		*Annual figures*							
1602–09	13.4	1602	6 (5)	1620	12	1640	11	1660	12
1610–19	12.2	1603	6	1621	10 (5)	1641	8	1661	21
1636–39	11	1604	23	–		1642	9	1662	8
1640–49	8.7	1605	7	1623	[1 (4)]	1643	5	1663	6
1650–59	4.9	1606	10	1624	[14]	1644	5	1664	15
1660–71	12.9	1607	16	1625	[1]	1645	13	1665	16
		1608	10	1626	[6]	1646	10	1666	9
		1609	21	1627	[6]	1647	11	1667	20
				1628	[1]	1648	10		
		1610	10	1629	[5]	1649	5	1671	9
		1611	11						
		1612	14	1630	[24]	1650	5		
		1613	12	1631	[35]	1651	6		
		1614	8	1632	[38]	1652	5		
		1615	13	1633	[38]	1653	1		
		1616	12	1634	[33]	1654	6		
		1617	17	1635	[34]	1655	8		
		1618	14	1636	14	1656	3		
		1619	11	1637	12	1657	4		
				1638	10	1658	5		
				1639	8	1659	6		

SOURCES: A. D. Charente-Maritime, I 86–7.
NOTE: Between 1622 and 1629, the register was poorly maintained "pour le malheur des guerres et la dispertion des enfans qu'on est bien souvent contraint de baptizer hors les lieux." The abnormally high figures for the years 1630–35 are probably to be attributed to the fact that many churches in the region were closed between these dates.

SYNOD: BASSE-GUYENNE

BORDEAUX (colloque du bas Agenais)

1616	3–400 families
1630	1000 people
1675	75 baptisms (=ca. 1875 people)

SOURCE: Paul Bert, *Histoire de la Révocation de l'Edit de Nantes à Bordeaux et dans le Bordelais* (Bordeaux, 1908), 3.

COUTRAS (colloque du bas Agenais)

Avg. baps. p.a.		*Annual figures*					
1600–09	14.1	1600	12	1620	10 (7)	–	
1610–19	15.6	1601	2	–		1641	16
1620–29	16.7	1602	20	1624	5 (5)	1642	15
1630–39	14.9	1603	19	1625	17	1643	17
1641–50	14.9	1604	9	1626	16	1644	9
		1605	16	1627	15	1645	22
		1606	12	1628	18	1646	8
		1607	22	1629	19	1647	14
		1608	14			1648	17
		1609	15	1630	18	1649	17
				1631	11		
		1610	13	1632	13 (9)	1650	5 (5)
		1611	18	1633	13 (9)		
		1612	25	1634	13		
		1613	18	1635	6		
		1614	8	1636	12		
		1615	10	1637	15		
		1616	8	1638	20		
		1617	20	1639	21		
		1618	14				
		1619	22				

SOURCES: Arsenal, Ms 6558; A.D. Gironde, Bibliothèque des Archives, Su 46/1.

LAYRAC (colloque du Condomois)

Avg. baps. p.a.		*Annual figures*							
1610–19	35.5	1610	49	1630	39	1650	20	1670	9
1620–29	27.3	1611	34	1631	17	1651	14	1671	2
1630–39	26.5	1612	34	1632	26	1652	1	1672	6
1640–49	26.1	1613	51	1633	35	1653	2	1673	7
1650–59	10.3	1614	13	1634	21	1654	6	1674	12
1660–69	11	1615	27	1635	26	1655	9		
1670–74	7.2	1616	40	1636	26	1656	11		
		1617	35	1637	29	1657	13		
		1618	35	1638	30	1658	17		
		1619	37	1639	16	1659	10		
		1620	21	1640	32	1660	11		
		1621	35	1641	30	1661	12		
		1622	19	1642	28	1662	6		
		1623	32	1643	27	1663	5		
		1624	30	1644	24	1664	11		
		1625	31	1645	28	1665	13		
		1626	25	1646	27	1666	10		
		1627	28	1647	17	1667	12		
		1628	28	1648	18	1668	17		
		1629	24	1649	30	1669	13		

SOURCE: A.D. Gers, Archives de l'Hôpital de Condom, H 80. Figures kindly supplied by Gregory Hanlon.

MUSSIDAN (colloque du Périgord)

Avg. baps. p.a.		*Annual figures*							
1600–09	22.6	1600	20	1620	17	1640	15	1660	12
1610–19	18.3	1601	23	1621	23	1641	19	1661	6
1620–29	19.8	1602	18	1622	2	1642	14	1662	12
1630–39	17.2	1603	18	1623	21	1643	18	1663	14
1640–49	16.5	1604	32	1624	30	1644	16	1664	16
1650–59	13.3	1605	27	1625	19	1645	16	1665	8 (10)
1660–65	11.5	1606	25	1626	25	1646	17		
		1607	27	1627	23	1647	20		
		1608	26	1628	21	1648	14		
		1609	20	1629	17	1649	16		
		1610	36	1630	26	1650	18		
		1611	22	1631	9	1651	9		
		1612	27	1632	18	1652	10		
		1613	11	1633	21	1653	15		
		1614	22	1634	21	1654	11		
		1615	17	1635	13	1655	13		
		1616	5	1636	13	1656	23		
		1617	6	1637	23	1657	12		
		1618	17	1638	16	1658	11		
		1619	20	1639	12	1659	12		

SOURCE: Arsenal, Ms 6561.

NERAC (colloque du Condomois)

Avg. baps. p.a.		*Annual figures*							
1603–16	407.5	1603	188 (6)	1619	253 (10)	1639	279	1668	155
1619–26	288.8	1604	475	1620	347	1640	291	1669	188
1639–50	270.6	1605	346 (10)	1621	222 (8)	1641	287	1670	154 (11)
1668–80	161.4	1606	419	1622	197 (10)	1642	300	–	
		1607	318 (10)	–		1643	320	1672	176
		1608	343 (11)	1624	260	1644	253	1673	164
		1609	415	1625	260	1645	226	1674	184
		1610	415	1626	266 (11)	1646	255	1675	155
		1611	354 (11)			1647	246	1676	164
		1612	358 (11)			1648	259	1677	168
		1613	415			1649	308	1678	144
		1614	285 (10)			1650	223	1679	98 (10)
		1615	310 (9)			1651	85 (6)	1680	146
		1616	416 (11)						

SOURCES: L.D.S. films 730829–31 (A.D. Lot-et-Garonne 4E 199/15–17).

ARTHEZ (colloque d'Orthez)

Avg. baps. p.a.		*Annual figures*			
1609–19	48.4	1609 11 (3)	1620 26	1640 28	1660 15
1620–29	23		1621 30	1641 16	1661 17
1630–39	19.9	1610 65	1622 25	1642 20	1662 15
1640–50	20.5	1611 51	1623 24	–	1663 20
1657–69	18.8	1612 65	1624 18	1645 27	1664 19
1670–78	28	1613 39	1625 28	1646 19	1665 25
		1614 39	1626 20	1647 18	1666 19
		1615 49	1627 12	–	1667 23
		1616 47	1628 25	1649 26	1668 27
		1617 38	1629 22		1669 22
		1618 42		1650 10	
		1619 50	1630 9	–	1670 24
			1631 15	1657 11	1671 24
			1632 18	1658 17	–
			1633 27	1659 15	1674 30
			1634 6 (4)		1675 29
			1635 7 (8)		1676 22
			1636 17		1677 40
			1637 24		1678 22 (10)
			1638 25		
			1639 31		

Source: A.D. Pyrénées-Atlantiques, 4 E 58.
Note: From 1668 onward, inhabitants of such communities as Lacq, Placis, and Arance begin to appear in the registers for the first time. Figures for the years 1668–79 reflect only baptisms involving residents of communities whose inhabitants previously worshipped at Arthez.

BELLOCQ (colloque d'Orthez)

Avg. baps. p.a.		*Annual figures*			
1580–89	76.8	1580 86	1600 77	1620 13 (3)	1640 21
1590–99	69.1	1581 93	1601 69	1621 40 (10)	1641 21 (4)
1600–09	73.2	1582 75	1602 77	1622 49	
1610–19	67.8	1583 68	1603 62	1623 55	
1620–29	58.6	1584 82	1604 81	1624 64	
1630–41	38	1585 79	1605 69	1625 65	
		1586 82	1606 68	1626 60	
		1587 63	1607 77	1627 50	
		1588 49	1608 66	1628 53	
		1589 91	1609 86	1629 53	
		1590 84	1610 78	1630 37	
		1591 80	1611 86	1631 16	
		1592 86	1612 76	1632 3 (1)	
		1593 64	1613 77	1633 19 (5)	
		1594 77	1614 47	1634 42	
		1595 59	1615 64	1635 27 (7)	
		1596 43	1616 64	1636 53	
		1597 89	1617 43 (6)	1637 50	
		1598 57	1618 55	–	
		1599 52	1619 54	1639 31	

Source: A.C. Bellocq (conserved at A.D. Pyrénées-Atlantiques), GG 1.

LAGOR (colloque d'Orthez)

Avg. baps. p.a.	
1600–09	45.7
1610–19	47.5
1620–29	29.6
1630–39	25.6
1640–50	25.6
1664–68	28.2

Annual figures

1600	51	1620	47	1640	34	1660	[14]
1601	43	1621	31	1641	30	1661	[17]
1602	51	1622	5 (2)	1642	22	1662	[21]
1603	36	1623	19 (10)	1643	23	1663	[22]
1604	46	1624	27	1644	29	1664	27
1605	33	1625	26	1645	27	1665	28
1606	56	1626	43	1646	17	1666	26
1607	43	1627	28 (11)	1647	33	1667	33
1608	57	1628	15 (4)	1648	27	1668	20 (9)
1609	41	1629	18 (6)	1649	24		
1610	47	1630	10	1650	16		
1611	49	1631	4	1651	[9]		
1612	58	1632	28	1652	[23]		
1613	50	1633	24	1653	[10]		
1614	37	1634	33	1654	[4]		
1615	47	1635	34	1655	[5]		
1616	60	1636	30	1656	[21]		
1617	31 (8)	1637	26	1657	[13]		
1618	45	1638	35	1658	[19]		
1619	35	1639	32	1659	[19]		

Source: A.D. Pyrénées-Atlantiques, 4 E 301.
Note: Registration may be incomplete 1651–63.

NAY (colloque de Nay)

Avg. baps. p.a.	
1618–29	23
1630–39	18.1
1640–49	18.4
1650–59	16.6
1660–69	13.1
1670–79	13.2
1680–82	15.7

Annual figures

1618	2 (3)	1630	16	1650	22	1670	12
1619	22	1631	18	1651	15	1671	16
		1632	19	1652	18	1672	12
1620	35	1633	14	1653	16	1673	15
–		1634	19	1654	14	1674	12
1622	21	1635	26	1655	18	1675	15
1623	25	1636	18	1656	18	1676	12
1624	24	1637	15	1657	17	1677	13
1625	19	1638	14 (6)	1658	18	1678	18
1626	17	1639	5 (7)	1659	10	1679	7
1627	32						
1628	20	1640	18	1660	14	1680	15
1629	19	1641	21	1661	11	1681	15
		1642	18	1662	15	1682	17
		1643	23	1663	12		
		1644	14	1664	15		
		1645	14	1665	10		
		1646	16	1666	16		
		1647	22	1667	9 (9)		
		1648	14	1668	12		
		1649	24	1669	14		

Source: A.C. Nay (conserved at A.D. Pyrénées-Atlantiques), GG 2.
Note: After 1667, the number of baptisms recorded in Nay's registers more than doubled, as inhabitants of such nearby communities as Beuste and Arros, whose temples were closed in 1667, began to come to Nay to worship. The raw figures have been reduced here by 52 percent to compensate for this change in the church's boundaries. The size of this correction was calculated by comparing the average number of baptisms in the five years before and after 1667–68. The notation of place of residence, which is nearly complete after 1668, corroborates that a correction of roughly this magnitude is appropriate.

ORTHEZ (colloque d'Orthez)

Avg. baps. p.a.		*Annual figures*					
1580–87	168.1	1580	193	1632	72 (8)	1650	95
1632–39	103.3	1581	162	1633	107	1651	77
1640–49	91.8	1582	182	1634	104	1652	92
1650–59	86.9	–		1635	99	1653	71
1660–63	95.8	1584	151	1636	110	1654	76
		1585	185	1637	99	1655	120
		1586	142	1638	106	1656	80
		1587	49 (4)	1639	95	1657	88
						1658	97
				1640	95	1659	73
				1641	87		
				1642	90	1660	93
				1643	78	1661	87
				1644	75	1662	101
				1645	88	1663	94 (11)
				1646	106		
				1647	103		
				1648	109		
				1649	87		

SOURCES: A.C. Orthez, registres protestants.
NOTES: Figures for the period 1580–87 have been corrected to remove the inhabitants of Sainte-Suzanne, where a separate temple was established early in the seventeenth century. Registers also exist for the years 1590–1603, but they seem poorly maintained.

SALIES (colloque de Sauveterre)

Avg. baps. p.a.		*Annual figures*					
1590–99	113.8	1590	119	1620	133	1655	16 (2)
1600–07	111	1591	127	1621	66 (8)	1656	113
1619–29	111	1592	135	1622	84 (10)	1657	90
1630–38	106.4	1593	114	1623	111	1658	132
1655–59	111.4	1594	109	1624	121	1659	85 (9)
1660–69	90.6	1595	127	1625	125		
		1596	87	1626	102	1660	75
		1597	131	1627	115	1661	103
		1598	91 (11)	1628	105	1662	90
		1599	88	1629	95	1663	92
						1664	95
		1600	117	1630	97	1665	83
		1601	47 (5)	1631	78	1666	95
		–		1632	110	1667	81 (10)
		1603	128	1633	109	1668	85
		–		1634	95	1669	24 (3)
		1605	95	1635	108		
		–		1636	120		
		1607	103	1637	108		
		–		1638	133		
		1619	16 (2)	–			

SOURCES: A.C. Salies (conserved at A.D. Pyrénées-Atlantiques), GG 15–16.

BRIATEXTE (colloque de l'Albigeois)

Avg. baps. p.a.		*Annual figures*			
1600–12	14.8	1600 16	1620 14	1654 8	1660 9
1620–24	10.2	1601 18	1621 21	1655 14	1661 12
1654–59	9.3	1602 14	1622 7	1656 5	1662 9
1660–67	10	1603 20	1623 13	1657 9	1663 13
		1604 12 (9)	1624 6	1658 11	1664 4
		–	–	1659 9	1665 15
		1608 7			1666 12
		1609 15			1667 6
		1610 12			
		1611 12			
		1612 18			
		–			

SOURCE: A. D. Tarn, E 5185.

CASTRES (colloque de l'Albigeois)

Avg. baps. p.a.		*Annual figures*		
1620–21	212.8	1620 95 (5)	1664 118	1675 136
1622–28	145.3	1621 206	1665 146	1676 140
1664–69	142.7	1622 146	1666 120	1677 136
1670–79	134.1	1623 167	1667 151	1678 130
1680–84	126.8	1624 174	1668 167	1679 127
		1625 164	1669 154	
		1626 125		1680 124
		1627 139	1670 150	1681 145
		1628 102	1671 151	1682 118
		1629 29	1672 134	1683 134
		–	1673 149	1684 113
			1674 138	1685 [178 (8)]

SOURCES: A.D. Tarn, E 5198 bis–5222.
NOTES: Registers also exist for the period 1630–63, but they are negligently maintained and appear to be incomplete. The entries for 1685 include many inhabitants of nearby localities whose temples had been closed.

MAS-GRENIER (colloque d'Armagnac)

Avg. baps. p.a.		*Annual figures*			
1600–09	21.8	1600 23	1620 33	1640 19	1660 8
1610–19	16.3	1601 11	1621 24	1641 9	1661 9
1620–29	15.8	1602 28	1622 11	1642 16	1662 5
1630–39	17.3	1603 20	1623 14	1643 17	1663 12
1640–49	13.9	1604 26	1624 24	1644 7	1664 2 (6)
1650–59	10.2	1605 29	1625 7	1645 17	
1660–64	8	1606 18	1626 4	1646 15	
		1607 23	1627 18	1647 10	
		1608 20	1628 6	1648 15	
		1609 20	1629 17	1649 14	
		1610 20	1630 12	1650 14	
		1611 25	1631 13	1651 10	
		1612 12	1632 17	1652 8	
		1613 14	1633 16	1653 5	
		1614 0	1634 20	1654 9	
		1615 8	1635 16	1655 13	
		1616 10	1636 18	1656 21	
		1617 27	1637 25	1657 6	
		1618 23	1638 14	1658 12	
		1619 24	1639 22	1659 4	

SOURCE: A.N., TT 252/34.
NOTE: There is no evidence of a gap in registration in 1614.

MILLAU (colloque du Rouergue)

Avg. baps. p.a.

1610–19	131.9
1620–29	132.1
1630–39	101.7
1640–49	106.2
1650–59	99.3
1660–69	93.5
1670–79	86.7
1680–84	83.2

Annual figures

1610	79	1630	117	1650	99	1670	85
1611	157	1631	86	1651	83	1671	91
1612	136	1632	75	1652	119	1672	94
1613	141	1633	113	1653	82	1673	87
1614	125	1634	102	1654	68	1674	108
1615	120	1635	103	1655	121	1675	86
1616	153	1636	70 (7)	1656	103	1676	66
1617	134	1637	90	1657	118	1677	95
1618	143	1638	119	1658	93	1678	88
1619	131	1639	100	1659	107	1679	67
1620	139	1640	108	1660	100	1680	84
1621	159	1641	115	1661	103	1681	80
1622	136	1642	119	1662	100	1682	84
1623	129	1643	106	1663	83	1683	93
1624	131	1644	90	1664	71	1684	75
1625	123	1645	108	1665	88		
1626	127	1646	115	1666	67		
1627	155	1647	94	1667	96 (9)		
1628	133	1648	69 (9)	1668	102		
1629	89	1649	111	1669	102		

SOURCES: A.C. Millau, GG 10–13. Figures kindly provided by Jacques Frayssenge.

MONTAUBAN (colloque du Bas-Quercy)

Avg. baps. p.a.

1600–09	672.7
1610–19	714.8
1620–29	530.1
1630–39	569
1640–49	553.1
1650–59	426.9
1660–69	481.6
1670–79	411.8
1680–84	382

Annual figures

1600	642	1620	650	1640	593	1660	518
1601	597	1621	742	1641	575	1661	508
1602	624	1622	237	1642	611	1662	484
1603	674	1623	524	1643	601	1663	468
1604	733	1624	460	1644	453	1664	500
1605	672	1625	607	1645	528	1665	495
1606	668	1626	461	1646	561	1666	466
1607	763	1627	566	1647	527	1667	474
1608	643	1628	617	1648	548	1668	474
1609	711	1629	440	1649	534	1669	429
1610	709	1630	371	1650	521	1670	470
1611	739	1631	502	1651	460	1671	486
1612	734	1632	494	1652	431	1672	448
1613	729	1633	589	1653	238	1673	432
1614	646	1634	603	1654	292	1674	445
1615	660	1635	627	1655	462	1675	395
1616	768	1636	597	1656	439	1676	356
1617	726	1637	642	1657	483	1677	388
1618	704	1638	599	1658	463	1678	350
1619	733	1639	666	1659	480	1679	348

1680	423
1681	340
1682	402
1683	32 (1)
1684	172 (6)
1685	278 (8)

SOURCES: A.D. Tarn-et-Garonne, 12 GG 8–27, 39–55.
NOTE: The register indicates that during the plague of 1653–4, the elders of the church left the city. The pastors, however, carried on with their duties "avec grand zele et ardeur." Baptisms were performed and subsequently recorded on the basis of "billetz" drawn up at the time.

PUYLAURENS (colloque du Lauragais)

Protestant population acc. censuses

	families	people
1630	390	
ca. 1640	369	
ca. 1665		1600
ca. 1680	356	1183

Avg. baps. p.a.

1632–41	65
1647–50	58
1669–72	56

SOURCE: Georges Frêche, "Contre-Réforme et dragonnades (1610–1789): Pour une orientation statistique de l'histoire du Protestantisme," *B.S.H.P.F.*, CXIX (1973), 368. G.E. de Falguerolles, "Les paroissiens de l'Eglise Réformée à Puylaurens (1630–1650)," *B.S.H.P.F.*, CXI (1965), 106, and "Les paroissiens de l'Eglise Réformée à Puylaurens (1669–1673)," *B.S.H.P.F.*, CXII (1966), 125, indicate a slightly different number of baptisms but a similar trend.

REALVILLE-ALBIAS (colloque du Bas-Quercy)

Avg. baps. p.a.

1618–21	49.3
1668–69	56

Annual figures

1618	26 (6)	1668	59
1619	49	1669	53
1620	40		
1621	29 (5)		

SOURCES: A.D. Tarn-et-Garonne, 6 E 2/3–4, 6 E 149/9–11.
NOTE: During the early decades of the seventeenth century, Réalville and Albias formed a single church, as both the baptismal registers and synodal records attest. At some point between 1626 and 1647 (gaps in the synodal records make it difficult to be any more precise), a separate church was established at Albias. Réalville's baptismal registers cover the period from 1618 through 1685 (with gaps between 1621 and 1631), but Albias's exist only for the years 1667–70. The figures for 1668 and 1669 given here combine those of Réalville and Albias. From August, 1670 onward, the number of baptisms celebrated at Réalville was swollen enormously by the arrival of numerous worshippers from Nègrepelisse, whose temple had been closed.

REVEL (colloque du Lauragais)

Avg. baps. p.a.

1600–09	67.6
1610–19	73.6
1620–29	64.6
1630–39	56.1
1640–49	59
1650–59	49.2
1660–69	50.4
1670–79	43.3
1680–84	40

Annual figures

1600	38 (7)	1620	64	1640	43	1660	54
1601	76	1621	83	1641	57	1661	52
1602	64	1622	56	1642	72	1662	37
1603	57	1623	59	1643	68	1663	42
1604	65	1624	71	1644	54	1664	40
1605	57	1625	61	1645	62	1665	53
1606	64	1626	56	1646	46	1666	61
1607	75	1627	71	1647	80	1667	42
1608	66	1628	61	1648	52	1668	68
1609	86	1629	64	1649	56	1669	30 (6)
1610	82	1630	52	1650	53	–	
1611	78	1631	47	1651	59	1671	59
1612	80	1632	46	1652	44	1672	54
1613	83	1633	70	1653	39	1673	52
1614	58	1634	67	1654	38	–	
1615	57	1635	56	1655	63	1676	39
1616	68	1636	64	1656	46	1677	36
1617	85	1637	52	1657	58	1678	39
1618	64	1638	52	1658	47	1679	24
1619	81	1639	55	1659	45		

1680	27 (9)
1681	41
1682	39
1683	47
1684	36

SOURCE: A.D. Haute-Garonne, 4 E 1716–23.

ROQUECOURBE (colloque de l'Albigeois)

Avg. baps. p.a.		*Annual figures*			
1614–19	49.6	1614 48	1630 52	1650 36	1670 36
1620–29	38.7	1615 40	1631 27	1651 4 (1)	1671 47
1630–39	42	1616 42 (8)	1632 29	1652 31 (10)	1672 30
1640–49	40.2	1617 55	1633 48	1653 17	1673 38
1650–59	33.6	1618 42	1634 49	1654 27	–
1660–69	33.3	1619 54	1635 47	1655 35	1677 38
1670–79	37.5		1636 28	1656 39	1678 29
1680–84	42.2	1620 38	1637 56	1657 34	1679 45
		1621 35	1638 35	1658 41	
		1622 43	1639 49	1659 38	1680 36
		1623 42			1681 32
		–	1640 40	1660 32	1682 62
		1627 29	1641 46	1661 29	1683 43
		1628 46	1642 56	1662 23	1684 38
		1629 38	1643 48	1663 30	
			1644 22	1664 40	
			1645 34	1665 39	
			1646 43	1666 23	
			1647 32	1667 44	
			1648 42	1668 46	
			1649 39	1669 27	

Sources: A. D. Tarn, E 5362–7, 5369–74.

SAINT-AMANS (colloque du Lauragais)

Avg. baps. p.a.		*Annual figures*			
1603–08	20.1	1603 10	1620 8	1640 24	1660 29
1618–28	21.6	1604 14	1621 13	1641 29	1661 38
1630–39	17.1	1605 22	1622 10	1642 15	1662 25
1640–49	22	1606 28	1623 8	1643 18	1663 27
1650–59	27.7	1607 20	1624 17	1644 14	1664 45
1660–69	34.9	1608 10 (2)	1625 38	1645 24	1665 11 (4)
1675–80	33.4	–	1626 16	1646 29	–
		1618 11 (4)	1627 26	1647 25	1668 39
		1619 40	1628 36	1648 26	1669 42
			1629 [0]	1649 16	–
					1675 27
			1630 8	1650 30	1676 31
			1631 10	1651 26	1677 36
			1632 20	1652 33	1678 30
			1633 14	1653 20	1679 40
			1634 17	1654 23	1680 28 (9)
			1635 10	1655 35	
			1636 27	1656 31	
			1637 25	1657 23	
			1638 13	1658 14	
			1639 27	1659 42	

Sources: A. D. Tarn, E 5379–81, 5384.
Note: "Depuis le vingt et quatriesme decembre 1628 n'ont point esté presantez aucuns anfans a babtesme a cauze que la ville fust le 26e du mois prinze pour les geans tenans le party de Monsieur de Rouan et a cause ausy de la maladie contagieuse quy a este en ceste ville quy est la cause qu'il n'y cy est point fette nulle predication par Mr de Lespinasse notre pasteur que jusques le seize mars 1630."

VABRE (colloque de l'Albigeois)

Avg. baps. p.a.	*Annual figures*			
1627–29 61	1627 59 (11)	1640 45	1660 61	1680 53
1630–39 61.4	1628 68	1641 79	1661 94	1681 61
1640–49 66.5	1629 51	1642 64	1662 88	–
1650–62 65.8		1643 78	–	1683 26 (6)
1668–77 62.2	1630 65	1644 53	1668 57	1684 58
1678–84 62	–	1645 53	1669 64	1685 12 (3)
	1633 65	1646 67		
	1634 55	1647 76	1670 43	
	1635 54	1648 66	1671 58	
	1636 83	1649 84	1672 69	
	1637 63		1673 71	
	1638 66	1650 93	1674 62	
	1639 40	1651 47	1675 45	
		1652 42 (6)	1676 79	
		1653 52	1677 74	
		1654 46	1678 76	
		1655 47 (10)	1679 67	
		1656 26		
		1657 27		
		1658 48		
		1659 75		

Sources: A. D. Tarn, E 5421-5, B 858.

SYNOD: BAS-LANGUEDOC

AIGUES-VIVES (colloque de Nîmes)

Avg. baps. p.a.	*Annual figures*			
1623–33 23	1623 18	1640 38	1666 31	1683 41
1637–49 28.8	1624 33	1641 29	1667 21	1684 32
1666–69 26.8	1625 32	1642 19	1668 31	
1673–76 36	1626 16	1643 37	1669 24	
1683–84 36.5	1627 15	1644 23		
	1628 17	1645 [14]	1673 39	
	1629 16	1646 26	1674 35	
		1647 [20]	1675 35	
	1630 30	1648 33	1676 35	
	1631 [17]	1649 31		
	1632 24			
	1633 29	1650 [13]		
	1634 23	1651 [20 (8)]		
	–			
	1637 37			
	1638 26			
	1639 18			

Sources: L. D. S. films 675459-60 (A.C. Aigues-Vives, GG 2-3).
Note: For the years in brackets, there appear to be gaps in the registers.

CODOGNAN (colloque de Nîmes)

Avg. baps. p.a.		*Annual figures*					
1600–09	5.8	1600	6	1610	8	1672	9
1610–15	8.5	1601	7	1611	2	1673	3
1672–80	8.9	1602	6	1612	7	1674	13
		1603	4	1613	10	1675	7
		1604	8	1614	11	1676	7
		1605	5	1615	13	1677	13
		1606	4	–		1678	10
		1607	7			1679	11
		1608	3				
		1609	8			1680	7
						1681	[14]
						1682	[38]

SOURCES: A.N. TT 241/12; A.D. Gard, 5 E 78/3. Figures kindly supplied by Jean-Noël Biraben.

LES VANS (colloque d'Uzès)

Avg. baps. p.a.		*Annual figures*					
1595–1600	40.9	1595	46	1650	43	1670	33
1638–49	44.8	1596	38	1651	53	1671	49
1650–59	35.9	1597	50	1652	41	1672	34
1660–69	41	1598	47	1653	60	1673	36
1670–79	40	1599	42	1654	26	1674	43
1680–85	35.8	1600	9 (8)	1655	20	1675	43
		–		1656	26	–	
		1638	42	1657	20	1677	39
		1639	52	1658	35	1678	38
				1659	35	1679	45
		1640	57				
		1641	43	1660	32	1680	34
		1642	61	1661	31	–	
		1643	39	1662	20	1682	41
		1644	37	1663	30	1683	31
		1645	52	1664	52	1684	41
		1646	44	1665	58	1685	11 (5)
		1647	33	1666	46		
		1648	27	1667	51		
		1649	50	1668	55		
				1669	35		

SOURCES: A.D. Ardèche, 5 E 59, 61–2. Figures kindly supplied by Jean-Noël Biraben.

LUNEL (colloque de Montpellier)

Avg. baps. p.a.	
1626–29	53
1630–39	50.9
1640–49	42.3
1650–59	43.1
1660–69	51.1
1670–79	53.7
1680–83	42

Annual figures

1626 42 (6)	1640 44	1660 57	1680 35
1627 37 (6)	1641 60	1661 49	1681 58
1628 45	1642 42	1662 44	1682 37
1629 35	1643 35	1663 57	1683 49
	1644 39	1664 45	1684 31
1630 60	1645 32	1665 60	
1631 46	1646 29	1666 48	
1632 55	1647 47	1667 57	
1633 49	1648 49	1668 48	
1634 46	1649 46	1669 46	
1635 55			
1636 52	1650 55	1670 59	
1637 52	1651 53	1671 48	
1638 37	1652 39	1672 63	
1639 57	1653 29	1673 54	
	1654 44	1674 54	
	1655 35	1675 64	
	1656 36	1676 49	
	1657 48	1677 49	
	1658 39	1678 58	
	1659 53	1679 39	

SOURCES: L.D.S. films 1334388–9 (A.C. Lunel, GG 28, 30, 32–48).
NOTE: Figures corrected for 1683–84 to eliminate the numerous acts involving inhabitants of Mauguio, Marsillargues, and Saint-Laurent-d'Aigouze, whose temples had been closed.

MARSILLARGUES (colloque de Nîmes)

Avg. baps. p.a.	
1600–09	55.4
1610–19	56.7
1620–29	62.7
1630–39	62.3
1640–49	50.5
1650–59	43.2
1660–69	47.3
1670–79	52.7
1680–84	47

Annual figures

1600 49	1620 61	1640 53	1660 38
1601 55	1621 67	1641 49	1661 36
1602 76	1622 40	1642 52	1662 31
1603 53	1623 40	1643 57	1663 42
1604 57	1624 70	1644 47	1664 52
1605 52	1625 73	1645 48	1665 51
1606 51	1626 69	1646 46	1666 58
1607 59	1627 67	1647 53	1667 57
1608 53	1628 72	1648 49	1668 53
1609 49	1629 68	1649 51	1669 55
1610 58	1630 73	1650 48	1670 50
1611 59	1631 62	1651 50	1671 54
1612 36	1632 66	1652 30	1672 52
1613 68	1633 64	1653 43	1673 67
1614 55	1634 67	1654 50	1674 53
1615 61	1635 60	1655 37	1675 59
1616 55	1636 62	1656 47	1676 53
1617 60	1637 46	1657 41	1677 46
1618 60	1638 68	1658 54	1678 53
1619 55	1639 55	1659 32	1679 40

1680	52
1681	46
1682	38
1683	52

SOURCE: L. D. S. films 1237044–5 (A. C. Marsillargues, GG 9–17). Jean-Marc Daumas, *Marsillargues en Languedoc, fief de Guillaume de Nogaret, petit Genève* (Marsillargues, 1985), pp. 49, 56, 69, provides slightly different figures.
NOTE: The number of acts was swollen in 1624 by inhabitants of Lunel bringing their children to Marsillargues for baptism. These cases have been eliminated here.

MONTPELLIER (colloque de Montpellier)

Avg. baps. p.a.		*Annual figures*							
1600–09	366.4	1600	420	1620	415	1640	239	1660	267
1610–19	394.2	1601	352	1621	415	1641	255	1661	260
1620–29	340.1	1602	357	1622	327	1642	264	1662	263
1630–39	258.1	1603	418	1623	222	1643	261	1663	240
1640–49	261.9	1604	311	1624	396	1644	274	1664	258
1650–59	262.4	1605	365	1625	365	1645	241	1665	262
1660–69	260.5	1606	355	1626	317	1646	291	1666	296
1670–79	259.6	1607	388	1627	350	1647	285	1667	241
1680–84	221.6	1608	354	1628	330	1648	254	1668	262
		1609	344	1629	264	1649	255	1669	256
		1610	374	1630	97	1650	297	1670	268
		1611	381	1631	258	1651	253	1671	255
		1612	374	1632	234	1652	262	1672	283
		1613	415	1633	301	1653	229	1673	299
		1614	358	1634	270	1654	246	1674	274
		1615	422	1635	299	1655	250	1675	239
		1616	413	1636	295	1656	265	1676	264
		1617	413	1637	270	1657	265	1677	247
		1618	407	1638	270	1658	288	1678	229
		1619	385	1639	287	1659	269	1679	238
						1680	273		
						1681	226		
						1682	198		
						1683	193		
						1684	218		

SOURCES: A.C. Montpellier, GG 320–1, 323–4, 326–7, 329–30, 333–5, 337–8, 341–54.

NIMES (colloque de Nîmes)

Avg. baps. p.a.		*Annual figures*							
1600–09	447.3	1600	463	1620	526	1640	315	1660	318
1610–19	514	1601	501	1621	561	1641	329	1661	342
1620–29	425.9	1602	471	1622	462	1642	399	1662	359
1630–39	345.8	1603	475	1623	437	1643	385	1663	352
1640–49	340.6	1604	442	1624	368	1644	322	1664	394
1650–59	346	1605	391	1625	413	1645	214	1665	398
1660–69	383.6	1606	467	1626	411	1646	351	1666	411
1670–79	435.9	1607	429	1627	430	1647	396	1667	399
1680–84	450.3	1608	444	1628	422	1648	382	1668	416
		1609	390	1629	229	1649	313	1669	447
		1610	479	1630	217	1650	306	1670	415
		1611	497	1631	350	1651	376	1671	413
		1612	485	1632	291	1652	374	1672	461
		1613	483	1633	318	1653	333	1673	407
		1614	511	1634	364	1654	362	1674	440
		1615	516	1635	352	1655	368	1675	451
		1616	554	1636	389	1656	351	1676	447
		1617	548	1637	369	1657	359	1677	451
		1618	525	1638	409	1658	316	1678	463
		1619	542	1639	399	1659	315	1679	411
						1680	430		
						1681	477		
						1682	445		
						1683	467		
						1684	431		
						1685	339 (9)		

SOURCES: A.C. Nîmes, UU 93–105. Figures kindly supplied by Jean-Noël Biraben.

SOMMIERES (colloque de Nîmes)

Avg. baps. p.a.		*Annual figures*					
1626–28	109.9	1626	82 (10)	1650	71	1678	89
1640–49	62.2	1627	103	1651	75	1679	65
1666–75	81.9	1628	126	–			
1676–84	87.3	–		1666	83	1680	120
		1640	65	1667	86	1681	102
		1641	59	1668	96	1682	85
		1642	69	1669	69	1683	79
		1643	70			1684	52 (7)
		1644	71	1670	39 (8)		
		1645	60	1673	83		
		1646	46	1674	96		
		1647	65	1675	75		
		1648	44	1676	81		
		1649	51	1677	76		

SOURCES: L. D. S. films 793710, 795202 (A. C. Sommières, GG 24–6).
NOTE: Registers also exist for the period 1652–65, but the registration appears to be incomplete.

UZES (colloque de Nîmes)

Avg. baps. p.a.		*Annual figures*							
1617–21	226.4	1617	247	1630	89	1650	145	1670	150
1622–31	199.5	1618	233	1631	140 (9)	1651	175	1671	181
1645–49	162.8	1619	264	–		1652	163	1672	151
1650–59	149.6			1645	44 (3)	1653	125	1673	173
1660–69	148.1	1620	188	1646	152	1654	139	1674	176
1670–79	166.5	1621	200	1647	158	1655	164	1675	155
1680–85	165.2	1622	127	1648	178	1656	148	1676	162
		1623	140	1649	160	1657	131	1677	174
		1624	178			1658	164	1678	188
		1625	194			1659	140	1679	155
		1626	203						
		1627	276			1660	120	1680	173
		1628	248			1661	147	1681	157
		1629	150			1662	152	1682	168
						1663	121	1683	164
						1664	139	1684	160
						1665	168	1685	128 (9)
						1666	147		
						1667	176		
						1668	157		
						1669	154		

SOURCES: A.C. Uzès, GG 32–42. Figures kindly supplied by Jean-Noël Biraben.

SYNOD: CEVENNES

ALES (colloque d'Anduze)

Avg. baps. p.a.		*Annual figures*							
1606–11	160.7	1606	173	1613	179	1662	150	1669	165
1612–18	178.3	1607	107	1614	172	1663	122	1670	180
1662–66	150.7	1608	162	1615	186	1664	171	1671	147(10)
1668–74	174.8	1609	163	1616	172	1665	159	1672	148 (11)
		1610	178	1617	199	1666	126 (10)	–	
		1611	181	1618	131 (10)	–		1674	169 (11)
		1612	179			1668	182		

SOURCES: L.D.S. films 667256–7 (A.C. Alès, E 1; A.D. Gard E 1, $5E^7$ 20–21).

ANDUZE (colloque d'Anduze)

Avg. baps. p.a.		*Annual figures*			
1600–04	189.9	1600 203	1620 181	1650 99	1670 127
1609–15	210.4	1601 193	1621 231	1651 119	1671 115
1616–23	191.4	1602 190	1622 175	1652 139	1672 138
1641–49	181	1603 169	1623 126	1653 150	–
1650–59	133.1	1604 130 (8)	–	1654 137	1674 163
1660–69	136.7	–	1641 151 (10)	1655 135	1675 110 (10)
1670–79	132.5	1608 51 (3)	1642 203	1656 144	–
1680–83	141.3	1609 180	1643 190	1657 121	1677 141
		1644 165	1658 149	–	
		1610 238	1645 175	1659 138	1679 111
		1611 205	1646 172		
		1612 224	1647 189	1660 127	1680 126
		1613 212	1648 188	1661 117	1681 137
		1614 192	1649 166	1662 151	1682 154
		1615 222		1663 106	1683 148
		1616 187		1664 135	
		1617 238		1665 144	
		1618 177		1666 143	
		1619 216		1667 158	
				1668 129	
				1669 157	

Sources: L. D. S. films 670775–8 (A.C. Anduze, GG 17–30).
Note: "Contagion" noted 1650.

AULAS (colloque de Sauve)

Avg. baps. p.a.		*Annual figures*			
1613–17	88.2	1613 93	1630 [47]	1650 [51]	1670 58
1664–76	75	1614 82	1631 [44]	1651 [55]	1671 72
		1615 76	1632 [48]	1652 [37]	1672 63
		1616 101	1633 [49]	1653 [40]	1673 76
		1617 89	1634 [57]	1654 [44]	1674 83
		1618 [69]	1635 [46]	1655 [41]	1675 65
		1619 [64]	1636 [69]	1656 [65]	1676 40 (7)
			1637 [52]	1657 [57]	
		1620 [67]	1638 [59]	1658 [44]	
		1621 [79]	1639 [54]	1659 [57]	
		1622 [50]			
		1623 [40]	1640 [45]	1660 [53]	
		1624 [75]	–	1661 [64]	
		1625 [66]	1644 [39]	1662 [46]	
		1626 [55]	1645 [24]	1663 [42]	
		1627 [70]	1646 [44]	1664 97	
		1628 [71]	1647 [44]	1665 73	
		1629 [39]	1648 [65]	1666 77	
			1649 [41]	1667 35 (4)	
				1668 82	
				1669 78	

Source: L. D. S. film 600436 (A.C. Aulas, GG 1–3).
Note: The earliest registers contain a substantial number of acts concerning the inhabitants of Bréau. At a date between 1613 and 1620 which I have not been able to determine with precision, a separate church was established there, which was closed by royal edict in 1663. On the evidence of the movement of the number of baptisms, I have estimated the date of formation of Bréau's church at 1617 and have only compared the number of baptisms prior to that date with those after the closure of the church.

LASALLE (colloque d'Anduze)

Avg. baps. p.a.		*Annual figures*			
1600–08	51.6	1600 71	1620 62	1640 55	1660 69
1610–19	55.8	1601 59	1621 63	1641 65	1661 64
1620–28	50.3	1602 52	1622 19	1642 74	1662 81
1631–39	62.7	1603 47	1623 26	1643 70	1663 66
1640–49	69	1604 55	1624 59	1644 66	1664 72
1650–59	60	1605 48	1625 58	1645 72	1665 70
1666–69	63.2	1606 34	1626 63	1646 67	1666 56
1670–78	75.9	1607 48	1627 55	1647 86	1667 33
		1608 50	1628 31 (8)	1648 69	1668 38
				1649 66	
		1610 54	1631 32 (8)	1650 72	1670 67
		1611 52	1632 60	1651 70	1671 84
		1612 48	1633 59	1652 75	1672 78
		1613 61	1634 71	1653 55	1673 83
		1614 51	1635 58	1654 70	1674 81
		1615 50	1636 67	1655 63	–
		1616 68	1637 63	1656 58	1677 87
		1617 59	1638 64	1657 51	1678 51
		1618 57	1639 70	1658 23	
		1619 58		1659 63	

Source: L. D. S. film 687553 (A.C. Lasalle, GG 12–19).

MONOBLET (colloque de Sauve)

Avg. baps. p.a.		*Annual figures*			
1600–09	43.8	1600 38	1620 31	1640 29	1660 32
1610–19	34.1	1601 32	1621 29	1641 31	1661 29
1620–29	50.6	1602 50	1622 26 (8)	1642 12	1662 39
1634–39	23	1603 30	–	1643 35	1663 31
1640–49	25.7	1604 50	1624 46	–	1664 28
1650–59	28	1605 46	1625 23	1645 22	1665 32
1660–69	31.9	1606 50	1626 30	1646 19	1666 29
1670–79	32.8	1607 46	1627 30	1647 28	1667 31
1680–82	41.7	1608 44	1628 26	1648 27	–
		1609 52	1629 11	1649 28	1669 36
		1610 49	1630 8	1650 31	1670 28
		1611 15	–	1651 28	1671 38
		1612 44	1634 24	1652 34	1672 32
		1613 21	–	1653 17	1673 37
		1614 36	1636 36	1654 35	–
		1615 33	1637 21	1655 27	1675 20
		1616 43	1638 13	1656 27	1676 45
		1617 37	1639 21	1657 22	1677 32
		1618 38		1658 25	1678 27
		1619 25		1659 34	1679 36
				1680 42	
				1681 47	
				1682 36	

Source: L. D. S. film 690951 (A.D. Gard, 5E 210–12).

SAINT-ETIENNE-VALLEE-FRANCAISE (colloque de Saint-Germain-de-Calberte)

Avg. baps. p.a.		*Annual figures*							
1600–09	50.3	1600	55	1620	36	1640	30	1660	50
1610–19	48	1601	56	1621	46	1641	26	1661	48
1620–29	38.5	1602	44	1622	31	1642	35	1662	44
1634–39	38.5	1603	39	1623	25	1643	32	1663	[24]
1640–49	36.7	1604	37	1624	50	1644	[6]	1664	[7]
1650–59	50.9	1605	56	1625	52	1645	38	1665	[9]
1660–62	47.3	1606	62	1626	45	1646	24	1666	[15]
1670–79	38.7	1607	45	1627	41	1647	44	1667	[27]
1680–82	46.6	1608	49	1628	31	1648	46	1668	[3 (8)]
		1609	60	1629	28	1649	55	1669	[20 (4)]
		1610	48	1630	45 (9)	1650	41	1670	38
		1611	66	1631	28	1651	56	1671	27
		1612	56	1632	39	1652	60	1672	40
		1613	45	1633	42	1653	41	1673	52
		1614	81	1634	40	1654	19 (4)	1674	38
		1615	46	1635	24	1655	61 (10)	1675	45
		1616	14	1636	38	1656	32	1676	33
		1617	49	1637	31	1657	51	1677	41
		1618	39	1638	40	1658	54	1678	38
		1619	36	1639	48	1659	52	1679	35
						1680	50		
						1681	43		
						1682	62		
						1683	31		
						1684	47		
						1685	[72 (9)]		

SOURCES: A.C. Saint-Etienne-Vallée-Française (at A.D. Lozère), GG 2–5; B.P.F., Ms 422, fol. 85. See also J. R. Armogathe, "Le diocèse de Mende au 17me siècle: Perspectives d'histoire religieuse," *Revue du Gévaudan des Causses et des Cévennes*, new ser., 17 (1971), 95.
NOTES: Registration probably incomplete 1644 and 1663–69. Number of baptisms swollen in 1685 by inhabitants of nearby communities.

SAINT-HIPPOLYTE-DU-FORT (colloque de Sauve)

Avg. baps. p.a.		*Annual figures*							
1600–09	99.4	1600	128	1620	149	1640	90	1660	125
1610–19	121.3	1601	103	1621	101	1641	81	1661	143
1620–29	116.9	1602	79	1622	88	1642	72	1662	151
1631–39	117.8	1603	74	1623	88	1643	103	1663	150
1640–49	100.1	1604	103	1624	140	1644	108	1664	137
1650–59	141.3	1605	108	1625	112	1645	121	1665	170
1660–69	141.6	1606	90	1626	100	1646	101	1666	127
1670–80	136.1	1607	89	1627	146	1647	139	1667	138
		1608	105	1628	131	1648	99	1668	138
		1609	115	1629	114	1649	87	1669	137
		1610	114	–		1650	103	1670	148
		1611	136	1631	96	1651	133	1671	174
		1612	114	1632	105	1652	141	1672	139
		1613	124	1633	115	1653	136	1673	158
		1614	115	1634	125	1654	141	1674	144
		1615	106	1635	119	1655	132	1675	140
		1616	117	1636	152	1656	160	1676	123
		1617	151	1637	98	1657	153	1677	120
		1618	100	1638	135	1658	176	1678	121
		1619	136	1639	115	1659	138	1679	109
						1680	124		
						1681	20 (2)		

SOURCES: L. D. S. films 692764–6 (A.C. Saint-Hippolyte-du-Fort, GG 3–7).

SAINT-JEAN-DU-GARD (colloque d'Anduze)

Avg. baps. p.a.		*Annual figures*			
1624–29	86	1600 [73]	1624 59 (8)	1640 99	1660 110
1630–39	85.3	1601 [93]	1625 97	1641 97	1661 91
1640–49	92.1	1602 [56]	1626 89	1642 108	1662 104
1650–59	91.4	1603 [45]	1627 88 (10)	1643 95	1663 80
1660–69	97.3	1604 [55]	–	1644 85	1664 102
1670–79	104.2	1605 [56]	1629 54	1645 77	1665 86
1680–84	94.8	1606 [57]		1646 88	1666 94
		1607 [61]	1630 56	1647 82	1667 99
		1608 [62]	1631 84	1648 102	1668 100
		1609 [31]	1632 88	1649 88	1669 107
			1633 91		
		1610 [44]	1634 73	1650 106	1670 88
		1611 [71]	1635 97	1651 105	1671 118
		1612 [29 (8)]	1636 102	1652 92	1672 103
		1613 [94]	1637 89	1653 82	1673 100
		1614 [75]	1638 89	1654 89	1674 132
		1615 [55 (8)]	1639 84	1655 101	1675 90
				1656 88	1676 97
				1657 87	1677 108
				1658 98	1678 118
				1659 66	1679 88
				1680 98	
				1681 109	
				1682 118	
				1683 65	
				1684 84	

Source: L.D.S. films 684507–8 (A.C. Saint-Jean-du-Gard, GG 16–20). My count here differs slightly for certain years from figures kindly provided by Jean-Noël Biraben.
Note: The extreme and unusual pattern of fluctuations in the number of acts per year between 1600 and 1615 has led me to eliminate the figures concerning these years from my calculations, even though the appearance of the registers offers no reason to suspect defective registration.

SAINT-LAURENT-LE-MINIER (colloque de Sauve)

Avg. baps. p.a.		*Annual figures*			
1610–19	26.7	1610 5 (2)	1630 27	1650 25	1670 41
1620–29	27.1	1611 42	1631 8	1651 23	1671 30
1630–39	11.2	1612 28	1632 3	1652 29	1672 40
1640–49	23.3	1613 34	1633 9	1653 26	1673 39
1650–59	23.2	1614 26 (8)	1634 7	1654 25	1674 30
1660–69	27.2	1615 31	1635 6	1655 24	1675 44
1670–79	35	1616 3	1636 2	1656 23	1676 32
1680–83	31.3	1617 8	1637 13	1657 23	1677 34
		1618 18	1638 21	1658 25	1678 28
		1619 41	1639 16	1659 9	1679 32
		1620 17	1640 32	1660 16	1680 33
		1621 29	1641 24	1661 15	1682 28
		1622 34	1642 31	1662 16	1682 32
		1623 27	1643 27	1663 21	1683 32
		1624 34	1644 16	1664 29	
		1625 30	1645 17	1665 35	
		1626 31	1646 26	1666 34	
		1627 23	1647 25	1667 37	
		1628 27	1648 24	1668 38	
		1629 19	1649 11	1669 31	

Source: A.C. Saint-Laurent-le-Minier, GG 1. Figures kindly supplied by Jean-Noël Biraben; verified against L.D.S. film 0701088.

SOUDORGUES (colloque d'Anduze)

Avg. baps. p.a.		*Annual figures*							
1619–28	41	1619	37	1630	43	1660	15	1670	36
1629–36	36.8	1620	46	1631	36	1661	18	1671	44
1660–69	29	1621	39	1632	39	1662	26	1672	22 (9)
1670–79	33.8	1622	25	1633	36	1663	22	–	
1680–83	29.8	1623	37	1634	32	1664	37	1674	34
		1624	50	1635	29	1665	34	1675	30
		1625	38	1636	37 (9)	1666	33	1676	36
		1626	53	–		1667	40	1677	31
		1627	46			1668	33	1678	35
		1628	39			1669	32	1679	28
		1629	33						
								1680	26
								1681	37
								1682	24
								1683	32
								1684	[83]

SOURCE: L. D. S. film 690965 (A.C. Soudorgues, GG 1, 3, 7, 9).
NOTE: The figure for 1684 includes numerous inhabitants of such nearby communities as Monoblet and Lasalle whose churches had been closed.

SUMENE (colloque de Sauve)

Avg. baps. p.a.		*Annual figures*							
1601–09	45.2	1600	20	1626	22	1650	56	1670	66
1610–17	44.2	1601	52	–		1651	67	1671	63
1632–39	56.2	1602	48	1632	36 (6)	1652	54	1672	56
1640–49	59	1603	43	1633	58	1653	45	1673	52
1650–59	57.4	1604	50	1634	64	1654	59	1674	52 (10)
1660–69	64.7	–		1635	64	1655	67	1675	53
1670–79	53.7	1608	38	1636	51	1656	53	1676	36
1680–83	44.4	1609	40	1637	42	1657	52	1677	54
				1638	37	1658	62	1678	43
		1610	49	1639	69	1659	59	1679	52
		1611	44						
		1612	46	1640	51	1660	72	1680	39
		1613	44	1641	76	1661	66	1681	46 (10)
		1614	36 (10)	1642	65	1662	54	1682	38
		1615	24 (8)	1643	65	1663	46	1683	40 (10)
		1616	39	1644	57	1664	70		
		1617	23 (5)	1645	49	1665	78		
		–		1646	54	1666	71		
		1625	54	1647	61	1667	70		
				1648	58	1668	59		
				1649	54	1669	55		

SOURCES: L.D.S. films 696660-1 (A.C. Sumène, GG 12-4).

ANNONAY

Avg. baps. p.a.

1600–07	93.7
1613–19	70
1620–29	66.7
1630–39	62.2
1640–49	53.7
1650–59	42.6
1660–69	47.5
1670–80	51.6

Annual figures

1600	119	1620	84	1640	64	1660	39
1601	100	1621	80	1641	68	1661	57
1602	108	1622	79	1642	64	1662	34
1603	93	1623	75	1643	55	1663	34
1604	99	1624	54	1644	53	1664	49
1605	80	1625	74	1645	38	1665	58
1606	50 (8)	1626	85	1646	60	1666	47
1607	38 (8)	1627	55	1647	37	1667	45
–		1628	43	1648	51	1668	57
1613	49	1629	38	1649	47	1669	55
1614	61						
1615	83	1630	47	1650	54	1670	54
1616	68	1631	30	1651	42	1671	61
1617	80	1632	43	1652	40	1672	45
1618	75	1633	48	1653	42	1673	55
1619	74	1634	63	1654	42	1674	52
		1635	74	1655	36	1675	58
		1636	84	1656	40	1676	42
		1637	70	1657	43	1677	50
		1638	81	1658	41	1678	50
		1639	82	1659	46	1679	49
						1680	50

Sources: L.D.S. films 1069212-3 (A.D. Ardèche, 5 E 37–40).

BOULIEU

Avg. baps. p.a.

1600–09	11.2
1610–19	11.2
1620–29	10.4
1630–39	5.5
1652–59	2.9
1660–66	3.1

Annual figures

1600	12	1620	13	–	
1601	8	1621	7	1652	2
1602	5	1622	11	1653	4
1603	14	1623	12	1654	2
1604	11	1624	10	1655	7
1605	19	1625	15	1656	4
1606	13	1626	8	1657	0
1607	4	1627	12	1658	4
1608	7	1628	6	1659	0
1609	19	1629	10		
				1660	5
1610	16	1630	9	1661	2
1611	9	1631	9	1662	6
1612	17	1632	7	1663	2
1613	10	1633	7	1664	2
1614	7	1634	8	1665	2
1615	14	1635	3	1666	3
1616	13	1636	1		
1617	6	1637	5		
1618	9	1638	1		
1619	11	1639	5		

Source: B.P.F., Ms E 64 (photocopy of original register in the Presbytère Protestant d'Annonay).

PRIVAS

1594–1613	110 Protestant baps. p.a. (=ca. 2750 people)
1663	310 Protestant families acc. census (=ca. 1400 people)
1665	115 Protestant families acc. census (=ca. 520 people)

SOURCES: Elie Reynier, *Histoire de Privas*, 3 vols. (Aubenas, 1941–46), I, 297, II, 187; Alain Molinier, *Stagnations et croissance: Le Vivarais aux XVIIe–XVIIIe siècles* (Paris, 1985), 247–50.

SYNOD: PROVENCE

LOURMARIN

Avg. baps. p.a.		*Annual figures*							
1619–29	37.5	1619	18 (5)	1630	38	1669	33	1680	27
1630–39	42.6	1620	38	1631	39	1670	31	1681	43
1669–79	35.5	1621	31	1632	36	1671	44	1682	39
1680–85	33.3	1622	37	1633	44	1672	31	1683	24
		1623	38	1634	54	1673	33	1684	39
		1624	34	1635	31	1674	32	1685	17 (8)
		1625	36	1636	46	1675	41		
		1626	41	1637	49	1676	37		
		1627	35	1638	41	1677	33		
		1628	46	1639	19 (4)	1678	46		
		1629	37			1679	29		

SOURCES: A.D. Vaucluse, E, Lourmarin; A.C. Lourmarin, Etat Civil 1, "Cultes réunies 1669–92."
NOTE: The annual figures are estimates of the number of baptisms concerning inhabitants of Lourmarin alone. The temple of Lourmarin also served the Protestants of such surrounding communities as Lauris, Cadenet, and "Sivergues." In 1620, two-thirds of all baptisms involved inhabitants of Lourmarin and one-third residents of nearby communities. The temple of Lourmarin was closed by decision of special royal *commissaires* in 1663, even though the church dated back to the 1560s and had a strong legal right to exist. The inhabitants of the town subsequently had to worship at Mérindol. Despite that, a "Registre des baptesmes et mortuaires des habitans de ce lieu de Leurmarin faisans proffession de la Religion P Ref." was still maintained, as if to assert the continued existence of the congregation. In this later register, virtually all of the acts concern inhabitants of Lourmarin–92 percent in the years 1675 and 1681. The total number of baptisms recorded has consequently been reduced by 33 percent for the years 1619–39 and by 8 percent for the years between 1669 and 1685.

BEAUMONT-LES-VALENCE (colloque du Viennois)

Avg. baps. p.a.		*Annual figures*			
1613–21	40.2	1613 12 (3)	1634 45 (10)	1650 48	1670 52
1634–39	53.3	1614 35	1635 55	1651 52	1671 20 (7)
1640–49	47	1615 31	1636 61	1652 50	–
1650–59	47.5	1616 44	1637 52	1653 47	1682 61
1660–71	55	1617 50	1638 46	1654 53	1683 33 (9)
1682–84	54.5	1618 40	1639 52	1655 40	1684 15 (3)
		1619 46		1656 48	
			1640 37	1657 50	
		1620 40	1641 50	1658 47	
		1621 20 (8)	1642 55	1659 40	
			1643 45		
			1644 44	1660 64	
			1645 51	1661 60	
			1646 47	1662 54	
			1647 47	1663 73	
			1648 52	1664 37	
			1649 42	1665 56	
				1666 52	
				1667 62	
				1668 53	
				1669 54	

SOURCE: L.D.S. film 0662512 (A.C. Beaumont-lès-Valence, unclassified).
NOTES: This church attracted worshippers from a wide area around Beaumont whose precise boundaries fluctuated over time, as did the number of inhabitants of Valence preferring to attend services here rather than crossing the Rhône to worship at Valence's church of Soyons, in the Vivarais. Fortunately, Beaumont's registers indicate the place of residence of nearly all couples presenting their children for baptism from 1613 onward. The figures provided here refer exclusively to the number of acts involving inhabitants of the core area of this temple: Beaumont and the immediately surrounding communities of Montmeyran, Montléger, Montvendre, Etoile, and Malissard. For 1650 and 1654, a page is missing in the register; figures are estimated based on the number of acts per page on the surrounding pages. For 1656, place of residence is rarely noted; the geographic distribution of the families bringing children to Beaumont for baptism is assumed to be similar to that found in the surrounding years. Registers also exist for the years 1624–32 and 1676–81, but the former is very incomplete and the latter is illegible in microfilm.

EMBRUN (colloque de l'Embrunais)

Avg. baps. p.a.		*Annual figures*			
1633–39	19.1	1633 6 (2)	1640 20	1660 16	1670 20 (10)
1640–50	13.7	–	1641 12	1661 16	1671 13 (10)
1659–68	14.4	1636 14 (9)	1642 21	1662 9	1672 [12]
1670–76	17.2	1637 17	1643 13	1663 13	1673 [7]
1680–84	12.8	1638 17	1644 11	1664 12	1674 8
		1639 21	1645 9	1665 10	1675 22
			1646 9	1666 22	–
			1647 12	1667 12	1680 5 (3)
			1648 13	1668 20	1681 15
			1649 18	–	1682 12
					1683 10
			1650 9 (9)		1684 5 (5)
			–		
			1659 1 (1)		

SOURCE: A.D. Hautes-Alpes, 2 E 507.
NOTE: Registers appear incomplete 1672–73.

GAP (colloque du Gapençais)

Avg. baps. p.a.		*Annual figures*			
1625–32	29.2	1625 15 (6)	1633 36	1668 23	1676 27
1633–40	29.6	1626 32	1634 28	1669 20	1677 29
1668–75	25.9	1627 38	1635 40	1670 28	1678 25
1676–84	27.2	1628 29	1636 29	1671 28	1679 22
		1629 23	1637 18	1672 29	1680 18
		1630 29	1638 39	1673 25	1681 27
		1631 26	1639 27	1674 25	1682 19
		1632 27	1640 10 (8)	1675 29	1683 29
					1684 20

SOURCES: A. D. Hautes-Alpes, 3 H supplément 114–18. Figures kindly provided by Jean-Pierre Bardet. René Debon, "Religion et vie quotidienne à Gap (1657-1685)," in Pierre Bolle, ed., *Le Protestantisme en Dauphiné au XVIIe siècle* (La Bégude-de-Mazenc, 1983), 163, provides slightly different figures for the years 1668–84.

NOTE: Registers also exist for the years 1643–46 and 1651–59, but they are poorly maintained and appear to be incomplete.

LORIOL (colloque du Valentinois)

Avg. baps. p.a.		*Annual figures*			
1614–19	56.3	1614 40 (9)	1630 28 (5)	1650 51	1670 61
1620–29	53.5	1615 66	1631 43 (9)	1651 42	1671 53
1630–39	47.4	1616 65	1632 46	1652 48	1672 61
1640–49	46.5	1617 62	1633 43	1653 39	1673 52
1650–59	44.3	1618 45	1634 39	1654 53	1674 61
1660–69	54.5	1619 46	1635 49	1655 38	1675 58
1670–79	53.6		1636 55	1656 50	1676 44
1680–84	61	1620 60	1637 42	1657 47	1677 53
		1621 64	1638 46	1658 35	1678 35
		1622 38	1639 44	1659 40	1679 58
		1623 21 (8)			
		1624 70	1640 44	1660 53	1680 59
		1625 67	1641 52	1661 43	1681 71
		1626 43	1642 48	1662 48	1682 43
		1627 49	1643 45	1663 40	1683 57
		1628 57	1644 47	1664 76	1684 58 (9)
		1629 22 (6)	1645 50	1666 57	
			1646 46	1667 68	
			1647 47	1668 54	
			1648 49	1669 66	
			1649 37		

SOURCE: A. D. Drôme, 6 E 19. Figures kindly provided by Jean-Pierre Bardet.

MENS-EN-TRIEVES (colloque du Grésivaudan)

Avg. baps. p.a.		*Annual figures*			
1604–07	42	1600 [14]	1645 37	1660 30	1676 78
1618–24	35	1601 [22]	1646 34	1661 58	1677 75
1645–55	41.7	1602 [18]	1647 44	1662 55	1678 82
1656–65	65.1	1603 [14]	1648 42	1663 79	1679 72
1666–75	75.9	1604 43	1649 35	1664 71	
1676–82	73	1605 36		1665 91	1680 55
		1606 38	1650 32	1666 97	1681 70
		1607 33 (7)	1651 40	1667 74	1682 79
		–	1652 44	1668 66	–
		1618 17 (5)	1653 43	1669 85	1684 [79]
		1619 30	1654 55		1685 [61]
		1620 36	1655 53	1670 74	
		1621 26	1656 62	1671 70	
		1622 30	1657 57	1672 67	
		1623 45	1658 75	1673 71	
		1624 26 (7)	1659 73	1674 74	
		–		1675 81	

Sources: A. D. Isère, 5 E 227 (2); Pierre Bolle, "Une paroisse réformée du Dauphiné à la veille de la Révocation de l'édit de Nantes: Mens-en-Trièves, 1650–1685," *B.S.H.P.F.*, CXI (1960), 109–35, 213–39, esp. 129.

Note: The low figures for 1600–1603 suggest incomplete registration. In 1684 and 1685, the number of baptisms was augmented by inhabitants of nearby communities bringing their children to Mens for baptism.

MONTELIMAR (colloque du Valentinois)

Avg. baps. p.a.		*Annual figures*		
1598–1601	110.9	1598 111	1668 38 (6)	1676 88
1668–75	100.1	1599 98	1669 108	1677 69
1676–82	74.6	1600 126	1670 100	1678 81
		1601 81 (9)	1671 98	1679 71
			1672 106	1680 70
			1673 90	1681 74
			1674 103	1682 38 (7)
			1675 108	

Sources: L.D.S. films 0614651–2 (A.D. Drôme 6 E 20/4 and 6 E 21). Figures for the early period kindly provided from the original registers by Jean-Pierre Bardet.

Note: A few of the baptisms in both 1598–1601 and 1668–82 involve inhabitants of such surrounding communities as Sauzet and Allan, which had a temple of their own for a brief period in the early 1600s.

MONTJOUX (colloque du Valentinois)

Avg. baps. p.a.		*Annual figures*					
1608–16	8.3	1608	7	1630	10	1650	5
1617–25	8.3	1609	7	1631	4	1651	2
1628–39	9	1610	15	1632	7	1652	13
1640–49	9	1611	8	1633	8	1653	3
1650–59	6.8	1612	14	1634	13	1654	1
1660–68	8	1613	5	1635	7	1655	13
		1614	5	1636	10	1656	10
		1615	5	1637	15	1657	7
		1616	9	1638	7	1658	6
		1617	17	1639	16	1659	8
		1618	8				
		1619	6	1640	12	1660	2
				1641	14	1661	5
		1620	7	1642	7	1662	6
		1621	5	1643	6	1663	10
		1622	5	1644	11	1664	12
		1623	10	1645	6	–	
		1624	7	1646	10	1667	9
		1625	7 (8)	1647	6	1668	12
		–		1648	11		
		1628	9 (9)	1649	7		
		1629	6				

Sources: B.P.F., Ms. E 50; Jean Sambuc, "Le registre des protestants de Montjoux (Drôme) 1608–1669 suivi d'un étude sur la famille des seigneurs dudit lieu," *B.S.H.P.F.*, CXV (1969), 93–112.

ORPIERRE (colloque du Gapençais)

Avg. baps. p.a.		*Annual figures*							
1633–39	47.3	1633	53	1640	44 (7)	1650	21 (5)	1672	[31]
1640–49	50.6	1634	44	–		1651	17 (4)	–	
1650–59	39	1635	49	1642	58	–		1674	10 (3)
1672–80	34.6	1636	60	1643	67	1658	13 (6)	1675	38
		1637	48	1644	51	1659	27 (9)	1676	41
		1638	39	1645	30	–		–	
		1639	38	1646	30			1679	22 (8)
				1647	45				
				1648	60			1680	16 (9)
				1649	49			1681	[9]

Source: A.D. Hautes-Alpes, 2 E 102^{1}.
Notes: Registration appears incomplete 1672, 1681. A register also exists for the years 1600–07 (A.N., TT 261/6), but it contains numerous gaps and appears unreliable.

PONT-EN-ROYANS (colloque du Viennois)

Avg. baps. p.a.		*Annual figures*							
1613–19	31.2	1613	32 (8)	1630	32	1650	22	1670	29
1620–29	33.2	1614	20	1631	26	1651	21	1671	21
1630–39	36.4	1615	32	1632	32	1652	32	1672	24
1640–49	32.6	1616	32	1633	40	1653	20	1673	32
1650–59	24.6	1617	28	1634	36	1654	29	1674	20
1660–69	29.7	1618	29	1635	42	1655	18	1675	24
1670–79	23.4	1619	35	1636	45	1656	21	1676	22
1680–81	25.1			1637	43	1657	26	1677	20
		1620	25	1638	33	1658	31	1678	25
		1621	43	1639	35	1659	26	1679	17
		1622	29						
		1623	33	1640	39	1660	35	1680	25
		1624	27	1641	32	1661	25	1681	17 (8)
		1625	29	1642	20 (8)	1662	33		
		1626	42	1643	12 (5)	1663	28		
		1627	39	1644	35	1664	37		
		1628	30	1645	31	1665	24		
		1629	35	1646	34	1666	27		
				1647	29	1667	35		
				1648	34	1668	24		
				1649	30	1669	29		

SOURCE: A. D. Isère, 4 E 261/GG 11–12.
NOTE: Prior to 1622, a separate church served the scattered Protestants of the Vercors. At some point between 1622 and 1635 (probably 1626, to judge by a sudden jump in the number of baptisms at Pont-en-Royans) this church closed and the Huguenots of this region began to worship at Pont-en-Royans. To compensate for this change, annual baptismal figures for the years prior to 1626 have been multiplied by 1.33, a correction derived by averaging the ratio of baptisms prior to and following 1626 with the ratio of all church members to inhabitants of Pont-en-Royans in 1672–73, the first years for which the registers systematically note the place of residence of those bringing their children to baptism.

VERCHENY (colloque du Diois)

Avg. baps. p.a.		*Annual figures*							
1633–39	12.2	1633	10 (5)	1640	[12]	1667	[2 (3)]	1681	11
1681–83	11.6	1634	15	1641	[15]	1668	[9]	1682	12
		1635	18	1642	[1]	1669	[17]	1683	8 (8)
		1636	13	1643	[5]				
		1637	8	1644	[14]	1670	[12]		
		1638	10	1645	[4]	1671	[11]		
		1639	4	1646	[10]	1672	[22]		
				1647	[6]	1673	[13]		
				1648	[11]	1674	[9]		
				1649	[9]	1675	[8]		
						1676	[1 (2)]		
				1650	[7]	–			
				1651	[4 (2)]				
				–					
				1655	[7]				
				1656	[1]				
				1657	[0]				
				1658	[3]				
				1659	[0]				

SOURCE: A.D. Drôme, 1 Mi 490 R 23.
NOTE: As the synodal records make clear, this small church had considerable difficulty staying afloat financially and was merged for part of the century with the equally precarious nearby churches of Saillans and Espenel. Because the synodal records do not appear complete enough to permit one to reconstruct the full story of these various mergers, and because Vercheny's registers record the place of residence of those bringing their children to be baptized with regularity only at the very beginning and end of the period for which these registers survive, these are the only years for which figures have been retained. In 1681–83, many of the recorded acts involve inhabitants of Espenel and Saillans. These have been eliminated; the figures retained refer exclusively to inhabitants of Vercheny.

INDEX

www.ingramcontent.com/pod-product-compliance
Lightning Source LLC
Chambersburg PA
CBHW061755260326
41914CB00006B/1115
* 9 7 8 0 8 7 1 6 9 8 1 5 5 *